The Knowledge of the Womb

Autopsychognosia with Psychedelic Drugs

By

Athanassios Kafkalides MD

Translated by Sandra Morris

1663 Liberty Drive, Suite 200
Bloomington, Indiana 47403
(800) 839-8640
www.AuthorHouse.com

© 2005 Athanassios Kafkalides MD.
All Rights Reserved.

No part of this book may be reproduced, stored in a retrieval system, or transmitted by any means without the written permission of the author.

First published by AuthorHouse 04/12/05

ISBN: 1-4184-8442-3 (e)
ISBN: 1-4184-8441-5 (sc)

Library of Congress Control Number: 2004097960

Printed in the United States of America
Bloomington, Indiana

This book is printed on acid-free paper.

This book was originally published in Greek in 1980 by Olkos Publishing House, Athens. Copyright © Athanassios Kafkalides

Throughout the history of human society, each older generation has been tragically aggressive towards the younger. And the vicious circle continues....

This book is dedicated to young people in the hope that, when some day they become parents, they will break that vicious circle.

The English version of "The Knowledge of the Womb" is dedicated to Dr. Albert Hofmann, a great scientist and humanist.

TABLE OF CONTENTS

PREFACE viii
AUTHOR'S NOTE... x
AUTHORS ACKNOWLEDGEMENTS xi
INTRODUCTION xii
PART ONE 1
Excerpts from and summaries of histories and pharmaceutical autopsychognosia sessions of some cases in Table 1................ 1
EXCERPTS FROM AND SUMMARIES OF R10's HISTORY AND SESSIONS 4
EXCERPTS FROM AND SUMMARIES OF R1's HISTORY AND SESSIONS 51
EXCERPTS FROM AND SUMMARIES OF R3's HISTORY AND SESSIONS 61
EXCERPTS FROM AND SUMMARIES OF R4's HISTORY AND SESSIONS 64
EXCERPTS FROM AND SUMMARIES OF R5's HISTORY AND SESSIONS 96
EXCERPTS FROM AND SUMMARIES OF R6's HISTORY AND SESSIONS 115
EXCERPTS FROM AND SUMMARIES OF R12's HISTORY AND 5th SESSION 123
EXCERPTS FROM AND SUMMARIES OF R16'S HISTORY AND SESSIONS 128
REMARKS ON THERAPEUTIC RESULTS OF PHARMACEUTICAL AUTOPSYCHOGNOSIA SESSIONS 155
PART TWO 159
General description of the subjective experiences and conclusions of the 16 cases of Table 1. 159

CHAPTER ONE: WHAT ONE MAY FEEL UNDER LSD-25 OR PSILOCYBINE 160

CHAPTER TWO: WHAT I BELIEVE ABOUT LSD-25 AND PSILOCYBINE 165

CHAPTER THREE: EXPERIENCES OF THE 16 CASES OF TABLE 1 DURING AUTOPSYCHOGNOSIA SESSIONS 167

CHAPTER FOUR: REALIZATIONS AND CONCLUSIONS OF THE 16 OF TABLE 1 174

CHAPTER FIVE: AUTOPSYCHOGNOSIA 187

PART THREE 199

Author's questions, conclusions and bioneuropsysiological interpretations of the experiences and conclusions of the 16 cases of table 1 199

CHAPTER ONE: MEMORY OF INTRA-UTERINE LIFE 200

CHAPTER TWO: A FEW NOTES ON BIONEUROPHYSIOLOGY 202

CHAPTER THREE A FEW NOTES ON STIMULI 217

CHAPTER FOUR: DEFINITION, CLINICAL PICTURES AND METHODOLOGY OF CLASSIFYING MENTAL DISTURBANCES OF THE 16 (TABLE 1) 226

CHAPTER FIVE: DEVELOPMENTAL MECHANISM OF MENTAL DISTURBANCE OF THE 16 230

APPENDIX: R17 239

GLOSSARY 243

INDEX 248

PREFACE

When I first became acquainted with the studies by the Greek psychiatrist and psychotherapist Athanassios Kafkalides in the late 1980s, I immediately realized that his use of LSD in psychotherapy signified a scientific breakthrough. From the 1950' onwards, scientific interest in the effects of psychoactive substances, in particular LSD, and the possibilities they offered for application in psychotherapy began to grow. Back in the 1960s, when Kafkalides began his research, considerable courage was required to establish the correlation between the states induced by LSD and our very earliest experiences from the time before, during and after birth, before we acquire speech. In addition, a strongly rational approach and scientific proficiency were needed to overcome the novelty and unfamiliarity of this field of research and to find an appropriate, coherent framework for investigation.

In this book Athanassios Kafkalides provides a summary of his work from 1960 to 1972 and gives an account of the re-enactment of very early experiences before and during birth in 16 patients, the majority of whom had severe neurotic and psychosomatic symptoms. LSD is able to bring our earliest experiences and our emotional states during such experiences into our consciousness; at the same time, with the appropriate expert support, an inner assessment and real understanding of these experiences becomes possible. On reading the case descriptions, it is astounding to see again and again how, in the course of an LSD session, the patient's problem turned out to stem from the dramatic early experience of a relationship - in the case of feelings of inferiority, for example, the experience of massive rejection and debasement in the prenatal stage of life. Kafkalides' findings thus enable us to achieve a new and direct understanding of the psychodynamics of neurotic and psychosomatic symptoms.

The statements made in psychotherapeutic research are often limited by the fact that such studies are restricted to individual cases. The framework used for research with LSD makes it possible to compare the re - enactment of experiences in several patients, allowing general statements to be made. The main point that Kafkalides was able to prove using this method was that a child's affective, positive or negative relationship with its mother before birth crucially determines its fundamental affectivity, its basic attitude towards life and the way in which it sees and experiences the world. Kafkalides' findings and the conclusions he draws from them seem to me to be so convincing that we cannot but accept this statement.

There is no doubt that this insight into the fundamental significance of prenatal affectivity presents a challenge for developmental psychology and psychotherapy as a whole, but in particular for psychoanalysis. Various psychoanalysts have suspected and begun to determine the significance of the prenatal mother-child relationship, but were unable to gain acceptance for their assumptions. Kafkalides' studies, which in a way furnish experimental proof of the importance of our earliest experiences of relationships, have provided a new basis for scientific discussion. Kafkalides also makes some initial remarks on this subject in the second part of the book, in which he introduces the basic categories of the "rejecting womb" and the "welcoming womb". He arrives at a new understanding of the roots and the psychodynamics involved in the development of neurotic, psychosomatic and psychotic symptoms of particular significance are his comments concerning sexual disorders and problems with relationships and their roots in prenatal disturbances. Of perhaps more general importance is the concept of "womb substitutes", which refers to the fact that re-enactments of the relationships experienced before birth play a much greater part in our personal relationships, our relationships to groups and the way in which we see and experience the world as a whole than had been previously assumed. In recent years, psychoanalytic theory and practice have become increasingly ready to accept the significance of our early experience of the mother; Kafkalides' findings challenge those involved to enter into fundamental discussion and probably revision of central psychoanalytical assumptions. It is my impression that in the present day and age the results of Kaflkalides' research are more likely to find acceptance than they were at the time he carried out his studies.

There is now a whole host of findings in prenatal and perinatal psychology and medicine that support Kafkalides' results. Accordingly, and especially in the interests of the patients, I hope that this book will reach a wide audience, as Kafkalides' findings may encourage many therapists who have made similar observations in different settings to take them seriously, so that they may provide better support for their patients while reassessing their early experiences.

Heidelberg 1995 　　　　　　　　　　　　　　　　　Ludwig Janus, MD.

AUTHOR'S NOTE

Comments and suggestions that followed publication of the Greek edition of "The Knowledge of the Womb" led to a differentiation of its presentation in the English edition. This means that, among other things, paragraphs and chapters have been changed around, a certain amount of new material has been added, some very little removed, and phraseology has been revised - all with the aim of making the English text flow better and therefore easier for the reader to follow. The basic ideas and conclusion incorporated in the Greek text, however, remain unchanged

AUTHORS ACKNOWLEDGEMENTS

I am deeply indebted to Ms Sandra Morris for her many contributions to this book. These include her excellent translation of the Greek text into English, her typing of the English manuscript, and her professional editing of both the Greek and English editions. During the writing of the manuscript Ms Morris also contributed significantly to the analysis of the material and to the clarification of concepts incorporated in this study. Throughout, her approach was supportive and sensitive, which proved invaluable to the development and completion of the work.

I am extremely grateful to Mr Arnold Crush who gave the English text its final and important brushing up. Mr Crush also made challenging suggestions which led me to rearrange the sequence of the main parts of the book.

I also wish to thank Mrs Eliza Stabekis for her assistance in the English translation of cases R4 and R5

INTRODUCTION

The field of experimental neuropsychiatry, which opens up through the scientific use of psychedelic drugs in special research centres, is as vast as an ocean. This book is but a drop in that ocean.

My endeavours to help cases who present symptoms and phenomena of mental disturbance through non-pharmaceutical psychotherapeutic analysis have, as a rule, resulted in an intellectual and emotional impasse. A typical example is the following excerpt from a non-pharmaceutical psychotherapeutic session with R6 of Table 1 (p.18) before she began autopsychognosia sessions[1] with psychedelic drugs:

R6: When I am with others, whether they're little children, young people, old people, male or female, I'm overwhelmed by a strong feeling of shame and I feel the need to run away and be alone, far from everyone.
Doctor: What exactly are you ashamed of?
R6: I feel I'm ugly. I'm ashamed of my ugly face. I feel that others will realize I'm ashamed and that only intensifies my shame.
Doctor: Do you feel that you're the ugliest woman in the world?
R6:... No, I don't feel that ...
Doctor: Do you believe that all ugly women should feel ashamed of their ugliness?
R6: I know that nature makes a person beautiful or ugly and so one shouldn't feel shame. But I feel ashamed even in front of new-born babies.
Doctor: Do you think that the new-born can perceive your ugliness?
R6: No, but that thought doesn't lessen my shame.[2]
Doctor: How do you explain this reaction of yours?
R6: I don't know ... I don't understand ... (prolonged silence).[3]
Doctor: Try to relax and say whatever comes into your mind.
R6: ... Honour thy father and thy mother ... (silence) ... that thy days may be long upon the earth ... (silence) ... The ten commandments are divine commandments ... They're the Word of God not of man ... He who

---

[1] See Part II, § 58.
[2] A typical example of a purely intellectual realization concerning irrational feelings: R6's rational conclusion that the new-born is not in a position to perceive her ugliness cannot alter her irrational feelings.
[3] Intellectual and emotional impasse.

violates God's commandments is punished by Him ... (silence) ... If you honour your parents, your days will be long upon the earth ... you'll live for many years ... What will happen if you don't honour them? ... You won't live long on earth ... you'll die young ... God will put you to death because you disobeyed His commandments .. God is a punisher ...

At this point R6 presented severe anxiety and refused to continue the free communication session.

Of great interest were the thoughts which R6 expressed with great anxiety during another non-pharmaceutical psychotherapeutic session.

The following is an excerpt from that free communication:

> ...I deserve to be punished. It's all my fault ... When I do something that I shouldn't, I'm punished ... When I go to church and kneel before an icon, I feel that God will punish me on the spot because I'm a sinner ... I don't know why I'm a sinner though. I feel that I've done something bad and must be punished for it ... I don't know what it is that I've done ... God will punish me with death ... I'm afraid because after my death I'll go to hell ...

This session, like almost all others of the same type, resulted in great anxiety and R6's refusal to continue. It is worth noting that the strong emotional reaction which accompanied the free communication sessions did not help her realize the cause of her mental disturbance. That realization was achieved during her 13th autopsychognosia session, an excerpt of which follows:

> I'm a sinner ... I'm guilty ... God is constantly threatening me with punishment. I'm just a weak, helpless girl and it's my fate not to be able to escape from Almighty God ... He wants to punish me. (despair) Why? Why?

At this point, R6 began to groan and then to cry out incoherently as her anxiety escalated, climaxing in a terror and agony very difficult to describe. Her body, which had assumed the foetal position,[4] presented alternating contractions of the abdominal and spinal muscles. Finally, after about twenty minutes, she calmed down and said:

> I was in the womb again ... My mother didn't want my existence or my sex in there ... She ordered me not to exist. (Note: She felt

---

[4] i.e. back and head arched forward, knees drawn up towards the chest and hands tucked under the chin.

her mother's wish as an order.) ... But I still exist and I'm not a male and that's why I feel a sinner ... That's my crime and that's why I have to be punished by Almighty God ... The hell I fear I'll go to after my death is the hell I lived in the womb, a hell I live every day, almost every minute.

Note: The cries and contractions of the abdominal and spinal muscles during the Session[5] were R6's reactions to the rejecting womb messages, reactions which, as a foetus, she had been unable to exteriorize and which had been 'stored' in her nervous system.

The colleague who remarks that my failure in the psychotherapeutic field could be due to lack of a dynamic psychotherapeutic personality may be right. Whatever the cause of the failure, the fact is that my cases came to the surgery in a state of anxiety and generally left feeling more anxious. Both the cases and I felt not only disappointment but exasperation at the quality of the psychotherapeutic results.

Amidst this gloom of negative psychotherapeutic results and of ignorance regarding the bioneurophysiological mechanism of emotional-intellectual symptoms, there appeared the hope-bearing message of d-lysergic acid diaethylamide (LSD-25).

LSD-25 began to be used as an aid to penetrating deeper into the unconscious in 1950. The first psychotherapeutic results encouraged many psychiatrists in various countries to experiment with the new drug. Influenced by the content of the scientific articles of that period and by my disappointment in psychotherapy, I decided that I too would try the new method.

From 1960 to 1970 I used LSD-25 with 43 cases who underwent autopsychognosia sessions at the Greek Hospital of Cairo. From 1970 to 1972, with special permission from the Ministry of Health of the Cypriot Government, I used Psilocybine Sandoz with six cases who underwent autopsychognosia sessions in the psychiatric wing of the General Hospital of Nicosia.

My clinical research from 1960 to 1972 is divided into three periods:
(a) *First period 1960 - 1965*: Characteristic of this period is my lack of experience with the new drug. My knowledge was purely theoretical and sprang from the scientific articles which had been published. During this period, the basic contraindications for autopsychognosia sessions were psychosis of any kind as well as organic lesions or

---

[5] 'Session' with a capital S - autopsychognosia session with psychedelic drugs.

functional or toxic disturbances of any system. On the basis of these criteria alone, 33 cases began Sessions with LSD-25. Of these 33, three cases have kept in touch with me till the present, 14 (aged 19-34) remained under my care until 1965 whereupon I lost trace of them, and 16 cases (aged over 35) discontinued autopsychognosia after one to three Sessions. I have lost trace of them as well.

(b) *Second period 1966 - 1970:* This period (as well as the following one) is characterized by a differentiation in the indications and contraindications for autopsychognosia sessions. The cases were selected on the basis of the criteria referred to in § 68. All ten cases of this period have kept in touch with me till the present.

(c) *Third period 1970 - 1972:* During this two-year period, six cases underwent autopsychognosia sessions with Psilocybine. Only three of these have remained in contact with me.

Before I close my short introductory note, I would like to stress certain points. The reader should know that the protagonists of this book are the 16 individuals of Table 1, (p.18). Without them, nothing would have been written. Although the 16 still frequently inform me of the evolution of their subjective state, this book does not mention the therapeutic results of their autopsychognosia sessions. This conscious omission has its basis in the following conclusions at which I arrived after many years of clinical study of the 16 cases in Table 1:

(a) Every effort to measure the subjective morbid condition of the 16 with psychometric tests was condemned to total or partial failure as their mental disturbance was not a measurable physical quantity.

(b) Many points which the 16 had written with 'complete' honesty in their history before embarking on the Sessions, altered with the progression of the Sessions. Thus, a new history or histories revealed new elements (e.g. womb rejection, womb acceptance) which I could not possibly have foreseen from the psychometric tests the cases took before they began the Sessions (see answers to R10's history questionnaire, pp.4-9, 46-50).

(c) Frequent clinical examinations of the 16 (sometimes two or three daily) revealed that the quality and/or intensity of any symptom or phenomenon might present periodic variations not only from day to day and from hour to hour but even from moment to moment. In other words, evaluation of the therapeutic results on a permanent basis I found to be impossible.

Because the experiences and conclusions of the 16 cases impressed me, I publish them here in the hope that they will be a spur to further experimentation for some colleagues; that they will arouse the well-intentioned curiosity of the public which thirsts for experimental scientific findings; that they will influence some pregnant women with positive results for the foetus. I must emphasize that in Parts II and III of the book it is not my intention to generalize the cases' conclusions. If, however, such an impression is created, the blame may be laid on my faulty style of expression.

The English edition of "The Knowledge of the Womb" is divided into three parts. Part I consists of excerpts from and summaries of the histories and autopsychognosia sessions of certain cases in Table 1. Part II is mainly concerned with a general description of the subjective experiences and conclusions of the 16 cases of Table 1 during their autopsychognosia sessions. In Part III, I present my theoretical views on the clinical classification of the 16 and on the mechanism of the development of their mental disturbance. I also propound certain bioneurophysiological conclusions, some of which are based on experimental data while others are theoretical conceptions which require experimental proof.

In 1972, the year I settled in Greece, I was obliged to discontinue my clinical experimental research with LSD-25 and Psilocybine because the Greek Ministry of Public Health rejected my repeated applications for provision of these drugs. I have, however, been able to continue my research with Ketamine. I should like to point out that the cases who underwent autopsychognosia sessions with Ketamine revived intra-uterine experiences and/or experiences of expulsion-birth and reached the same general conclusions as did the 16 cases of Table 1.

The emotional experiences of a foetus, whose nervous system was stimulated by the emotions of his mother, are expressed in the pictures painted by R17 after his 8th and 13th Sessions with Ketamine (see Appendix). The emotional-intellectual interpretation of the symbolism of the paintings is given by R17 himself.

To avoid confusion or misunderstanding, I would like to point out that the meaning of many terms as given in the glossary does not correspond to the meaning given them by traditional psychiatry.

PART ONE

Excerpts from and summaries of histories and pharmaceutical autopsychognosia sessions of some cases in Table 1.

Athanassios Kafkalides MD

TABLE 1

The Cases	Sex	Age	Symptoms and Phenomena [S & P]	Intra-uterine Acceptance		Womb Rejection		Unclear Localization of Womb Rejection
				Constant	Periodical	Sub-category of Intra-uterine Rejection	Rejection of Expulsion-birth	
R1	male	33	nervous tension, neurotic S & P, psychoticlike S & P	-	+	Periodically Existentially Unwanted and Periodically Unwanted	+	-
R2	male	23	nervous tension, neurotic S & P, melancholia	-	+	Periodically Unwanted	-	-
R3	female	24	nervous tension, neurotic S & P, melancholia	+	-	-	+	-
R4	male	22	nervous tension, neurotic S & P, psychoticlike S & P	-	+	Periodically Unwanted	+	-
R5	male	21	nervous tension, neurotic S & P, melancholia	-	+	Periodically Unwanted	+	-
R6	female	20	nervous tension, neurotic S & P, psychoticlike S & P	-	-	Existentially Unwanted, Unwanted because of her Sex, Periodically Unwanted and Hereditarily Unwanted	-	-
R7	female	26	nervous tension, neurotic S & P, melancholia	-	+	-	-	+
R8	female	25	nervous tension, neurotic S & P, psychoticlike S & P	-	-	Unwanted because of her Sex	-	-
R9	male	23	nervous tension, neurotic S & P, psychoticlike S & P	-	-	Unwanted because of his Sex and Periodically Unwanted	-	-
R10	female	26	nervous tension, neurotic S & P, psychoticlike S & P	-	-	Existentially Unwanted, Unwanted because of her Sex, Periodically Unwanted and Hereditarily Unwanted	±[A]	-
R11	female	29	nervous tension, neurotic S & P, melancholia	-	-	-	-	+
R12	male	30	nervous tension, neurotic S & P, melancholia	-	+	Periodically Unwanted	+	-
R13	female	27	nervous tension, neurotic S & P, melancholia, depressivelike S & P	+	-	-	+	-

A   For interpretation of ± of R10's rejection of expulsion-birth , see § 31.

R14	female	20	nervous tension, neurotic S & P, depressivelike S & P	-	-	Existentially Unwanted	-	-
R15	female	28	nervous tension, neurotic S & P, melancholia	-	+	Periodically Unwanted	-	-
R16	female	24	nervous tension, neurotic S & P, melancholia	-	+	Periodically Unwanted because of her Sex	+	-

EXCERPTS FROM AND SUMMARIES OF R10's HISTORY AND SESSIONS

R10's ANSWERS TO THE HISTORY QUESTIONNAIRE BEFORE AUTOPSYCHOGNOSIA SESSIONS

History Female, 26 years' old, university degree, social worker, single, brother eight years' younger, state of health of parents and brother very good.

Question: What are your complaints?
Answer: Frequent periods of dizziness and great physical fatigue since childhood; insomnia and loss of appetite for the last year.

Question: Describe any pharmaceutical therapy or any other therapy you may have undergone.
Answer: I have been using cortizone ointments for severe dermatitis for many years. This allergy broke out at age 19 when, for the first time, I decided to and did overcome (consciously, at least) the terror I had always felt for exams. The allergy is exacerbated when I have metal on my skin - earrings, bracelets, necklaces and so on.

Question: What events in your life can you remember? Which of these events do you consider important? What emotions did these important events produce in you?
Answer: I remember that at age two I asked the girl next door to play with me. She refused. I felt that she didn't want to play with me because there was something wrong with me. From about that age, I can remember having a feeling of isolation. I vaguely felt that it was my lot to be left out of good things. My experiences with other neighbourhood children made me feel that I was something dark and evil that nobody wanted around. Thus, I was afraid to visit them to play or to see them in the street. I became afraid of even stepping outside the front door.

At ages six and seven I contrived certain rigid patterns for ascending and descending the stairs in our house. The most common was two steps up and one down or vice versa, depending on whether I was going up or down. I felt compelled to perform the pattern perfectly till the very end every single time I used the stairs. This compulsive behaviour drove me mad with anxiety and was exhausting.

At age seven I suddenly began to cough. The cough was very dry, harsh and aggravating. I felt that something was choking me and I had to get it out. But whatever it was, it would never come out. I could never get to the bottom of the cough. It lasted for many months.

At about that age, 7 - 8, I really began to live in a fantasy world. I daydreamed a great deal, although I don't remember clearly about what. By age nine, some of the fantasies had become sexual in content (see below).

At age seven, a feeling that had long been lurking in the background, became fully conscious - never expect anything good regarding anything at all, never get your hopes up about anything because nothing will come of it. This feeling of hopelessness or pessimism has been with me ever since.

From 11 - 17 I spent almost all of my time on school and homework - both of which I loathed with a passion - and rhythmical gymnastics. Gymnastics was not just a hobby for me: I adored it and took it very seriously. I wanted to reach the very top. I was certain, however, that I never would. Unfortunately, I had not a shred of self-confidence. This was part of the reason why, when I turned 17, I suddenly decided to stop gymnastics - a decision which I still bitterly regret.

I then began to eat a great deal and put on a lot of weight. My weight exacerbated a feeling that I had long had, but which had by now become torturous for me - the feeling that I was ugly in face and body. Other feelings which I had long had about myself also became much stronger from this period: I realized completely that I was an idiot, I lacked intelligence in academic matters and my common sense was non-existent; I felt that I was an extremely bad and selfish person and this made me feel unbearable guilt, everything I did I felt guilty for; the fears and shyness I had felt in public places (shops, buses and so on) since the age of about six also increased unbearably. In general, I felt I was rubbish, a nothing.

Since very young (about four), I have so often been tortured by the fact that I feel people around me (whether I know them or not) watch me. I feel they watch and pass judgement on me because I'm stupid, ugly, shy, strange, awkward, some sort of freak or whatever.

Answers on myself: There seems to be no contact between me and other people. Almost nothing from the external world penetrates me and what little does, I am suspicious about and have no faith in my emotional and intellectual reaction to it. The old romanticism, the faith and hope I once had in other people and things, has gone. In its place is deep cynicism and a question which has long haunted me but which now becomes even more burning: "What is true? What is real?" The answer is: "Nothing." Not even my own inner thoughts, ideas and emotions, not even myself.

Answers on my sex: I cannot call myself a woman. When someone first called me a woman at 21, I felt embarrassed because it was a lie. Since then, I've never been able to consider myself a woman. I also believe that anyone who calls me a woman doesn't know what he or she is talking about. If I ask myself what a woman is, all I can say is that it's something that I'm not. Perhaps it's because I feel that I haven't really grown up. I still feel a child.

As far as men are concerned, I feel aggressive towards them because they consider women inferior. But I also feel aggressive towards women because they are stupid. Of course I know well that men have made them so. Androcratic society has done a 'good job' of degrading women to the miserable creatures that they are.

Answers on my sexual activity: At age four I had an experience of sexual play with a boy of the same age. I was with a girl, also of the same age, when he proposed to her that they lie down on the grass and play 'grown-ups'. Since the girl refused, he then made me the same proposition. I accepted. I felt pleasure when he rubbed his genitals against mine. Then my girlfriend's older sister appeared. I suddenly felt that I had been doing something very bad. I felt very ashamed, embarrassed and afraid that she would tell my mother and father what I had done.

At the age of nine, I began to masturbate. This continued till I was 24. The masturbation was accompanied by sexual fantasies which only very slowly became explicitly sexual, for example at the age of ten the fantasy concerned a naked man and woman simply lying beside each other. (My ignorance of matters sexual, even until last year, was appalling.)

From the onset of adolescence till 24, you could say I was very puritanical. I absolutely excluded the idea of my having sex, the thought of it revolted me. In fact, I did not even feel the need for it. But if anyone else - female or male - wanted to and did make love, I could not judge them negatively, that was their business. When I was 19, I had my first kiss on the mouth. I had never permitted such a thing before. It was a terrible shock to me. The utter revulsion, the terrible guilt it caused me lasted for many months. Revulsion and guilt was a pattern to be repeated many times after that, though not always - it depended on the man, the circumstances.

At 24 I suddenly began to feel strong sexual desires and the need to satisfy them. This put me into a terrible dilemma, considering my fears and taboos concerning sex. However, after some months I did make love.

I felt pleasure but also great apprehension that the man would think me a whore. I did not reach orgasm.

As my sexual experiences increased, I found them more and more painful. The tragedy is that while on the one hand I feel the need to satisfy my sexual desires, on the other hand making love is hell. Whenever I feel my excitement increasing, my body breaks into spasms. The stronger the excitement, the more painful the spasms. Somehow I do reach orgasm with clitoral stimulation, but I cannot when the man is in me (there the pain is too great). At orgasm, the emotional and physical pain is unbearable.

In the meantime, in my everyday life, I have been suffering from insomnia, loss of appetite, and emotional numbness. These began some months after my first sexual experience and have been deteriorating since then. What caused them in the first place, at least in part, was the negative behaviour of my sexual partners towards me. On one occasion, when one ignored me, my body broke into strong, lengthy and uncontrollable spasms.

Question: Do you always understand the motives of you behaviour? If not, give a specific example.
Answer: (a) I strive to reach perfection in everything I do but I always feel I'll fail. Why do I need to be so perfect?

(b) On a few occasions, I have dared to express my desperate need to talk to someone about how terrible I feel. I especially need to talk to my mother. I want her to listen and answer with understanding and sympathy. I want her to recognize and accept the fact that I'm in a mess. I don't understand how or why her accepting this would help.

(c) I have reached a point of tremendous emotional control which does nothing but eat me up. I go into long and deep depressions which are interspersed with strong feelings of anger and aggressiveness directed I'm not sure where. I can never really express this aggressiveness, not even when I'm alone. I know I want to do something violent - smash something, tear something down - but I can't. So the feelings remain inside me, sizzling and bubbling.

Question: What do you desire most in life?
Answer: I need to be free - free of my emotions, free of my self-control, free in my thinking. I want to move, to dance freely but it seems that my mental rigidity extends to the muscles of my body.

Question: What are your ambitions?
Answer: I have none. I have said that I'm nothing. So what ambitions can I have?

Question: What are your expectations?

Answer: I once hoped I would achieve the freedoms I mentioned some day. I know now that I never will. If I broke out of my control to speak, what would I say? - that I'm stupid? - that all that I say is stupid? - that what others say is an act and/or stereotyped? I see through them and me - I see the emptiness. I expect nothing. With no hope, no faith, no patience, with this despair and desperation, what is the purpose of living? I just want to fade away.

Question: What do you fear most?

Answer: (a) Life. (b) I had always been afraid that God would punish me for being a bad person. When I turned 17 I lost all my belief or faith in the existence of God. But while I have openly denied the existence of God since then, within me I am terrified that, if He does exist, He will punish me for denying Him by sending me to hell and hell-fire.

Question: What are your other fears?

Answer: Spiders, spiders' webs, cockroaches, grasshoppers and suchlike terrify and repulse me.

Question: Describe your recreational activities.

Answer: To relax, I must drink, and a lot. So I drink, get drunk and then I can dance and sing freely. But then I crash down into a terrible depression.

Question: Are any of your dreams repeated in a stereotyped fashion?

Answer: I frequently have dreams about repulsive insects, especially spiders. The spider's very presence (in the dream) is threatening. I feel terror that whether I try to kill it or run away from it, it will strike first - it will inevitably jump on me and inject me with its poison. I wake up shuddering.

Question: What are your feelings for your mother?

Answer: I feel that my mother worries for and helps relatives and friends who have problems but she doesn't want to know about mine. I desperately needed to talk to her but when I tried she didn't want to listen. I don't think I've ever loved her.

Question: What are your feelings for your father?

Answer: I feel love and tenderness for my father although I've only just realized that I've never tried to really talk to him. It had never entered my head that I should or would.

Question: What are your feelings for your brother?

Answer: I love him very much.

Question: Your feelings about the interpersonal relations of you mother and father?

Answer: My father appreciates my mother's qualities and he loves her. My mother in one way appreciates my father's qualities, but in another way she dominates him and looks down on him. She becomes irritated and scornful when he expresses his feelings for her - and he does that often.

Question: Your feelings about the interpersonal relations of your mother and brother?

Answer: I feel that my mother oppresses my brother and that makes me sad.

Question: Your feelings about the interpersonal relations of your father and brother?

Answer: I feel that their communication is only superficial. My father is to blame for that. He can't open up.

Question: Do you feel that you have concealed anything in answering the above questions?

Answer: Not that I can think of.

Recapitulation of my problems: I feel like a vegetable, a strange vegetable which lives in pain.

Question: Do you have anything else to add?
Answer: Nothing.

R10's SESSIONS

Session 1 The Session begins with nausea and a dry, aggravating cough.

R10: I remember when I was seven, I had this same cough which lasted for many months. I was later told there was no physical basis for it. It was a nervous cough.... I remember how everyone else's problems were always bigger and more important than mine - at least that's what my friends showed me. They'd talk to me for hours about their problems and I'd keep quiet about mine and let them have their say, but this was not reciprocated. They were not prepared to listen to me. They took advantage of me. (A sudden rush of strong feelings makes her cry out and burst into tears.) ...

Doctor: What is it? What do you feel?

R10: ... I don't know ... I just feel it's something horrible I saw, but I don't know what ... (crying continues) ... I have cried like this many times before because I'd be in agony. I wanted someone to see me to know what I was going through. But I'd always hide it. I had to. Why? I keep feeling who cares anyway? ... (sarcastic laugh) ... I laugh because I'm ludicrous

... I often get very depressed and I used to cry a lot ... (silence) ... I can't live up to what others and I expect of myself. I set very high intellectual standards which are impossible to reach.

Doctor: Why should you be so clever?

R10: I don't know why. But I have always striven for it. I can't reach it. It's like there's a solid wall around me that restricts me, a wall I can't get out of because it's there ... (She presents strong, painful contractions of the abdominal muscles which oblige her to curl up.) ... I want to break through that wall.

Doctor: Who put the wall there?

R10: I suppose my mother did. (This is not said with much conviction.) ... I have to endure these restrictions, to endure everything, just endurance, always endurance. I'm tired of enduring ...

Doctor: Who obliges you to endure everything?

R10: I do. Because I'm always told I have no patience and have a bad temper.

Doctor: Who told you that?

R10: My parents. I have a bad temper and I explode, so I have to control it ... (the muscular contractions reappear) ... I can't stop these convulsions. They make me tired. Something must have happened to me, but I don't know how and when. It's ridiculous having my legs curled up like this. I'm very restricted. It gives me cramps. I want to stretch my legs, but I can't. The blankets restrict me too ... (silence) ... People - my mother, relatives, friends - were always complimenting me, telling me I was something when I knew I was nothing. Why tell me I'm clever when I'm not? I'm tired of saying the same old rubbish. I don't get anywhere in saying I'm not clever. It doesn't untie me. They put the restrictions on me by telling me those things. I wasn't that person they wanted me to be. I wasn't clever enough to be what they wanted me to be. I didn't dare tell them because they didn't want to hear that. They helped make matters worse. I am a perfectionist but my perfectionism stops me from being a perfectionist. It makes me go round in circles. All that terrible studying helped me get my degree. For my parents, that was nice. What a joke! They didn't realize what a failure I felt. I was judged by the system That doesn't say much for me and I was so aware of it. I can't lie like that ... Doctor, I feel such responsibility for wasting your time. I don't like imposing myself on people because I'm afraid they'll reject me ...

Doctor: Have you been rejected?

R10: Yes, by many people. It doesn't take much. People were always bringing up their own problems and I have a good listening ear. But they never sensed my need to speak. My mother didn't listen. I had so many problems, I was so mixed up but she wouldn't accept this. She didn't see the reason for it. She just didn't want to know, so she closed her eyes.

R10's thoughts after Session 1: In this Session I did not learn much that was new about myself. I was, however, able to express feelings I had either not been able to express at all before, or not been able to express so clearly.
Concerning rejection: People don't want me around for much because I am a bad person, bad-tempered and moody, selfish, stupid and boring. I don't like to impose on people's time because I'm afraid they'll see how I am and will want to get rid of me. I can't flatter myself that people really care for me as I am.

Session 2 The Session begins with very strong contractions of the abdominal muscles which oblige R10 to curl up. Periodically she presents a dry, aggravating cough. During this Session, R10 vividly revives her obsessional behaviour on the stairs of her house when she was a child (see History p. 21). There is a virtual absence of emotion in this Session which is practically a repetition of the first (signs of strong resistance).

Session 3 The Session begins with very strong contractions of the abdominal muscles and a dry, aggravating cough which is repeated periodically.
R10: I can see an enormous hawk hovering threateningly over a small, helpless chicken embryo which is trying to run and hide from the hawk. The hawk won't leave me alone, its shadow is always over me, its claws are outstretched, threatening. My mother wouldn't leave me alone. She'd impose her ideas on me and I'd listen and be affected but also frustrated because often I felt that it wasn't the way she said it was. I saw a situation differently. I got frustrated because I didn't dare contradict her and because I couldn't express myself anyway. How I hate hypocrisy! Just because someone is in a position of power, being older, stronger, bigger, the parent, he thinks he can impose on the child, ignoring its needs, as if the child is not an individual too. My mother is an hypocrite ... (silence) ...
... I feel you're wasting your time, Doctor. I don't want to impose myself on others because of my insignificance in their eyes. Any other person is more significant than I am. When I tried to talk, nobody listened. I needed to be heard ...
R10 then sees the following image: Although the doctor remains beside me, I imagine that he leaves the room, abandoning me, and that I get up from the couch and quickly slam the door on him before he can

close it on me. (Symbolism: R10 rejects the doctor before he can reject her.) Almost simultaneously, I see myself crouched alternately in a tiny cave and an egg-shell. (First momentary revival of R10's intra-uterine life which was caused by the doctor's imaginary rejection of her. After the Session, R10 rejected this intellectual interpretation put forward by the doctor. Despite the fact that during the 4th, 5th, 11th and 12th Sessions R10 also relived intra-uterine rejection, after these sessions she could not accept that the experiences were real. It was the 13th Session which permanently convinced her that her intra-uterine rejection was a real experience.)

Session 4   R10: I remember my mother telling me that she had financial difficulties before and after her wedding. I feel that deep down she didn't really accept her marriage, nor did she want children ... (R10 suddenly presents violent and painful contractions of the abdominal muscles which oblige her to curl up.) ... I feel rejected. I see a flash of a foetus in the uterus. I feel that I'm that foetus ... (long silence) ... I feel very sensitive, everything affects me. I feel rejection at the slightest thing, the most insignificant word, the most insignificant event. The rejection makes me feel insignificant, rubbish. I built a wall against this rejection, an impenetrable, strong wall of steel or concrete. I am alone. I have a strong need to share - especially music, gym and relationships with people. But I can't share anything because of the wall. So everything turns in on myself. I keep going round in a vicious circle behind my wall. I'm all alone, for and to myself.

R10's thoughts after Session 4: Although for a fraction of a second I felt rejection from the womb in the Session, although I felt I was reliving something that had actually happened to me, this feeling has not remained with me. I do not and cannot fully accept or believe it now. I cannot trust what I said in the Session.

Doctor's observation: The fourth Session is characterized by a slight diminuation in R10's resistance to reliving unconscious states.

Session 5 Throughout this entire Session, the dry, aggravating cough alternates with painful contractions of the abdominal muscles.

R10: I know and feel that I wasn't meant to exist. I was meant to be a nothing, a void. This is why I feel I'm nothing, insignificant, strange and aloof, and people sense this. Every single cell in my body has and eye and a mind of its own telling me I'm nothing. My mother didn't want me, nor the sexual act which produced me. Yet I ended up being born. How I hate her for not wanting me! What a farce! She didn't want

The Knowledge of the Womb

me and she got a live baby on her hands. What a cold woman. I don't remember her ever as a positive, warm force. I don't think she's ever had emotions. She has such fantastic control. She passed her great control of her emotions onto me. My self-control blocks me from expressing my feelings and communicating with people. I hated her and I hated school because education was the thing she held dear. I spent hours and hours studying because I would procrastinate. My procrastination really used to irritate her. That was my revenge on her, the only way I could punish her. I realize now that even the fact that I stopped gym was to punish her. How I hated her and how I hated her orders! But I obeyed all her orders ... I have an image of the blood circulatory systems of two persons being intertwined. The image is powerful and awesome. The blood of the one person mixes with the blood of the other. I felt a part of her. We were part of each other. I understand now very clearly why she has affected me greatly throughout my life, why I have obeyed her orders. I cannot forget such a powerful influence as that. (R10 means the intra-uterine influence.) I feel guilty when I don't obey the orders ... What a life!! Life is a farce. It stinks. Why do I live? Nothing is true. Actions and thoughts are acts. Everyone acts. This falsity of life always preoccupies me - from big-game politics to interpersonal relations ...

R10's thoughts after Session 5: In the first Session, I said that I wanted to get beyond the restrictions, be free of them. The restrictions are the womb. The solid wall around me, which I mentioned in the fourth Session, is the womb even though I had said then that I built a wall. I can still only half-believe most things I've said in the Session so far. As for the thoughts I noted above and after the previous Sessions, I have the feeling that they all sound rather stupid. Perhaps the only thing I really do believe is the feeling that I'm trapped permanently behind a wall which surrounds me.

Session 6 Strong nausea. Strong contractions of the abdominal muscles. R10 makes the same complaints as in past Sessions about her mother's coldness. She gives the impression that she is not allowing the Session to evolve.
Doctor: You have said that your mother was a cold figure. What about your father?
R10: What about him? There's nothing much to say[6] except that he showered me with warmth and love. But I didn't deserve such great love because I was nothing. So I would hurt him purposely to show him I

---

6   Doctor's note: R10's words here show severe repression of her fixation to her father.

didn't deserve it. He needed to pour love onto me because my mother was cold to him. I was his outlet.

Doctor: What sort of relationship did your mother have with your father?

R10: I can't explain Mother's relationship with Father. I can't think of the two together. I don't want to think of the two together ... I felt my father holding me in his arms when I was a very small baby. I felt his warmth, his tenderness, his power, and sex vibrations that were coming out of him and flowing through me. I became sexually aroused. But this is all wrong. It's not morally right. He's my father. My arousal needed gratification. I feel that that's where the masturbation stemmed from. But this was wrong also, not allowed. I always masturbated while having the fantasy of two unknown people - unknown to me - having sex. I feel I could never be a sex object. I am not sexy. No man would want me ... (silence) ...

Doctor: Why?

R10: I suppose because I was not and should not have been a sex object for my father. (After the Session, R10 explains that this was an intellectual, not emotional, interpretation.) I've talked about my control which makes me seem cool, aloof. But I have and have had very strong emotions. Emotions which I have felt since I was very young I came to feel were not right and had to be controlled. I was somehow made to feel shame or guilt for them, ludicrous ...

R10's thoughts after Session 6: In this Session I became aware of unconscious sexual desires for my father. I feel that the unknown woman in my sex fantasies symbolized me while the unknown man symbolized my father. But why were the two people making love in the fantasies unknown to me? - because I considered everything in terms of myself, and I knew my father. Because it was wrong, perhaps prohibited, to want to make love with my father, the man in the fantasy had to be unknown to me - repression of my desires for my father. But the fact that the woman in the fantasy could not be me, the fact that she too had to be unknown to me, shows severe repression.

Session 7 During this Session R10 revives an experience she had at the age of six.

R10: ... I'm at home, alone in the house. I'm sitting near the top of the stairs. I hear someone coming though the house. It's a neighbour of ours and he's drunk. He comes up the stairs. His breathing is heavy. He sits down and makes me caress his genitals. I feel pleasure, excitement, revulsion and shame. I'm afraid that my parents will suddenly appear and see what I'm doing. I feel that the compulsive acts on the stairs (mentioned in the History, p. 4) began after this experience with the man. The shame I feel because of my desire for the drunken man symbolizes the original shame I felt for wanting my father. I also feel shame because I'm betraying my father ... (silence) ...

Doctor: What do the patterns on the stairs - the two up and one down - symbolize?

R10: Two testicles and a penis ... My hand is becoming smaller. It feels like the hand of a very small baby, very sensitive and weak. This hand is being pulled away from something and smacked ... (She then clenches her fist so hard that the doctor hears the squeaking noise.) ... (silence) ...

Doctor: What's happening?

R10: I'm squeezing something very hard, as hard as I can ... (silence) ...

Doctor: What's that?

R10: It's my father's penis. This is my revenge because I couldn't have it, and it's punishment for the shame he made me feel ... (From this point on R10 resists by speaking of irrelevant matters.)

Session 8   R10:   ... At orgasm, I expose myself physically and emotionally. I'm exposed as if by a flash of light where the man suddenly realizes my feelings for him and he can then use this against me. He could dominate me absolutely and I can't allow this because of the emotional pain he'd cause me. He'd ignore my feelings, step on them and have me only for sex ... (silence) ...

Doctor: What are you thinking of?

R10: ... My mother was cool, calm, logical, perceptive, far-seeing, assessing the end result of things whereas my father didn't so much. He was hot-headed and emotional, he was guided by his emotions. My father appreciated my mother's qualities and cared for her very much ... I have an image of them, close to each other, looking at each other. I can see the look in my father's eyes - it's full of devotion, adoration. I was ludicrous in my desire for him because the feeling was only one-way. And I felt helpless because of the way he felt for my mother and because I was too small. I would have liked to have replaced my mother in that image, to have him look at me as he looked at her - with warmth, tenderness, love and desire in his eyes, which would lead to making love. But to replace her was impossible, ridiculous, and I was left feeling ludicrous in my strong arousal which wasn't meant to be seen, but it was ... (silence) ... As a small baby, I was caught aroused by a sudden flash of light. I was masturbating in the darkness and suddenly the light was turned on. I felt terribly ashamed and guilty and ridiculous because I was exposed, I thought they'd know why I was so aroused. My mother made me feel that it was very bad to masturbate. But it was even worse that I was masturbating out of strong desire for my father ...

R10's thoughts after Session 8: Orgasm exposes my strong feelings for my father which are morally wrong, not allowed, making me feel guilty and ludicrous. It seems that the small, weak and sensitive hand (mentioned in Session 7) which was pulled away and slapped was the hand that masturbated and was slapped by my mother.

Session 9   R10: ... Right now, I feel I would like to do gym as a man, to do his steps and movements with the muscles, the power and the strength that go into them. I feel mannish in the legs. They feel very big and muscley. I just don't know what I am. I could almost be a man. I hate this feeling. It frightens me. Maybe that's why in gym I couldn't express the lyricism, the femininity I loved and wanted to express so much. I had it inside me but it couldn't come out. (R10's bipolar desires - on the one hand to do gymnastics as a man and on the other as a woman - reveal for the first time unconscious confusion concerning her sex identity.) I could only 'express' powerful, manly movements. I had fantastic power for them because my legs had become so huge and muscley. But at the same time, my legs gave me a huge complex. I never want to have legs like that again. This is one big reason why I don't want to return to gym. (R10 is strict with her diet. So she loses weight and the dimensions of her legs decrease.)

I feel I am mannish in other ways too - in the way I dance various folk dances, in the way I walk, the way I sit. I was mannish in my being domineering in my childhood, thinking I was the only one who could do things properly and taking over. I am mannish when I stand up for myself, I don't like to be fooled. What's femininity? Helplessness? Prissy-prissy stuff? I can't stand those things!   I must do! act! ... I can understand why it would be nice to be a man - I'd have someone to care for me as much as I cared for my father. By being a man I'd be wanted, very much. (See also Session 12 where her mother wanted her to be a boy.) ... (silence) ... Often I feel I have no feelings. I feel that I was born cold of a cold woman, as if she gave birth to a stone, and that around this cold stone feelings are arbitrarily added. This is a problem when confronting society because the role of the human is to have feelings, and I feel society would scorn me for

The Knowledge of the Womb

not being human. Coldness to me means asexuality because I don't have the feelings appropriate to either sex.

Session 10 R10 begins by recounting a dream she had had three nights before this Session.

R10: In the dream I see my brother at about age one. He can walk and he has long locks. My brother is being forced to approach a female singer. The singer is well-known for being butch and, normally, she looks it with her mannish attire and short cropped hair. In this dream, however, her hair is shoulder-length and styled, she is wearing make-up and a long gown. She is trying very hard to be charming and feminine. (The dream then becomes confused and R10 does not remember what follows.) ...

Doctor: Do you identify with anyone in this dream?

R10: Yes, with my brother[7] ...(silence) ... I feel like a man. My chest is broad and muscley. I feel strange in the genitals - a horrible, horrible feeling ... (She starts to resist by talking around the subject and the Session ceases to evolve. Only towards the end does she allow the drug to take its effect.) ... I feel strange pressures in my breasts. I remember when I was at home I was shy of myself and couldn't look at myself naked in the mirror. It was somehow wrong that I should have breasts, I should cover them. I vaguely feel that it's morally wrong to have breasts. Having breasts means they'll be touched and that means sex. They're flesh and flesh means physical contact, sex. Having them means I'm a woman and I shouldn't be ... The pressures make me feel that my breasts are disappearing. I'm flat-chested ... There's a split in my feeling like a boy. First, I feel like a boy in having a flat chest. Second, ... I don't know. This is all very confusing. I can't grasp what's going on, what it means and why ...

Session 11 The Session begins with the dry, harsh cough.

R10: I remember now that my cough at seven was when my mother was pregnant with my brother. But what were the reasons for it? ... (contractions of the abdominal muscles begin) ... I want to smash something but I'm too weak to. I'm such a nothing, it doesn't matter if I pursue the road to self-destruction. It's my fate and I am my own witch. I'm not worth it as a human being. I want to turn my back on my parents to complete my

---

[7] R10's note: Why didn't I mention in the Session something which is so obvious? I not only identify with my brother in the dream, but also with the female singer who in reality looks like a man, but in the dream was trying hard to look like a woman. There is strong identification there. (Realization made a few days after the Session).

self-destruction ... I see strange patterns on the wall. I don't want to look at them. They're somehow coming out of the wall, threatening ... (She tries to avoid the patterns by closing her eyes. The doctor tries to coax her to look at them.) ... I see a spider's web and now three big spiders in it. The whole thing revolts me. The web alone terrifies me. To be caught in it, with a spider waiting at one end to catch me - ugh! And the spider on its own repulses me. It will inevitably attack me. Its legs are phallic symbols which insert poison into my body ... (Again she begins to resist. Again the doctor coaxes her to express what she sees.) ... I can see eyes in the web looking at me ... I see geometrical patterns, intricate, but cold and calculated. I don't like things that are cold and calculated. They coldly calculate whatever they want ...

Doctor: Can you give an example of this?

R10: My mother discarded me, rejected me. That was calculation on her behalf. I'm not very sure about that though ... (silence) ...

Doctor: Try and return to the period of rejection.

R10: How can I do that? I can't.

Doctor: Try, for example, by thinking about the convulsions when they appear. What causes them?

R10: ... It must have been claustrophobic in there. I was forced to lie in a certain position and I hated being small surrounded by something enormous which was commanding me against my will. What was this thing against my will that I hated so much? Why am I resisting so much when I feel that this will give me the answer to my feelings of not being human, of nothingness, and of feeling like a boy? My hatred was so strong but I was not able to do anything about it, being so restricted. If I could have torn at the walls of the uterus, I would have. This feeling is exactly like the feeling I've had all my life of wanting to explode, to give vent to my aggressiveness, but not being able to ...

R10's realization after Session 11: One form of resistance in this and the last Sessions has been consciously to control the convulsions by lying on my stomach. In this position, the convulsive movements which normally throw the upper and lower halves of my body forward are greatly hampered. (See development in Session 12.)

Session 12 R10: These strong convulsions are drawing me into the foetal position, in the womb. I'm crying because they're putting me into a position where my mother didn't want me. I feel so bewildered and hurt. Why shouldn't she want me? Ether - I can smell it. It's in my throat, being pushed against my nose, makes me feel so sick, so nauseous. I'm helpless, can't push it away. It's something inevitable I can't do anything about. My legs are paralyzed. (At this point her legs are extended.) I can't draw them into the foetal position even though I know that's where I'll find the answers to my nothingness and my feeling a boy ... (silence) ...

Doctor: Are you paralyzing your legs so that you won't take the foetal position, perhaps?
R10: Yes. I was just thinking the same thing.
Doctor: Flex your legs.
R10: (As she flexes her legs, she sees a horrible image and bursts into tears.) ... Oh no! No! ... The image is of a baby curled up in the womb with big, muscley bottom and thighs. The image is grotesque. The baby looks like a satyr. There was supposed to be a boy in that womb. My legs, especially my thighs, feel huge and muscley. Huge, muscley thighs surrounding a penis. I am a boy ... (silence) ...
Doctor: Try to understand why you feel a boy.
R10: That's what I was meant to be. Every message coming into me from my mother was telling me to be a boy. If she'd known there was a girl in there, she would have willed me to change into a boy.
Doctor: It was an order?
R10: Yes, a very strong will. It's like the ether, it controls you and you're helpless, can't get away from it ... (silence) ...
Doctor: Why should you worry that you're a girl and she wanted a boy?
R10: She wouldn't treat me properly if I were a girl. She'd be disappointed and I'd be nothing in her eyes. She wouldn't treat me as a human being. Her will, her wish, her desire was so strong for a boy, so positive for a boy, that as a girl I was negative. I wasn't wanted as a girl at all because she wanted a boy. I wasn't even a human being, as it was a human being - something living - that was in the uterus, but that living being was supposed to be a boy. So I was negative and I was nothing. I was terrified my mother would realize I was a girl. I wasn't meant to exist, I wasn't meant to be living, so I wasn't meant to feel. That's why in everyday life I become cold, numb, I have no feelings, I'm non-human, I cease to exist ... (silence) ...
Doctor: You say that when you reach orgasm through clitoral stimulation, you also become numb. What does orgasm symbolize for you?
R10: When I have an orgasm, it means that I'm female, that I'm a human being - something that my mother doesn't want ... (long silence) ... I don't want to speak ...

Doctor: You've said that you wanted to talk to your mother but she wouldn't listen, she paid no attention.

R10: This is symbolic. I wanted to tell her I was a girl, not the boy she wanted. And I couldn't talk to my father as a girl and tell him I wanted him ... My mother was always telling me what to say, what to do, which is telling me what to be. What a bitch!

R10's thoughts after Session 12: In this Session I was able to make what I think are important discoveries because my resistance was considerably less than in previous Sessions. I feel, however, that there was some control. I made a conscious effort to stop my crying and I controlled my aggressiveness towards my mother.

Session 13 R10: ... I know some interfering, domineering mothers. I identify with their oppressed children. The mothers are my mother. I'm very angry with my mother. She could see she had an obviously troubled child and she didn't do anything about it. She'd never try to talk to me about it, never asked me, never tried to help. She didn't want to know or accept I was troubled, mixed up. And I always had to act and think as she wanted. Never any discussions. If I dared make any remarks that clashed with her thinking, I was told I was absolutely wrong and not to be so stupid; she knew what was right. Who told her she was a god? ...

I don't want to be my mother's child. Our relationship, with its authority, discipline, distance and injustice, was the same as in a school. No, I don't want that kind of relationship, I don't want her to be my mother. It's just too incongruous. (As she says this, she feels the muscular contractions beginning and becoming stronger and stronger. She has absolutely no control over her body. The convulsion draw her, by sharp contractions in the ribs and belly, into the foetal position; then sharp, jerking movements in the bottom and thighs thrust them up and out so that she arches back. Her whole body is in pain) ... This is like being in hell, in hell-fire ... This continuous pain is unbearable. I'm trying to ease it by telling myself it's not so bad, but it's always there! ... It had to be endured ... endurance ... endurance ... It's driving me crazy ... Can't stand it ... Bitch!! ... Can't think, I'm in such agony ... And this is how it's always been ... This pain has always been there, all those years, now. I'm exactly the same now as I was then ... I haven't left my mother ... She's still around me ... permeating me physically and mentally ... in every molecule. I hate her! I could just tear her womb out, scratch it away! (She makes furious scratching movements at the air.) ...

The Knowledge of the Womb

This pressure which is making me act like this, which is all around me, is so big and powerful and oppressive, it's as if it's beyond human proportions ... It's like some great, heavy, oppressive ghost or power ... I can feel it. I can almost see it in all the air in the room ... My mother's will was a tremendous power in itself ... I feel weak, despondent, hopeless. It's as if I'm having a conversation with my mother: "So you're in pain? Why? So what?" "But I'm in pain." "But you aren't a boy." So I'm not a boy and haven't the right to be in pain. If I'd been a boy and in pain, there would have been justification to complain and ask for sympathy. But I was a girl, so I had no right to suffer because only boys have rights. Being a girl I was nothing, not a human being, so it was even more illogical to say I 'suffered' because, being nothing, I couldn't feel. An unreal situation in which a non-entity was feeling nothing. This is why I don't deserve sympathy and why it's unrealistic to give it to me ...

R10's thoughts after Session 13: In this Session, my resistance was much less and on the whole I was able to go wherever the drug took me. This was the first Session in which I gave full vent to my aggressiveness towards my mother. Another important factor for me is that this Session finally drove home the point that I was supposed to be a boy. Session 12 almost convinced me, but I was still left with the feeling that my intelligent mother could not have been so stupid and so old-fashioned in wanting her first-born to be a boy. In everyday life the aggressiveness I feel, which reaches a point where I want to explode, is because my mother's will was for a boy. I couldn't explode with fury in reaction to the womb's pressure on me because I was inside it and too small and weak. I had repressed the memory of the awful experience in the womb, but the aggressiveness, unfulfilled and seemingly without direction, remained within me in my life thereafter.

It's very clear now why my mother affects me so greatly till this day. Actually, I've never left her, I'm within her, she is still around me, through me, permeating my mind and body, torturing me as she did then, without trace of mercy.

Session 14 At the beginning of this Session R10 presents resistance each time her unconscious feelings for her father tend to become conscious. Towards the end of the Session, she realizes more clearly than in past Sessions how fixated she is to her father and how indifferent she thinks he is towards her. She also realizes more fully the degree of and reasons for the guilt she felt (and feels) for her sexual desires for her father which were expressed through masturbation.

R10: The aggravating cough I had when I was seven symbolized (a) a protest against my mother being a mother, (b) an attempt to tell her I'm a girl, (c) identification with my mother so that I could cough out the new baby in her womb, (d) an attempt to spit out all the aggressiveness I felt towards her.

Session 15 The Session begins with muscular contractions which pull R10 up into the sitting position. This makes her wonder, because in previous Sessions the muscular contractions had obliged her to assume the foetal position. When she tries, out of curiosity, to curl up, the muscular contractions again force her to sit up. For R10's interpretation of this muscular activity, (see p.37.)
R10: (anxiety) My legs feel aroused, aroused but helpless ... (silence) ...
Doctor: Aroused sexually?
R10: Yes. Just before, I felt very aroused in the genitals. Now that arousal has gone down to my legs ... (silence) ...
Doctor: What does arousal of the legs mean?
R10: It's a sort of tension, a tension that they want to act, to move, but they won't ... They're not allowed to move. Something is stopping them ... (anxiety increases, she begins to cry out) ... (silence) ...
Doctor: What is it? What do you feel?
R10: I don't know ... pain. There's such pressure in my bottom - I'm pulling it so hard together. When I was young, I'd do the same thing - I'd hold everything in tight to stop myself from shitting. I also remember bashing my head against walls when I was young, trying to run through them. I feel like putting my head through the wall now (the wall beside the couch) ... (silence) ...
Doctor: What was the purpose of trying to run through walls?
R10: To get through something ... I'm scared ... (silence) ...
Doctor: What are you afraid of?
R10: (anxiety increases) ... There's something ... a big power ... (cries) ... I think I'm small and I think it's something big and I think I'm going to be punished ... I'm not in the womb ... I really would like to bash my head through the wall. (She knocks her head against the wall very hard.)
Doctor: What does the wall symbolize?
R10: My mother's womb ... (Anxiety increases strongly. The cries become screams of absolute terror. She moves about restlessly on the couch trying to find some way to hide from whatever it is that is causing her terror. She covers her head with her hands screaming, "Oh no!" Finally, a vision appears before her eyes:) A horrible creature ... I see a creature ... He's going to attack me ... He's so ugly ... He's looming over

me with a fierce look on his face ... arms outstretched threateningly ... His face is white like a mask ... his eyes green ... hair thin and white, sticking out tattily all over his head ... He's wearing a green robe which fades into the air ... He's a green monster ... (silence) ... I'm afraid ...

Doctor: Afraid of what?

R10: I don't know ... I feel really cheap ... I'm aroused ... I feel like a prostitute. I feel as if I'm dressed and painted like a prostitute ... I feel ashamed ... Somebody aroused me sexually and I responded. Then he just abandoned me scornfully and made me feel cheap for having the feelings I'd shown him ... I remember my relationship with the first man I had sex with. He humiliated, degraded me, treated me with contempt. All men treat women like that ... (silence) ...

Doctor: Who was the first to behave this way?

R10: My bastard father ... I hate him ... He was cold towards me ... I feel very cold towards him too, that'll show him. He plays his little game. We must all play our little games, mustn't we. My legs hurt, they're closed so tight ... (silence) ...

Doctor: That means?

R10: They'll never open to anybody. I can be just as cold and just as cruel as he towards me ... I'll put a knife in my father, and mother. I hate them. I'll do everything I can to hurt them, to make them squirm and feel pain, everything I can ... I had a dream last night that my mother was dead (hysterical laughter) ... She looked like the green creature - her face was white, her hair white and untidy. She wasn't dead but she looked it. She was in cobwebs and she looked like a witch. Further away my friend and I were making love. I was terrified that my mother would wake up and see I was making love. My friend's hair was combed in the style of my father's. I have just realized that my friend is a father substitute. That depresses me. I won't and don't accept it ... From the waist down I feel like a dummy, like those plastic mannequins they have in shop windows. Where the thighs join, there aren't any genitals. That means I'm cold, asexual. When I hold my bottom in tight, it makes my thighs stick together. By doing this, I make sure I keep all my desire inside, not allowing it to come out, to be shown ... (silence) ...

Doctor: Desire for?

R10: My father. That has something to do with running through walls when I was two ... My desire for sex makes me feel insane. The arousal makes my mind cancerous, it makes me crazy, sick. I just don't feel as if I'm normal. After masturbating, I felt I had cancer in the brain. My mother had told me that people who masturbate get cancer in the brain, and I thought I had it. I really felt I was going crazy. The cancer makes you feel aware of your guilt - guilt because the arousal stemmed from my father ... (long silence) ... (crying) ... I feel helpless ... and I really need comfort ... I want my father to hold my head, to hold it and rock it. My crying is numbed, my whole body is numbed now. I just want to sleep. I want to forget. I want to forget the feeling of sexual desire for my father, but it doesn't work, the feeling is still there. It feels like a volcano. I feel pressure in the genitals and there are internal pressures which tear my emotions apart, which shake my whole body, violently. I'm like a volcano that's never allowed to burst ... I don't recognize my father now. He's become ugly, distorted, bigger. He fades into the ghost region. He's become the green creature, just like my mother. My father doesn't even seem to have genitals. But I remember that he does have genitals ... (silence) ...

Doctor: How do you remember that?

R10: I saw him. That has something to do with my trying to run through walls when I was young ... (silence) ...

Doctor: You saw him? You saw his genitals?

R10: Yes. I walked into the bathroom while he was having a shower ... (silence) ...

Doctor: On purpose?

R10: No. I didn't think there was anyone in the bathroom ... (silence) ...

Doctor: How old were you?

R10: I was two.

Doctor: Was your mother there too?

R10: No, just my father standing up having a shower. I remember how big his genitals seemed to me ... I can see that green monster again. The look in his eyes, I feel it in my eyes too, that nasty, cruel look of evil intent ... (silence) ... My father's genitals are flesh. Flesh disgusts me. It's like they're not human. And they're conspicuous, something that can't be hidden. A man standing naked just can't hide his genitals no matter what he does. It's like a vulnerable point ... Now my father has become a plastic dummy without genitals. I can see the green creature. He's small now. He's evil. He is the penis ... (For some time, R10's words seem to have no clear emotional content.) ...

Again I see my father as a plastic dummy. Everything is so distorted, so gross. My mother's hand is in this image now. It's as if she grabs my father's penis, she takes it and she does what she likes with it: she squeezes it, she gets rid of it. She controls the penis, she abuses it. Just by having it she's abusing it, letting it go to waste. It should be me who has it. I'd know how to use it properly - through my physical need and emotional attachment. I think that by hanging onto the penis, it's just a way of hanging onto an emotional attachment, because physical desire and emotional attachment go together. But the arousal and emotional attachment I had for my father wasn't returned and so I felt the pain of rejection. Any penis reminds me of that pain. My desire is ludicrous because it's revealed ...Yes, I touched my father. That's why I feel cheap. I think I put my hand on his penis, on his trousers, of course. That's forbidden territory. To my touch it felt big, full ... Maybe my father ... I don't know. I don't know. (angrily) I don't know ... (silence) ...

Doctor: Why do you feel upset now?

R10: Because I feel like an idiot talking about the penis all the time. How can I say that my father had an erection? It sounds like a fantastic thing, doesn't it? I don't know if it was fantasy or reality. When the penis is erect, it's ready to attack, it's so agile and quick and strong. It makes me want to run away. It hurts me. It's evil because it hurts me. It hurts me because it doesn't have feelings ... (silence) ... My father doesn't have feelings for me ... (There follows a long series of thoughts which give the impression that R10 is going round in circles without reaching any conclusion - a clear indication of resistance.) ...

... My mother caught me once when I was masturbating. I felt that she realized my desire for my father and she punished me ferociously. But that's not the only reason why my mother terrifies me. She's a superpower. She's the hawk. She threatens my existence. My mother is the green womb around me. (The green womb is associated with the green creature.) She consumes me, distorts me, dissolves me. I disintegrate in there. I'm sick, mentally sick, warped, I mean not sane. I don't know what I am. I lose my inner equilibrium ... (Again R10 goes round in circles - resistance.) ...

Before orgasm I feel physical excitement and emotional pain. I try to escape from this by not concentrating on the genital area. But when I tell myself not to escape and I push myself to concentrate on the genital area and the excitement, that's when I reach a point of unbearable pain, of terror for myself. I feel I'm going to disintegrate. I feel trapped (anxiety increases) ... I disintegrate as a person. The destruction, the distortion that comes with orgasm is a distortion of every form of my very being. Orgasm is a threat to my life. It's the green creature, which symbolizes anything to do with sex. Orgasm takes me back to the womb. That's how I feel it. It means going back to the womb because both threaten my existence ... Orgasm exposes me and also my sick feelings to my sexual partner, the feelings of the volcano which should never be revealed. I should never expose my physical or emotional desires.

Doctor: Does the exposure of you physical and emotional desires mean that you're a woman and that you need sex?

R10: I don't accept that, that I'm a woman and I need sex ... (silence) ... I can see myself aged two running up to touch my father's penis and that I'm pushed away. He pushed me away like a fly. He made me dissolve, he made me feel like a shit. His rejection made me feel disintegrated, just as I felt in the womb. That's why my father is also the green creature ... And I'm the green creature because I'm evil too. I kill my mother and father. I kill my father because even though I'd said that I'd never open my legs to any man, I have opened them, I have had sex. So I betrayed my father. And I kill my mother by taking my father away from her in the form of my friend. (See dream, p.34-35) ...

When I reach orgasm with clitoral stimulation, it consumes my whole body emotionally and physically - just like being in the womb. It's like a shattering of my very being. My whole body shakes violently with the same convulsions I had in the womb when I was receiving the rejecting messages from my mother. Orgasm with penetration of the penis into my vagina - with my father's green penis - would make me experience double rejection. That's why I can't reach orgasm when the man is in me.

R10's conclusions from Session 15: What was the significance of the convulsions drawing me into a sitting position at the beginning of the Session? I mentioned then that I was not in the womb because of this position. There are two answers to the question.

Firstly, I was resisting returning to the womb or I was already in it and wouldn't accept it. When I felt great anxiety at the big power, I said I was not in the womb and yet a few seconds later I said I wanted to break through the walls of the womb. Also, the words 'power' and 'superpower' which I use in the Sessions, always refer to the womb.

Secondly, in this Session, I spoke in detail about my sexual problem with my father which obviously began after my birth, when I could sit, or at least try to. The convulsions which drew me into a sitting position symbolized the paternal rejection whereas the convulsions which draw me into the foetal position symbolize my intra-uterine rejection.

This was the first Session in which I felt terror of the womb. The feeling that I am a plastic dummy is a defence against my very strong (volcanic) desires for my father which I must never reveal because he rejected me. Saying that I'm not a woman and that I don't need sex is a defence against the inevitable paternal rejection. As well, my mother rejected me as a female. Thus I haven't the right to feel anything, especially sexual desires. My sexual desires make me feel insane, sick, distorted, cancerous, both because I had already felt insane, sick, distorted from the womb, and because my mother told me that masturbation (sexual desire for Father) causes cancer in the brain.

Another problem concerning my sexual desires is that they make me feel cheap, a whore, both as a result of my mother's punishing me for masturbating and my father's abrupt rejection of my sexual approach to him. When I was two, I saw my father in the shower. Later, I tried to touch his penis, thinking that he had an erection. My father rejected me and this rejection was associated with my rejection in the womb from which I tried to break out by trying to run through walls which symbolized the walls of the womb.

Interpretation of the dream mentioned in Session 15: I was afraid that my mother would wake up and see that I was making love with my father, in the form of a father substitute, and that I was taking him away from her. As well, I was afraid she'd see that I was a female because I was making love as a female.

Session 16 R10: I feel great fear. I don't know why. I have to calm down because with the fear I can't think, I have no control over myself. From the last Session I know that the cause of the fear is the green creature which symbolizes many things including sex and punishment. The fear of sex comes from the fear of punishment, punishment by my mother. She's going to make me feel terrified of having any sexual arousal. It's not supposed to exist. I have to stamp it out. When she caught me masturbating she made me feel terrible ... I'm not expressing what I want to say. I can't talk. That often happens to me. Many times I want to say things but they don't come out, I get stuck, my tongue gets tied. It reminds me of times when I feel very excited in sex and I want to pull the man's hair, dig my fingers into him, but I can't. I can't seem to move. So all the tension remains within me. It just goes round and round inside me. It doesn't come out anywhere - through my hands, my mouth ... I'm afraid ... I'm afraid of being a man ...

Doctor: Why should you be a man and how can you be a man?

R10: ... (silence ... Instead of answering, she asks to go to the toilet. Walking there and back becomes increasingly difficult till it is almost impossible. Her legs are stuck hard together. The pressure in her thighs and knees which keeps her legs together becomes enormously painful.)
... If I could press my legs harder together I would. I absolutely have to because if I start opening my legs, it's as if the walls of a dam break down and everything comes out all jumbled up, there's no order in it. As I said

in the last Session, everything is a mess. It means destruction ... of me. Where am I? Where are my pieces? They're scattered all over the place. How do I pick myself up from there? How can I put the right pieces back into the right places? I can't. Keeping my legs so hard together means I change sex. I can't open my legs, so it means I'm not a female. With my legs in this position I'm in the position of a man making love and I'm making the appropriate movements. I don't want to be a man, not even for my mother. I'm not a man. I'm not a man! I can't talk, I can't express what I feel, I can't do anything. I'm stuck. I'm not a man. I don't want to be a man. I'm not a woman. I'm not a woman because I'm a man. (R10's contradictions reveal once again her unconscious confusion concerning her sex identity.)

Doctor: When you say you're a man, are you expressing your desire to be a man?

R10: I am a man. I can feel it in me. It's part of me ... (silence) ...

Doctor: Is it your desire to be a man?

R10: No. It comes from my mother. Her will for me to be a man becomes part of my thinking. How else can I feel so much that being a man is part of me when I don't want to be a man ... (silence) ...

Doctor: Can you recollect any signs during your life of tendencies towards male behaviour?

R10: I was very domineering. (R10 considers this trait of hers to be a sign of active homosexual tendencies.) I believe that being domineering is a male quality. My mother is domineering. She domineers my father. It's not my father who wore the pants in the house, it's my mother. She's humiliated him ... (crying) ... I identify with my mother and feel I'm a man ... (silence) ...

Doctor: What did you mean when you said that being a man is part of you?

R10: My flesh is male, my blood, my molecules. I don't feel I have a penis at the moment, but I can feel my male molecules.

Doctor: What do you feel as a man?

R10: I feel that I'm a weak person. I'm like my father who's weak. Now I'm not identifying with my strong mother as a man but with my weak father. I'm feeling that my mother takes the lead role in everything. I'm seeing my father as being passive in sex. I can see him at my mother's command. I have an image of my mother lying on top of my father and directing the sex act. In the last Session I saw my father's genitals as plastic, powerless, immobilized. My mother got rid of them, in other words she castrated him. My mother is the king and queen. Both roles are male. And I in the last Session had plastic genitals too. That means I identify with my weak father. Now I feel I have a penis and testicles, and they're fleshy - not plastic -, soft, weak, helpless. Oh, how humiliating!! ... My mother has cast-iron genitals. She is imperious, imperial, the ruler. Behind her cast-iron genitals is the womb. What do they want of me? - that I be a boy. That's her order, the law as given by Mother. It's my mother's will, the will of the womb which I've felt in past Sessions as some strange, strong force, stronger than anything else. You can't bend that iron will ... (silence) ...

Doctor: You said before that if you opened your thighs, there'd be a catastrophe.

R10: The catastrophe is if I'm female ... (silence) ...

Doctor: Is it if you're female or if you have sexual contact as a female?

R10: Sexual contact will make me female. If I don't have sexual contact, I'm ignoring my sex, there's nothing to worry about ...

Doctor: But doesn't sexual contact also include orgasm?

R10: I'm thinking simply in terms of sexual contact without orgasm. Even that's painful because it forces me to play the role of a female and that means catastrophe, crumbling, disintegrating into countless pieces. Sexual contact becomes so painful because I want to be female but I don't want to dissolve. Sometimes when I'm making love I think, "I want, I want, I want to be female but I can't, I can't, I can't."[8] As many "wants" as I say, that's how many "can'ts" I say.

But why do I want to be a female? Is it because I am female? No, that isn't sufficient reason. I want to be wanted by my father as a female. I want it very much. That's why I remained a female in many ways. My father actually saved me from swinging towards being a man, towards active homosexuality. My mother's will for a boy was the most powerful thing of all and my wish that my father should want me as a female was the counterbalance that I was holding onto by a thin thread which could have so easily snapped. Till now, it's more or less counterbalanced my mother's will, but not quite. In past Sessions I said that I felt there was a void under me and that what saved me from falling away into the chaos was my father. Wanting my father kept me quite feminine, superficially at least.

Just imagine, wouldn't my mother have an absolute shock if she had an openly homosexual child. Serves her right, bitch! She deserves

---

[8] R10's note: This is the first time I realized that the "wants" and "can'ts" that I say to myself during sex refer to my wanting but not being able to be female during sex.

everything she gets. It's punishment for her. I'd show her exactly what a mess she made, instead of all the cover-ups I made, acting the opposite to what I really felt. I had to present a good face for my mother because she's a prig, puritan, conservative, a supporter of the status quo. She may have wanted a boy but she got a girl - so if I look like a girl, I should act like one too. So if I started to exhibit my homosexual traits, it would have meant immediate punishment by my mother. I wanted to punish her, but she punished me. Who always got there first? She did. She's always dominated and oppressed me ... I need to return to the womb as a boy or return and become a boy in there. Only as a boy would going back not be hell.

Doctor: To return to the uterus means to pass through her vulva and vagina and so into the uterus?

R10: Yes, that's what I saw before - a male baby in the womb and a man making love with the mother are exactly the same thing. I would like the male baby and the man to be me ... (R10 then hesitantly and vaguely relates her homosexual interests.) ... I feel that the arousal I feel for certain types of women is a refuge to which I flee. I'm running away from feeling for my male friend so that I can escape the danger of disintegration - because sexual contact with my friend forces me to be female.

Session 17 The Session begins with chills and movements from the waist down similar to the movements of a man during the sexual act. Simultaneously, R10 feels that she is a naked, emaciated man with a limp penis. She feels like a concentration camp victim. This feeling alternates with the feeling that she is a hideous creature which was born burnt and half-dead of an ostrich. R10 identifies with the ostrich which tries to escape from deadly danger by hiding only its head in the sand while the rest of its body is exposed to the enemy's attack. She also identifies with the ostrich in her unsuccessful attempt to hide her distortion (caused by the intra-uterine fire) which makes her feel ludicrous. (In her everyday life R10 feels unbearably ludicrous at the slightest thing. She also feels that she is hideously ugly.)

R10: ... My mother's womb was a blast furnace, like a furnace in a German concentration camp that they throw bodies into. This blast furnace that contains the fire is made of steel. It's too strong, you can't fight it. My mother is a Nazi torturer ... Now I can see myself at the age

---

9 R10's note: My mother confirmed to me that when I was two, she was again pregnant. During the fifth month of her pregnancy, she suffered a miscarriage and this upset her greatly.

The Knowledge of the Womb

of two. I can see my mother with a big belly. She's telling me that she's pregnant.[9] Immediately I become the weak, helpless, half-dead foetus in the womb again.[10] Now I can see the concentration camp man curled up in the foetal position. He keeps being thrown into the fire, one time after the other. Everything in life throws me back into the fire of the womb. I can't stand it inside the womb but I go back because I can't stand what's outside the womb either - life. I don't want life. It's like life is the unnatural. I keep going back to the womb because it's the only thing I know. I also feel that it's my mother's will that I be in the blast furnace ...

Session 18 R10: I don't exist for the next person when I'm not being used as their tool. I don't have any meaning for them except for use, and at the time of use. Only then do I exist for them. And if I'm not being used, then I don't exist. My mother uses me in the womb. She acts on me blindly and does whatever she wants with me. She doesn't consider me at all. I'm fed with rejecting stimuli and when I'm not fed with such stimuli in everyday life, I don't exist. Why don't I exist? Because I only exist through my mother. I have to exist in pain. The pain is within me and all around me. She puts unbearable pressure on me in the womb, bombarding me with her rejecting messages - makes me feel I'm going to die ... (R10's description here shows her agonizing everyday reference to the womb. See also Session 17 and 19. During her 18th Session R10 also realized that the man with whom she had a relationship at that time symbolized her father and her father the womb.)

Session 19 This Session is almost a repetition of the 18th. R10 again realizes that she can exist only under one condition: that she revive almost incessantly the conditions of the rejecting womb. Thus, in her everyday life R10 unconsciously creates conditions of rejection. A typical example from this period is the evolution of every meeting with her friend which R10 unconsciously steers to what she feels is his inevitable rejection of her.

Session 20 The Session begins with the usual muscular contractions and cough. R10 sees images of a spider's web which traps and immobilizes her so that the spider can penetrate her body, and particularly her vagina, with its legs. R10 feels that the web is the womb and the spider's legs the rejecting messages.

---

10 R10's note: I felt my mother's second pregnancy as a total rejection of me, which instantly reactivated my intra-uterine rejection.

R10: ... There should not be any pulsating of my bodily organs. There should not be any contractions of the vagina. The contractions of my vagina mean that I'm a female and I don't want to be anything. I just want to be a neutral. I don't want a vagina with a penis in it. I don't want pulsations of my bodily organs which show that I'm pulsing with life, that I exist. I don't want contractions of my vagina which show that I'm a female. And I don't want close contact. Those three things are connected. In the womb I existed, I was a female and I had close contact with my mother ... (silence) ... I'm a nothing. I don't have a personality of my own. To get some sort of personality, I have to take somebody else's. That means through my life I try on different styles, different personalities because I don't know what myself is. When my partner reaches orgasm, I identify very closely with him. That way, someone - myself - shows me love and I become a man, so then my mother accepts me...(silence) The emotional pain which comes from having the vagina excited - because excitation of the vagina makes me feel female - comes from the womb because the same thing happened in the womb. Can you believe that, Doctor?

Doctor: How do you feel about it?

R10: That's what I feel. The pain now comes because of the pain then, and that's why I can't get rid of it now. Oh, I'm fed up. I don't want to think of anything ... (She goes to the toilet. When she returns:) I know I've been avoiding facing something because I'm terrified. Can I face it now? Is it too late?

Doctor: The pharmacodynamic activity of the drug is still working fully. Try and follow it wherever it takes you, despite your terror.

R10: Oh God! I feel as if my heart is going to stop if I face it. But I have to face it. How do you feel when you go down those long, steep Luna Park slippery dips? I went down one once and I really felt that my heart was going to stop. That's how I feel now. I feel something like that when I'm approaching orgasm. Oh, the terror of it ... Can I do it?

Doctor: You mean let yourself revive the cause of your terror?

R10: Yes.

Doctor: It's up to you. You have to decide whether you'll go through the terror, no matter how strong it is, in order to feel its cause.

R10: ... (crying) ... I can't ... (silence) ... Maybe it's better if you leave for a while. I don't want to be alone, really. I want you to stay because I'm afraid and your presence is a comfort. But if you do stay, I'll feel inhibited. So it's better if I'm alone. (The doctor leaves the room.)

R10 then recounts her feelings and actions: As soon as the doctor leaves the room, I feel the need to go to the toilet again. When I return, I see the doctor and tell him that it's the terror of something I'm trying to avoid which makes me want to urinate constantly. I enter the room and lie down. The convulsions begin immediately. One minute I contract forward into the foetal position and the next my back, neck and head are thrown backwards, my body forming an arch, as if I'm trying to get out of the womb. My face has great pressure on it, as if it is being squashed in . My head aches terribly. My impulse is to lie on my stomach to impede the convulsions, but I force myself not to do so and let the process continue to see where it will lead me. The cough periodically interrupts the convulsions.

This whole process continues for a long time, becoming stronger and stronger. The groans become cries, then shouts and screams of terror and pain ... Stop! ... Stop! ... No more! ... No more! ... (speaking to the air, my mother the big power). In desperation I beat the wall with my fists and I feel the convulsions becoming stronger, more painful. It's as if my mother is punishing me for trying to react to her. I see octopuses' legs and human hands, especially the fingers, extended over me ... I call out for the doctor. The doctor enters but his presence doesn't stop the convulsions which continue to increase in intensity. I groan loudly from the unbearable pain of the convulsions and the pressure in my head.

R10: (screaming with pain) ... Oh, it hurts! Bitch! ... Why doesn't it stop? Why? ... Why doesn't it stop? ... Oh, it kills me! ... It kills me! ... Will it stop? ... It's so-o-o painful. Ooooa ... Oh, I feel like I'm going to break in two. Oh, my back, for God's sake, my back! She's going to break my bloody spine! ... Ooh, ooa ... No mercy, she has no mercy ... The pain has to come out! ... (Eventually, she calms down somewhat for a little, but then:) I see the teeth, sharp shark's teeth. The spider's web is filled with sharp teeth ... Inside ... ooh! (extremely strong muscular contractions, cries) ... Inside the teeth ... torture! ... The teeth are the door to hell! ... (Immediately before her eyes, the teeth open wide revealing fire within the shark's mouth. She screams:) The fire! The fire! No, no, no! ... (lengthy screaming of great intensity) ... The fire's everywhere ... The fire's inside the mouth. The shark's teeth open and you have fire! ... It's full of fire! An oven! An oven! ... You put a live foetus into the fire and you bring out a burnt foetus! All charcoal and charred and brown ... (sobbing) ... You put the foetus in the oven with a shovel and you take it out when it's burnt with a shovel ... The handle of the shovel looks like a penis. The penis propels me into the oven like a shovel ... I keep seeing fire all the time, everywhere ... I keep living in it all my days ... The fire is in the womb ... and with sex I return to the fire ...

Session 21 The Session begins with the usual muscular contractions. R10 feels that she is trapped in a spider's web. The legs of an enormous black spider penetrate her body and transmit an electric current of tremendous voltage which causes her violent spasms of the whole body and the feeling that she is exploding and disintegrating into countless pieces. Screaming and extreme terror and panic accompany this lengthy subjective state which R10 characterizes as the revival of her intra-uterine rejection.

R10: ... My mother wants to kill me, but unfortunately I didn't die. I feel that she kept me alive just to torture me. She didn't want me to exist, nor did she want my sex. She distorted me and then she deliberately gave birth to me so that my distortion could be seen by everybody. That's unbearable. I prefer the hell of the womb ... I feel I'm in the womb again ... I do anything and everything you want, Mum. If you don't like sex, then neither do I. If you think that sex is bad, then so do I. If you don't like your vagina being penetrated by a penis, then I don't like being penetrated either ... (silence) ...

Doctor: How do you know that she doesn't like her vagina to be penetrated by a penis?

R10: I can feel it. I know it. I can feel her reaction when her vagina has a penis in it. The walls of her vagina become cold to it. The walls of that vagina don't want that visitor at all. I can feel all her abhorrence at having her vagina penetrated and her abhorrence becomes mine. Whatever happens in her vagina, I can feel it happening in mine. Whatever she feels, I feel. I know everything that's going on inside her. I'm the exact copy of my mother, like a print from a negative ...(This explains why R10 could never conceive of her mother having sexual desires) I see my mother not very far from me. I see myself opening my arms and stretching them out to her, trying to reach her. I feel that I want to love my mother. Loving my mother is like the situation of a slave who is whipped and beaten by his master and loves his master. If I love my mother, I neutralize her in a way, I try to lessen my pain and weakness by identifying with her and getting some of her power. The womb is dominant and overpowering and I am submissive. Being submissive means being in agony. Or do I like that? I have to like being submissive, I have to accept it. If I like the submissiveness and the agony, then my pain is lessened ...

Session 22 R10: ... I see lightning. It's in the shape of a spider. It's a spider of lightning. It's going to put an electric current through me. I don't want to get an electric shock ... (silence) ... (At this point R10 admits that she neutralized the image because it caused her unbearable fear. The doctor encourages her to return to the image.) ... It's very dangerous to get an electric shock through water. The walls of the womb are a spider which sends electric shocks through the amniotic fluid that hit me (long silence - resistance).

Doctor: Follow the image. Don't stop it.

R10: ... No, no, I don't want to see wombs, foetuses. Why can't we just have a pleasant chat? (giggle) - (R10 continues her resistance. Although she speaks about the rejecting womb, it is purely intellectually. There is not a trace of emotional element.)

R10: ... I feel I'm a white mass, very small and soft. I'm not properly formed yet, nothing is defined. I'm given electric shocks. I feel that my mother realized she was pregnant very, very early. That's when she began to bombard me with her rejecting messages. I feel that after the initial assault, I didn't develop any more. The way I feel I am reminds me of the way schizophrenic children depict themselves. I've seen drawings of schizophrenic children. The drawing of themselves is like a shadow or a ghost of themselves. They're not finished and they're not formed. They don't know how to draw themselves with a proper body, proper limbs and facial features. Their drawings remind me of the skinny concentration camp man ...

R10: The first knowledge I ever had was of my mother's rejecting messages. It was the knowledge of poison and evil. I'm like Eve. The devil made Eve eat the apple. (giggle) ... Anyway, the devil is not the devil. The devil is God. God's the devil. My mother is a god, a god in male form, of course. Nobody ever thought that God took a female form, did they. Why didn't they? Why does God have to be a bloody man? Why couldn't God be a woman? Because women are just contemptible little worms ...

Session 23 In this Session, R10 realizes that there is nothing good about her because her existence and her sex did not satisfy the womb. She also realizes that she is not allowed to expect anything good from her environment because she did not experience anything good in the intra-uterine environment. R10 feels sever anxiety and tries to scratch her face with her nails.

R10: (to the doctor) Why don't you hit me? Why don't you destroy me? I don't have the guts to destroy myself ...

Doctor: Why should I destroy you?

R10: I'll kill her some day, I'll kill her! Bitch! Monster! ... I can see the grotesque green face of a dragon. Its wide mouth is open and all its sharp teeth are exposed. There's fire within the mouth ... (screaming) ... She's eating me, she's tearing me to shreds ... (to the doctor) Please, don't let her eat me ... (At this point, R10 obstructs the evolution of the Session.)

(After the Session R10 mentions that the green dragon with the sharp teeth symbolizes the rejecting womb and combines the symbolism of the green creature of Session 15 with the shark's teeth from Session 20.)

Session 24 During this Session R10 feels ludicrous because of her presence in the womb contrary to the latter's will. Consequently the feeling of ludicrousness is generalized to every sphere of her everyday life. "There's nothing I can feel, there's nothing I can do without feeling a fool for it," says R10.

R10: ... I remember a scene from a movie where a woman is raped by three men. I can see one of the men from the backside fucking the woman while the other two hold her down ... You bastards! ... Three big strong men against a defenceless woman ... Oh God ... I hate ... I hate ... I hate ... I just hate men! You fuck![11] ... (sobbing, feeling of helplessness) ... I hate the injustice of man being endowed with more physical strength than a woman. The woman can't fight back. He imposes himself on her, he does whatever he likes. I identify fully with the woman in the movie ... agony ... torture ... I hate ... Oh God, I hate ... Those three powerful men symbolize my mother's all-powerful womb. Men with their rape send me back to the hell of the womb[12] ...(sobbing) ... I can't fight the womb. If I give her one, she gives me a hundred. Her blows are horrifying. They make me break down into pieces, like the bodies are in pieces all over the place in Picasso's 'Guernica' ... I want to kill myself because I have to finish what my mother started ...

Session 25 R10: ... When I drink alcohol, I always overdo it. At first I feel high but then I go into a depression, I get nauseous and often end up vomiting. I understand now why I drink so much. I want to create inner conditions (intense nausea) just like the inner conditions the rejecting womb caused me. Drunkenness takes me back to the womb and that's where I want to go so that I can smash it! I want to kill my mother but I only end up feeling sick as a dog. Yet my sole purpose in getting drunk is to kill my mother. My sole purpose in everything I do in life is to kill my mother. I have to break out of the little dark prison cell she's put me into.

---

[11] R10's note: I mean rape.
[12] R10's note: I consider penetration of the penis into my vagina as rape because "it forces me to play the role of a female and that means catastrophe" (p. 39).

It's made of the strongest materials in the world. But even if I put a bomb to it, I'll only end up buried under the rubble ...

Session 26 R10 presents severe anxiety.
Doctor: What is it?
R10: (screaming with terror) The womb! The womb! ... I'm on fire ... the fire ... the fire ...Do you understand, Doctor, Fire! (screaming continues) ...
Doctor: Describe what you feel.
R10: (pained crying) ... There's nothing left of me. My voice is just an echo from something that was ... (screaming-crying) ... I'm destroyed ... burnt destroyed ... by fire ... (screaming-crying) ...
Doctor: Where is the fire?
R10: It's everywhere ... It's the walls. Look, the walls are fire.[13] Everywhere fire ... Everything I touch is burning ... (sobbing) ... That's why I get old[14] and I become distorted and deformed ... from the fire ... I feel like I've been thrown through the ages, ages of fire ... one fire after another ... too many fires, Doctor, too many fires ... Everyone ... Everyone before me[15] went through fire ... I walk through a sea of fire ... and I become a fire myself ...
... I'm the most revolting monster on this earth. You stupid woman, you gave birth to a freak! Yes my dear mother, you gave birth to a monster spider. I'm the spider now[16] ... Oh no! (She screams with horror at having become a spider.[17]) ... I'm a spider. I'm revolting. Ha ha ha. I get revenge on you, you bitch! - by being a spider[18] ... Now what's happening? Now I feel as if I'm spinning in a washing machine. I'm at my mother's mercy. I stopped being the spider. I'm burning again ... (screaming) ... If I become a spider, I stop burning ... (screaming) ...
Doctor: Become a spider then.
R10: (screaming) Be a spider? I'll kill! I'll Kill her![19] ... I can't do it. I can't ... (screaming) ... I feel so nauseous. I want to vomit ...

---

[13] R10's note: The walls of the room represent the walls of the womb.
[14] R10's note: I have said many times in previous Sessions that the intra-uterine experience wore me out and made me old.
[15] R10's note: I mean my female ancestors.
[16] R10's note: Here, I am identifying with the womb which I frequently see in the Sessions as a giant black spider.
[17] R10's note: The horror is because, though I am identifying with the spider, I am simultaneously identifying with its victim.
[18] R10's note: Now I am fully the evil spider, no more its victim.
[19] R10's note: Just as she wanted to kill me when I was in her womb.

(R10 has calmed down somewhat and says:) When I was a foetus, before the rejecting messages came in, I was not completely calm, but tense, waiting. It's as if I knew that something terrible was going to happen because it had happened before. That's why I said I've been through ages of fire. As if there was a fire before me and before that and before that; my mother a fire, my grandmother and so on, back through the centuries. So if you have a pattern established, then you know there's going to be another fire. The pattern is that there will be another one and that's what you're waiting for. You're petrified waiting because you can't avoid it. It's as if I were a fire born of a fire born of a fire and so on. I think that's why I can't find a moment of calmness in the womb. Before the rejecting messages come in, I'm in a certain position in the womb, the foetal position, the same position my mother and grandmother and great-grandmother and all the others before them were in. I know that position and I know what it means and it can't mean good, it can't mean calm. There's going to be a terrible shock that'll make me convulse and burn. The first time my mother bombarded me with her rejecting messages, I felt an electric current of tremendous voltage passing through my body ...

R10's observation after Session 26: In this Session I identify with the spider (my mother's womb) in order to escape the burning I suffer in the womb. This identification, however, is only brief because the womb easily overpowers me. I become its victim again and start to burn.

Session 27 R10: ... I feel tremendous pressure on me, from all sides. It's coming from the womb. I feel squashed ... I can't stand it ... I don't want to live ... The legs of the huge black spider are touching my fingers. Ooh, they're sending electricity through me. (At this point, her arms are extended out from her shoulders, her body is straight. Arms and body form the shape of a cross.) I'm Christ on the cross[20] ... I feel so helpless, so weak ... It's the end ... Doctor, I'm dying ... I can't breathe ... I'm staring straight into the most unbearably terrifying vacuum ... (terrified screams) - (Because R10's terror is lengthy, the doctor is obliged to stop the Session with an intramuscular injection of 50 mg chlorpromazine. Shortly after the injection R10 says:) The womb is the beginning and the end of my life ... I'm stuck forever in a deep cavern of darkness.

Session 28 The main characteristic of this Session is R10's neutralization of the pharmacodynamic activity of the psychedelic drug.

---

20 R10's note: In other words, I am the victim of God-womb-spider.

After the Session, however, R10 wants to continue the Sessions because (a) only during the Sessions can she express the pressure, pain and terror of the rejecting womb and thus feel some sort of release and (b) only during the Sessions can she express her aggressiveness towards her mother, something which also gives her some feeling of release.

Session 29 R10: I feel great pressure inside me and all around me. I feel distorted. I'm hiding under the blankets because I don't want anybody to see me ... (muscular contractions, anxiety which increases leading to lengthy screaming) ... I'm in hell ... I'm going to die ... I can't stand it ... I want to die. (The last phrases are repeated continuously for a long time.) ... Somebody please kill me, put me out of my misery ... I'm getting electricity through my hands. (Her body and arms have formed the shape of a cross.) I'm Christ on the cross in the womb, in an Easter egg that's all bloody ... The electricity has paralyzed me ... (screaming continues) ... I'm a robot ... The spider (the womb) fucks and distorts me ... The electricity is coming up my legs, reaches my genitals. I'm a man with a penis that's vibrating. I'm a male robot. Now I feel like a (female) doll ... Now I don't know what sex I am ... (silence) ...

Doctor: As a robot, do you feel that all your movements are under someone else's control?

R10: Yes! ... I'm a robot that's been dismantled. I'm a doll that's been thrown into the rubbish because nobody wants me. I'm very tired. I don't want to feel. My feelings exhaust me. My feelings are sick and the only way to get rid of them is to die. Every molecule in my body is rotten (repeated many times). What my mother did to me cannot be changed. She caused irreparable damage. I can't live with a body that's rotten. It's unbearable. I have to live with it every day, every second. I can't. Really, my mother has to take the first prize for ultimate destruction. That's what she wanted and she accomplished her goal. I feel I'm useless in this world, that I shouldn't be here. Why is my form, my body in this world? Why does it take up space in this world? It's taking up space, it shouldn't. Where I am should be a vacuum. I am a nothing and I'm forced to drag around this body with its stupid, sick emotions. It's a burden to be here in this world and carry all this pain, but that's what she wanted. My mother is a universal law that distorts me. If you go against the law, the law is so powerful it pulverizes you ...

Session 30 R10: ... I feel the convulsions right up in my chest. They make me very aware of my breasts. I want to tear my breasts off. That way, I won't have problems. The convulsions make me feel ludicrous. I'm ludicrous because I have breasts and female genitals. My mother doesn't accept my being female in the womb. In there, she examines and distorts my every cell because I'm female. She terrifies me with her microscopic examination and distortion. Now I can understand why all those school and university exams terrified me out of my mind. Going into the examination room was like being put under the microscope in the womb. It's as if those exams we examining every molecule in me. Going into the exam room was like stepping straight into the green dragon's mouth with the fire burning ...

R10: ... I can see (in an image) and feel a knife which is up in my vagina and which is mutilating it ... (silence) ...

Doctor: Who put the knife there?

R10: ... The spider and the penis that enters my vagina when I make love ... The penis rapes me ... I see the open mouth of the shark and webs ... I feel so sick, so nauseous (very strong contractions of the abdominal muscles) ... (silence) ...

Doctor: Don't avoid the image. Don't neutralize what you feel.

R10: ... I feel I'm in the shark's mouth ... She's pulverizing me, the bitch ... (weak pained cries) ... Oh Go-o-o-o-od ... (At this point, R10 presents uncontrollable vomiting. It is worth noting that despite very strong nausea in all the previous Sessions, she had never vomited.) ... I'm getting pressure in the top of my head ... I'm going through my mother's vagina ... Pressure, pain, it's unbearable ... Why doesn't it finish? It's never-ending ... Oh Go-o-od ... I'm cold ... Now I'm back in the womb again. (R10 again presents the usual muscular contractions.) ... I prefer to be in the womb. It's warmer because I'm in her, with her. I feel it's my place ... I'm going through the vagina again. I'm upside down. I feel helpless and ludicrous because my legs have fallen apart and my mother is examining my genitals. I feel all alone surrounded by chaos in this world. But I felt the same thing in the womb - chaos. I was with her but I was all alone because she didn't want me ... I don't want to become pregnant. I don't want to become a mother. I don't want to become myself. If I become pregnant, the foetus inside me will be rotten, just as I was in my mother's womb. All my female ancestors were rotten embryos inside their mother's womb ... (R10's double identification, should she become pregnant, with her mother and the foetus within her [R10's] womb.)

R10: ... My aggravating cough symbolizes my identification with my mother. I try to cough out what is in the womb, that is, myself. It's a vain attempt to be free of the hell of the womb ...

R10's DESCRIPTIONS OF HER PSYCHOTICLIKE S & P[21]

Depressivelike S & P The agonising symptoms leading me towards suicide before I began the Sessions were virtually indescribable because they were incomprehensible and I was ignorant of their cause. Through my experience and knowledge from the Sessions, I can now set them down as: (a) The feeling that I am being watched almost constantly by the green creature . (b) The feeling that others reject me because I am nothing. (c) The feeling that I am utterly ludicrous. (d) The feeling that I cannot communicate with others. (e) Other mental and physical symptoms.

Rejection by others Rejections, big and 'small', explicit or implied, enter me like a shaft and shatter me. At this point, I feel a chaotic horror for the rejection and particularly for the intention behind it. I feel that the rejector is deliberately hurting me and wants to reduce me to the nothing he or she thinks I am (this even in the case of close friends). Simultaneously, I feel intensely that yes, I am nothing, and this too is a horrifying feeling.

The above leads instantly to and is then accompanied by the urgent wish to die on the spot - the only way to escape the horror of the rejection of my nothingness. "Oh God, I can't live like this, I don't want to live like this, I don't want to live, I shouldn't live."

The horror is unbearable and does not last very long. I sink down into a deep gloom where I feel extremely hurt, sad and bitter about the deliberate rejection which makes me feel more worthless than I usually do. (I am almost constantly reminded of my worthlessness and other negative qualities, such as ludicrousness, in my everyday life by the presence of the green creature.) I would like to fight against the person's rejection, to stand up for myself in order that he/she retract his/her rejections and replace it with apologies and acceptance. But I feel too weak to fight and anyway it's pointless. The truth is that I am nothing, and you can't fight the truth.

The person who rejects me is absolutely right. I have no qualities. I cannot grasp what 'me' is. It is a vacuum. Or if I do have some 'qualities', they are anything negative you can think of - I'm bad, boring, ludicrous, stupid, selfish, etc. In short, I am shit, and shit is also nothing, a despicable nothing. Feeling nothing is an agonizing, bitter sensation.

I cannot live with all this pain. It is unbearable and I feel desperate because nothing can change, can break this deadlock. I cannot wipe that

---

21 For meaning of term 'psychoticlike' see § 127.

rejection out of time, out of existence, and I cannot alter my nothingness - I will continue to be a prisoner of it. Death is the only way to break out of this deadlock and get release, relief.[22] Why does a nothing live? It's incongruous, it's wrong. Why do I waste space on this earth?

The reactions I have described till now may be modified in various ways:

(a) Sometimes in the presence of the rejector, the bitterness of the gloom stage becomes aggressiveness and I may lash out at the rejector. This behaviour, however, so horrifies me, makes me feel such a monster, that the hurt for the rejection is overshadowed by an intensified feeling of being a despicable nothing accompanied by unbearable guilt.

(b) Other times, when I am alone after rejection, the bitterness of the gloom stage alternates with or is accompanied by aggressiveness towards the absent rejector in the form of an imaginary argument where I stand up for myself. (This happens when I have not felt or have not dared express my aggressiveness in his presence.) Finally, however, it is the rejection of myself as a nothing which prevails. Sometimes the aggressiveness ceases to be directed towards the absent rejector and becomes aggressiveness without clear direction, without a (conscious) target and is thus very frustrating.

(c) Other times during the gloom stage, the chaotic horror periodically resurfaces and alternates with the gloom.

The feeling of ludicrousness Whether I have been rejected by somebody or not, I often feel extremely ludicrous.

In the presence of others, my behaviour is characterized by an effort to make a highly favourable impression on them; that I am highly intelligent, interesting, perceptive, feminine, sexy, beautiful, strong, masculine, etc. etc. This effort is accompanied by highly exaggerated speech content and intonation as well as hand and facial gestures. Simultaneously, I feel sometimes vaguely, sometimes fairly strongly that my behaviour and its motivations are ludicrous. While my ludicrous behaviour is taking place, I feel the green creature watching me. My awareness of its presence, its mocking 'comments' and its derisive 'laughter' is sometimes vague, other times very strong. I don't actually hear its voice but I feel it. I have

---

[22] R10's note: Actually, I feel there are two possible ways to break the deadlock - death or utter insanity where the ego is so shattered that it ceases to feel anything, permanently. Because I have not reached this state, death is the only plausible alternative for me.

no doubt of its existence. The more loudly it 'laughs' at me, the more horrified I feel.

When I am alone after a gathering, the green creature makes me realize and feel fully how utterly ludicrous I was at the gathering. It 'tells' me that I was trying to fool others and myself that I am 'something' when I know I am nothing. The feeling of utter ludicrousness and nothingness and the chaotic horror they cause, reach their peak with my conviction that others perceived my ludicrousness, the full extent of it. "Fool! You made an impression alright, but it wasn't the one you wanted. How can people accept or even tolerate a fool like you?" Death is the only escape from these excruciatingly painful feelings.

The feeling that I cannot communicate Another factor which causes me bitter gloom is my feeling that I cannot communicate with people around me because I am stupid, empty, nothing. Though people have said nothing to this effect, I'm convinced that they think me stupid and suchlike and that it's a waste of time trying to communicate with me. Though it is my feeling of nothingness which drives me to try to be 'something' accepted by others, it is this very feeling of nothingness which dooms my effort to failure. Failure of communication is further ensured by my strong feeling that there is a certain space between others and myself across which words have to get. But my words don't get across. They get lost somewhere in that space which is like a vacuum, an emptiness which swallows up words and the feelings behind them. I am left feeling isolated and lonely.

Other mental and physical symptoms The bitter gloom, which is accompanied by general physical exhaustion, robs me of any will for physical activity. It also causes intellectual lethargy - it is particularly difficult or impossible for me to concentrate on anything intellectual.

Because all the symptoms mentioned till now are so painful, I frequently escape from them by becoming numb. The numbness often occurs automatically, that is, it takes place without any conscious will or effort, but sometimes I evoke it deliberately. In this state of numbness, my emotions are anaesthetized and so, frequently, is my body. I feel utter indifference towards others and myself. I feel dead inside. I feel as if I don't exist in this world.

I feel this numb state as one of only partial death. Intellectually, I know that I am still alive. I don't want this partial death. I desire total death. When I am obsessed with the thought of death, the green creature disappears. This is because his goal has been accomplished - in wanting to die, I have submitted to the will of the womb (the green creature). The only other occasion in my everyday life where the presence of the green creature watching me is non-existent or almost non-existent is when I'm occupied with housework. At that time I go through the movements like a robot - I do not feel or think much or at all and thus the creature cannot very well 'criticize' me.[23]

Example of schizophreniclike and paranoiaclike state Very frequently, as I'm walking alone in the street, I feel very strongly like a man in the way I hold myself and walk, in my feeling that I am sure and strong, powerful, not to be fooled with.

At the same time, however, there are vague feelings, which sometimes become clear and strong for a second or two, of being very unsure of myself, feeling scared and helpless and weak lest any man comment on my femaleness. I want to hide my head and run away, out of everyone's sight.

These mainly vague feelings explode to the surface fully and clearly when any man does make an obscene or ridiculing comment on my femaleness. For a moment or two, I feel as if transfixed by a chaos, by a paralyzing terror. But then, though I continue to feel utterly at their mercy, impotent and somewhat chaotic, I am also overcome by a violent desire to kill these men in the most violent way I can think of, such as swiftly snapping their necks, tearing knives through their bodies or tearing their flesh and limbs apart with my bare hands so that in the end they would be severely and unrecognizably mutilated. I feel this passionately and also feel that I could perform this act mercilessly, completely cold-bloodedly.

The emotional-intellectual interpretation of the above is as follows: The men who comment so negatively on my femaleness are instantly and totally identified with the all-powerful womb, my mother, who wanted me a boy. Their degrading, humiliating and ridiculing comments make me feel as nothing, as weak and powerless as I had felt in the womb where my femaleness was at the mercy of my mother's constant attacks. The ridiculing remarks as well not only point out to me all too clearly the ludicrousness of my being female, but also my distortion, my ugliness in face and body (I have felt in the Sessions that the womb distorted me beyond repair).

---

[23] Doctor's note: For the interpretation of R10's depressivelike S and P, see pp.53-54)

The Knowledge of the Womb

The men's comments, as well as their touch, also affect me so greatly because, as I discovered in a Session, I feel any negative comment or touch by a man as deadly rape. In the Sessions, I have felt the womb as a spider raping me with its evil black legs (the rejecting messages) in its endeavour to kill me - a terrifying, chaotic feeling. The womb's rejecting messages make me disintegrate, adding to the feeling of chaos and terror.

I react to all these unbearable feelings with the violent desire to kill mercilessly and cold-bloodedly those who cause me these unbearable feelings, that is, the men, but more basically my womb-spider-mother. At this point, I am identifying fully with my mother - I want to kill her just as she had wanted to kill me when I was in her womb.

However, though I am identifying with my mother, I am still at the same time the weak, helpless and terrified female and thus my violent desires are not acted upon. When, as sometimes happens, I try to return a verbal attack or hit out at the men, they always foil me and ridicule me even more.

All the above helps explain why, when I walk alone in the street, I feel like a strong, powerful man and, simultaneously, a weak, helpless female. I feel the latter because I am afraid of an attack by the men who symbolize the womb. My only defence against these awful female feelings is to react to them be feeling and behaving like a powerful man - like the men who would comment on me. The actual attack by the men momentarily breaks down my defence but I soon react again with the violent feelings.

Doctor's comment: The very rapid alternation of the functioning of R10's sex identity and the reactivated rejecting womb makes her feel as if her bipolar feelings occur simultaneously.

R10's sexual problem Here is a fairly full description of my sexual activity before, during and after orgasm with a male partner. First of all, I point out that the only way I can reach orgasm is through clitoral stimulation. The whole process, then, is as follows:
(a) When the tongue first touches the clitoris, I feel sharp pleasure-pain-fear - like a shock.
(b) As the stimulation continues, I try to avoid the pain and fear by neutralizing the pleasure which causes them. I achieve this by thinking of some non-descript event that happened very recently.
(c) When orgasm begins I feel pleasure.
(d) The pleasure is very quickly dissipated by painful convulsions in the abdomen which are periodically interrupted by a dry, aggravating cough; pain in the genital organs; feeling that I am a whore; feeling

that I'm going to die. The feeling of impending death is horrifying and leads to deep depression and sobbing.

(e) After this, I feel emotionally and physically drained. I don't want to feel anything at all and so I feel nothing, I feel numb. Of course, this is purely self-defence against all the previous and unbearable pain.

R10's ANSWERS TO THE HISTORY QUESTIONNAIRE AFTER AUTOPSYCHOGNOSIA SESSIONS

Question: What are your complaints?

Answer: (a) Since I was very young I have suffered from sharp, stabbing pains which can occur in any part of my body. (The pains are due to the reactivation of the memory of the rejecting intra-uterine messages - in the Sessions, I often felt the rejecting messages as the stabbing of knives or spider's legs.)

(b) The cough.

(c) In the last years of gym, I frequently had to stop training a few minutes after I'd begun because of intense pain in my calves. (When I was in the womb, my mother wanted me to be a male. Thus, only a male is perfect. Unconsciously, I thought that through gymnastics I could become that perfect male. In other words, I was trying to satisfy my mother's wish. As a result, I tried, with my female body, to do perfect gym as a man. Thus, the muscles of my legs eventually became overdeveloped and looked like a man's, but they hurt me terribly because I was trying to transform their female nature.)

(d) The green creature.

Question: Describe any pharmaceutical therapy or any other therapy you have undergone.

Answer: I have realized that my allergy is exacerbated not only by metals but by the hot summer sun. (The heat of summer reactivates the rejecting womb which I felt as a metal blast furnace.)

Question: What events in your life can you remember? Which of these events do you consider important? What emotions did these important events produce in you?

Answer: I now remember some events and state from my early life which I had repressed, but most basic and important among them is the experience of the rejecting womb (see Sessions).

Answers on myself: The Sessions speak for themselves as far as my existential problem is concerned.

The Knowledge of the Womb

Answers on my sex: Again, the Sessions speak for themselves on the problem of my sex identity.

Answers on my sexual activity: I had forgotten to mention in the previous questionnaire - clearly because I wanted to forget - that some time before I began the Sessions I had momentarily felt sexual attraction (in a passive capacity, as I later realized) for a 45-year old woman I knew. The attraction occurred during a conversation when she suddenly said to me very sensually, "I'm going to eat you." Some time after I began the Sessions, I frequently felt sexual attraction in my everyday life for a certain type of woman. (I realized that if ever I had sexual activity with such a type, I would be the passive partner.) This woman gave me the impression that she felt sure of herself and free to do anything, particularly in sex which I imagined she would have with any man or woman she wanted. I considered such a woman a whore. I felt her behaviour was like a man's. The interpretation of my attraction in this : Because heterosexual sex takes me back to the hell of the womb, I try to avoid this by replacing men with women who behave like men. I also had dreams where I, with male genital organs, was making love with a young woman or girl. It is clear that in these dreams I was trying to become the man that the womb wanted.

Question: Do you always understand the motives of your behaviour? If not, give a specific example.
Answer: I realize now that before the Sessions I really had no idea as to the motives of my behaviour as a whole. For example, the reason for my perfectionism is that my mother wanted a boy and so only a boy can be perfect. To satisfy my mother's wish, I try to become a boy, I try to be perfect. But, of course, I can never be perfect because I'm a female.

When I want my mother to tell me that she sees how terrible I feel, I really want her to recognize and accept that she's the one who put me into this mess. My depressions, my aggressiveness and the motives of my behaviour in general have their roots in the rejecting womb.

Question: What do you desire most in life?
Answer: I want to feel calmness which I feel only the love, affection and protection of a man can give me.

Question: What are your ambitions?
Answer: The same as before the Sessions.

Question: What are your expectations?
Answer: I have none.

Question: What do you fear most?

Answer: (a) Rejection, which is part and parcel of my very existence and of life. (b) I know that the God I was so afraid of is the rejecting womb.

Question: What are your other fears?
Answer: I still have the same terror of spiders, webs, etc. as before.

(Question: Describe your recreational activities.
Answer: I still drink as I did before the Sessions but now I understand what's happening within me at such times. At first drink gives me the chance to express things I really want to express. (Without it I'm so inhibited and stiff.) However, sooner or later it reactivates the rejecting womb.

Question: Are any of your dreams repeated in a stereotyped fashion?
Answer: I often dream that the love of a man could make me feel calm. But there's always a big crowd between us which prevents me from approaching him and touching him. (The dream expresses not only my pessimism but also the real impossibility of my approaching and grasping calmness I want so much. Because I did not have a moment of calmness in the womb, so I do not have the right to have it now or ever - For interpretation of the spider dreams I had before, and during the Sessions,(see pp. 40-43)

Question: What are your feelings for your mother?
Answer: Although I now know the cause of my aggressiveness towards my mother, I often can't control the aggressiveness.

Question: What are your feelings for your father?
Answer: I'm still fixated to him. I also feel aggressive towards him although I realize why (see Sessions 6, 7, 8, 14 and 15).

Question: What are your feelings for your brother?
Answer: I realized in the 14th Session that when my mother was pregnant with my brother, I felt aggressive towards the baby in her womb. However, since his birth, I don't remember having any unpleasant feelings towards him.

Question: Your feelings about the interpersonal relations of your mother and father?
Answer: On this subject, I think and feel exactly as I did before the Sessions (see Sessions 8,15 and 16).

Question: Your feelings about the interpersonal relations of you mother and brother?
Answer: The same as before the Sessions. Their 'communication' reminds me of mine with my mother, but I'm very glad to see that my brother reacts positively to her attempts to dominate him.

Question: Your feelings about the interpersonal relations of your father and brother?

Answer: Their 'communications' reminds me of my father's and mine.

Question: Do you feel that you have concealed anything in answering the above questions?

Answer: Now, no. Apart from the intra-uterine rejection, my father's rejection and so on, which I could not possibly have remembered, I had not mentioned a few factors in the original questionnaire - such as the sexual attraction for the 45-year old woman - either because I had forgotten them or because I had not realized they were relevant. An illustration of the latter is the following letter I wrote when I had taken the decision to commit suicide, just a couple of days before beginning the preparation for autopsychognosia sessions.

> "This is not going to be an abortive attempt. It is going to succeed. I have reached a blank wall in my life which seems to me to be impossible to get past and for this reason my desperation has reached a point such as I have never known before. Its burden is intolerable. I feel so very, very alone and I see absolutely no hope for the future. I did hope once, tremendously, even in my darkest moments. I had faith in other people and, I suppose, vaguely hoped that I would have more faith in myself and perhaps be able to achieve something. Now I realize very clearly and cold-bloodedly that there's no faith and no hope. Yes, I'm still young but I feel like a vegetable, and I'll grow older only to be the same, but older, vegetable. I cannot change what is so deeply embedded inside me. I know myself well, and I know I'm so locked up inside myself, I'll never get out. I have no faith in myself and never will have. I'm inadequate."

Recapitulation of my problems: I cannot bear this continual rejection coming at me from everybody and everything. I cannot bear the painful emotions- rejections of any type or magnitude cause me.

Question: Do you have anything else to add?

Answer: My everyday feelings of rejection, ludicrousness, being a nothing, not being able to communicate, not being a woman, all stem from my rejection in the womb. I project the womb to the green creature and to people around me who, in the final analysis, all reject me as the womb had done.

As a foetus in the womb, I felt my mother's rejection as an attempt to kill me. The chaotic terror her rejection caused me was not only because I felt her threatening my existence and my sex, but also because I felt her rejection as deliberate. Because I was so weak and tiny and she all-powerful and enormous, I had to believe what she believed - that I was a nothing. If I did not, she would punish me with stronger and more painful rejecting messages, as I learned when I tried to react to her.

Her rejection made me feel that I should never have been conceived in the first place, that both my existence within her and my sex were ludicrous. My feeling of ludicrousness was intensified by the fact that I felt her rejection distorted me physically, mentally and emotionally.

As well, I felt not a trace of communication between us. I felt her attacking me blindly, mercilessly, without any consideration of me, as if I were an object, a piece of rubbish. I could not get the message to her across the amniotic fluid to leave me alone. I was in pain, but she didn't care. She kept up her attack then and she's still attacking me now. I don't feel I've grown up. I don't feel I've left her. I'm still living in the womb.

EXCERPTS FROM AND SUMMARIES OF R1's HISTORY AND SESSIONS

"OBSESSIONAL MOTIVES OF MY POLITICAL ACTIVITIES"

R1 has written: The following deals with the interpretation of my political activities during the dictatorship in my country (a Latin American state) based on the knowledge I obtained from eight autopsychognosia sessions.

I feel that I should particularly emphasize the fact that some principles, which I had formerly considered basic and irrefutable, altered during the course of my autopsychognosia. I must also stress the fact that any tendency on the part of the reader to make generalizations from what follows is hazardous. My intention is not to evaluate politics or violence but to present and interpret my own particular involvement with them from an obsessional point of view. If the reader is not amongst those who - motivated by fear to which they give ideological dimensions - have conditioned themselves to hide what is false or difficult, then he or she might find that this text contributes in a small way towards the effort to recognize the relationship between political activity and mental health. I considered the rather detailed references to my parents and past necessary for a better understanding of the interpretation of my political activities.

Mother She had not known her father who left home at the time when she was born (for reasons that were not revealed to her) and did not ever reappear. Any wish for her father is forbidden. When, at the age of five, she asks for him "as a Christmas present", her mother slaps her. She grows up in an atmosphere of double matriarchy (that of mother and grandmother) in a house haunted by the absence of and desire for a man's presence. The principle which prevails is: the woman is the one who stays and preserves; the man is the one who goes away, who is forbidden. Sex is forbidden. At the age of thirteen, she is publicly humiliated by the teachers with the consent of her family because she was seen speaking to a boy.

Her father's absence deprives her of the ability to recognize a father substitute. She oscillates between *good* men (harmless homosexuals) and *evil* men (*gorillas* with very manly features and characteristics), the latter becoming the great passions of her life. The principle *good-evil* motivates her and I inherit this.

Artistic by nature and active in many fields, she abandons an artistic career in order to find security with an industrialist from whom, however, she quickly separates. A few years later, she marries my father and they leave for France where my father's mother lives. At the beginning of World War II, my father becomes a volunteer in the French army and my mother a volunteer nurse. She feels almost erotic gratification in nursing the invalid (that is, impotent-permissible) soldiers. She then becomes her husband's nurse when he becomes bedridden because of a war wound. She becomes pregnant many times but has miscarriages. During the third year of the war, she becomes pregnant again. The foetus within her uterus is me. After my birth, we return home to Latin America and stay with her mother. Immediately afterwards, my father abandons her.

Father He is very dependent on his oppressive and overprotective mother whom he nevertheless punishes by squandering her vast fortune. He possesses an absolutely androcratic mentality. His point of reference is his male ancestors, "three generations of men of science", not his female ancestors. During World War II, he is wounded in the head. My mother nurses him. His recovery coincides with my birth and our return home. As soon as we return, my father abandons my mother just as her father had abandoned her mother when she was a baby.

My father's frequent disappearances disturb my mother. She imparts this mental conflict to me: the father is the one who is absent, the deserter. His character lends support to this image I have of him: Mother is the one who speaks, who accuses; Father remains silent. I hear that my father is profligate, financially irresponsible: because of him, my mother and I live in fear and insecurity. Nevertheless, my father teaches me through his words or, more frequently, his silence the affirmation of the dangers of love, the love of poetry, the power to smile in adversity. However, it is the security my mother teaches that I more frequently choose. Within the matriarchal atmosphere where I grow up with the order, "Father does not exist", her own anguish about the lack of a father takes root in my soul. I feel as if I too have never had a father. Her fear of and desire for a man impregnates my being. Thus, throughout my life I pursue strong father substitutes (the most intelligent, richest, most powerful men) who, for me, are friends, teachers, rivals or opponents, or frequently all those things combined.

After the 7th Session, I realize that by identifying with my mother, it had not been possible for me to have a father or to be a father (that is, a man) and thus I was caught up in a life dominated by false identity and illness. Realizing that I differ from my mother, I shout, "I'm very sorry, but I did have a father."

Some facts about my life During my childhood, I feel that my family sometimes rejects me totally while at other times it is fiercely possessive of me. I'm constantly plagued by illnesses, real and imaginary, which are 'cured' by my mother. When my mother is absent from the house, I go through hours of unbearable agony, afraid that I will die.

When I am five, my mother catches me touching my penis. She admonishes me very gently, saying that I must not touch my penis or else I'll turn into a monster. Then, at my mother's suggestion, a friend of the family appears before me half naked and wearing an anti-gas mask (where did they find it?) on his face. "Look, that's how you'll end up." The message of the man with the fly-like head is all to clear: castration or death. The memory of the monster neutralizes all conscious sexual desire for many years.

It is during the following years that I can pinpoint the time when my first fantasies begin, which gradually shape themselves around the double principle *good-evil*: the *good* submissive woman (whom I must nevertheless torment) and the *evil* man who threatens my existence and who I must compete against and defeat.

At the age of thirteen (I am a boarder in a Jesuit college) I experience my first ideological crisis. I question the existence and goodness of God, the motives of one's faith in God, I question family love and its value. This crisis does not progress very far because during this period I find relative security in a series of father substitutes. From then on I believe in a God-Father substitute who blesses my relationships with *good* (submissive) women and forbids relationships with *evil* women (women who are not submissive and who have many sexual relationships).

Between 16 and 20, I become attached to a political leader, *D*, who becomes a father substitute because he makes me feel particularly accepted (till then I had always felt that I was the black sheep of any group I belong to). *D* is an insecure man, a phallocrat, but cultured, a mixture of the bold avant-guardist in intellectual matters and the religious conservative. I believe in and embrace *D*'s principles. Before the military coup occurs in my country, *D* threatens that he will take to the mountains with his followers should there be a dictatorship. However, when the dictatorship actually takes place *D*, after a few days' imprisonment, becomes a law-abiding citizen.

During the same period (16 - 20 years old) I become conscious of the fact that sex is prohibited and this is combined with a peculiar feeling of social guilt. I feel, in other words, that *evil* men and *evil* women are free to have sex. However, *evil* people are rich. My sexual desires make me feel that I possess some of the ingredients of a rich man. Therefore I must be punished, castrated (become impotent) and become poor.

At the age of fifteen the following thing happens to me. During a storm my thoughts turn to my father. I feel he is alone. I weep for him and through my tears I identify with my forbidden father (forbidden by my mother). This feeling of loneliness compels me to declare my love to my best friend's girlfriend with whom I had been secretly in love for two years.

Between 18 and 23 I swing from one parent to the other. They have separated and live in different countries. A period characterized by fickle emotions.

When I am 23, my father dies. My mother forbids me to see him "so that I won't get a fright". In the days immediately following his death she goes about dressed in red, as if celebrating over the red male blood that had been shed.

At this time I begin to have my first sexual experiences with *evil* women, women who have many sexual relationships. Simultaneously I have a 'platonic' relationship with another girl, the ideal girl, who must remain chaste, but whom I must also torment.

The fragile equilibrium between the *good* and *evil* relationships is broken when the ideal girl goes abroad with her family so that her father can get away from the collaborators of the junta that is preparing for a coup. I interpret the girl's departure as a punishment for my sexual relations with the *evil* women. The effect is immediate: I become temporarily impotent, something which, at the time, I consider to be 'accidental'.

How I function during the dictatorship in my country The democratic government is overthrown by a junta consisting of the military and landowners. I am 26 at the time. I witness a scene of violence that causes me terror, anger and guilt. (Till then I had been politically involved only at a superficial level.) I feel that the dictatorship has deprived me of the ideal girl.

The following principle crystallizes in my mind and becomes an obsession: "Fight the junta!" (*good* must fight *evil*). *Good* is our oppressed and tyrannized poor people, the 'descamisados' who are threatened with death by the junta. *Evil* is the collaborators-junta[24] who threaten the people with death because they refuse to bow to their will. *Good* will inevitably crush *evil*. I side with *good*.

After somewhat briefly participating in the struggle against the junta, I go abroad thinking that I would be able to fight it more effectively from there. The real motive for my flight, however, is my wish to see the ideal girl again. I go to the same country and city where her family has taken refuge. I do in fact see her but when I try to make love with her, I find I am impotent. How is it that the ideal girl is castrating me?

Eventually, the ideal girl, frustrated, deserts me and returns to our junta-ruled country. This second rejection of hers throws me into a world of political fantasies. The *evil* men (the collaborators-junta) prevent me from returning home and once again deprive me of the ideal girl. (I deny my own responsibility for her flight.) Thus, confined and isolated for months on a deserted farm, I spend my time 'killing' the *evil* men by throwing a dagger at a target hanging on the wall, expecting the ideal girl and the revolution to knock at my door.

A few months later I become obsessed with the idea of carrying out bomb attacks. I meet other self-exiled resistance men and work as a chemist in underground networks. This activity utterly thrills me. I feel that I really exist only when I'm preparing explosives. Plans are laid for my return home to participate in a guerilla group. My return, however, is constantly postponed for a 'more propitious' time and never comes about. Yet, although I act in accordance with my credo, my activity doesn't bring me any satisfaction nor does it free me from the constant anxiety simmering within me. I renew my pursuit of a father substitute, particularly in the field of politics. International political leaders and close comrades fill me with enthusiasm at first but later their image crumbles before my eyes. I live in a world where the pursuit of practical results makes serious introspection and direct expression impossible. The world of the Resistance which I give myself to tends to become the same as the world of the hateful junta which I'm fighting. Deprivation, oppression and aggressiveness often prevail amongst the members of the conspiracy group and are manifested uncontrollably, degrading our relationships as human beings.

I isolate myself on the farm again and 'punish' myself by depriving myself of any serious scientific activity and by inflicting incredible torture on myself in order to compensate for the tortures being inflicted on the

---

24   Doctor's note: For R1 collaborators, junta and the German S.S.(p. 60) are closely associated because they all symbolize the rejecting womb which strikes ruthlessly and unawares.

resistance members at home, tortures which I feel guilty for because I am not experiencing them first-hand. The use of an assumed name helps me not to be myself. During the same period I constantly have dreams in which I cannot cross the frontiers of my country because my passport doesn't have a photograph. Avoiding all my basic problems, love, creativity, I live the life of someone else. I am a person without an identity.

I hear that the ideal girl has married in my country. Within my acute pain I feel deep creative powers awakening, as if I have savoured a sublime moment of existence. Thus I experience a new period of temporary intellectual growth which is combined with a sexual relationship with another girl who resembles the archetypal image of my mother rather closely. Yet I don't find peace with her because she is *evil* (she is also having relationships with other men). We separate and I slip back into a world of political fantasies again. During this period my soul is filled with indifference and callousness but also guilt towards my home, my mother. I hear that my mother's mother has died but I do not get in touch with my mother for 'security reasons'. I hear that my mother is approaching financial ruin and I feel deeply satisfied. Now I am truly poor. I will be free of my guilt.

During the same period I feel that the fanatical and unwavering convictions expressed by my comrades is alien to me. The world I live in and the world I desire prove to be conflicting and opposed to each other. Seeking a solution to the emotional confusion that overwhelms me, I become increasingly involved in the activities of the guerilla network. Finally, I myself 'manage' to become the victim of an explosion, something which fills me with deep satisfaction. Fortunately I am unharmed by the explosion but I become a target of the foreign police. I go into hiding and then, for the first time in my life, I discover masturbation. A little later I have an affair with and then marry a woman older than myself with whom I identify because she is socially deprived and therefore *good*. This woman becomes pregnant. I am overcome by ever-increasing fear. I feel that I cannot be a father. Basic elements of my mother's pregnancy with me are repeated. The woman tries without success to get rid of the foetus. Finally, a girl is born. Almost immediately after, I compulsively abandon my wife and daughter and return to my country, no longer involved in politics.

EXPERIENCES OF MY INTRA-UTERINE LIFE WHICH I RELIVED DURING MY AUTOPSYCHOGNOSIA SESSIONS

The Knowledge of the Womb

Within the uterus I am accepted by my mother (I am a substitute for the husband and father who are forbidden to her but whom she desires). During the 5th Session I assume the foetal position and experience the bliss of security and acceptance. However, in every Session I also relive the fear that I will die, which I had felt when I was in my mother's womb. (The fear of death is something that I feel in my everyday life as well as in my frequent nightmares.)

I am threatened with death from without. Every external stimulus removes me from the state of acceptance-security and generates terror and aggressiveness within me. The facts confirm that both mother and foetus are faced with multiple threats of death. My father's mother tyrannizes my pregnant mother and hopes I die in the womb. During the 2nd Session I am terrified at the sight of a woman dressed in black who threatens me with death. In her dress and appearance this black-clad woman reminds me of my father's mother, who really did hope that I would die.

During the 8th month of my mother's pregnancy, the German S.S. and their French collaborators burst into our house to search it. My mother faints. She is saved because the German officer in charge, moved by her pregnant condition, orders his men not to disturb her. I feel that this terrifying experience for my mother left deep traces within me. In everyday life, the sight of a collaborator dressed in a typical trenchcoat and trilby hat produces feelings of terror and aggressiveness within me. The sight of a collaborator reactivates my pregnant mother's terror which my nervous system has retained to this day.

Together with the threat from without, I feel I am also threatened from within. I feel that my mother's acceptance of my foetal existence is followed by rejection. My mother wants me dead to be free of her mother-in-law's hounding and to take revenge on my father, as my presence in her womb reminds her of him. A typical example of the threat of death that comes from within is the dream I have the night that 'B' rejects me. (B is a woman with whom I had a relationship and to whom I was totally attached.) The subject of my dream is fear in various forms: fear of the void, fear of *evil* women, fear of *evil* men, fear of dogs, fear of collaborators. I overcome them all. Society, represented by television, congratulates me on my victory. My mother appears crying and suddenly her sweet face crumbles and in its place appears a terrifying mask whose mouth and eyes emit destructive energy. I wake up howling.

During the Sessions, when the psychedelic drug reactivates the rejection from within, I am overcome by an unbearable and paralyzing terror which forces me to stop the Sessions from evolving further.

During the first Session I feel the need to hold my breath till I am on the point of fainting. I realize that in this way I am reliving the danger of strangulation by the umbilical cord which was coiled around my neck at delivery. (This fact concerning the umbilical cord was verified by my mother after the first Session.)

THE EMOTIONAL MOTIVES OF MY BEHAVIOUR DURING THE DICTATORSHIP

Question 1:	Why do I become sexually impotent with the *evil* women when the ideal girl goes abroad with her family?
Question 2:	Why am I impotent with the ideal girl when I meet her abroad?
Question 3:	Why does the principle: "Fight the Junta!" (*good* must fight *evil*) become crystallized in my mind?
Question 4:	Why do I side with *good*?
Question 5:	Why do I become obsessed with the idea of explosions?
Question 6:	Why do I compulsively deny my daughter and wife?
Question 7:	Why do I abandon politics?

Answer to questions 1 and 2 I consider (emotionally) the departure of the ideal girl as punishment for my sexual relationships with the *evil* women. The ideal girl symbolizes my mother. My mother forbids me to have sexual relations. To regain the acceptance of the ideal girl, I must stop all sexual relations. Solution: I become impotent. It is at this point that my subjective confusion begins. The womb-mother rejects me when I have sexual desires and/or relations. The womb-mother accepts me only when I do not have sexual desires and/or relations (but how can I return to the womb that I yearn for without sexual desires and/or relations?). Under such conditions my return is out of the question. Thus, when I meet the ideal girl abroad, it is impossible for me to have sexual intercourse with her.

Answer to question 3 *Evil* is any power that threatens me with death. *Evil* demands that I submit to its will. *Evil* causes me terror. *Evil* is the collaborators-German S.S.[25] who threaten my foetal existence with death; the collaborators-junta that threaten me with death because I do not

---

[25] See footnote, p. 55.

The Knowledge of the Womb

want to submit to their will; the collaborators-junta that deprive me of the ideal girl (womb substitute) and so threaten me with death; the woman in black (my father's mother) who wants me to die; my mother's *gorillas* who take the womb-mother away from me and so threaten me with death; my mother, each time she rejects me (whether I am in her womb or whether I do not submit to her will).

Before the Sessions, I consider that the main characteristic of *evil* people is that they can make love whenever they like. All *evils* combine and form a *common evil*. *Evil* provokes in me terror and anger and activates my aggressiveness towards it. *Good* is whoever is threatened with death by *evil* (the people, myself). Each time I am threatened, I wish to return to the uterus, the place where I had felt bliss. This return is achieved through orgasm.

My mother rejects sex. She makes me submit to her will, not to have sex. If I disobey, she will reject me (a death threat). I submit and am castrated (I become impotent), I become *good* in her eyes. However, because I have sexual desires, I am *evil* and feel guilty. She will punish (reject) me. I can satisfy my sexual desires with *evil* women (paid prostitutes, as well as women who have many sexual relationships). However, this kind of sexual gratification is pure misery because it has nothing in common with the return to the ideal, accepting womb.

Answer to question 4 I have in me some elements of *evil* because of my sexual desires. By helping *good* defeat *evil*, I am purified, I annihilate the *evil* man within me, erase my social guilt and win the ideal girl who abandoned me because of the *evil* in me (my sexual desires).

Answer to question 5 During the 6th and 7th Sessions, I recollect that from early adolescence I had been tortured by *explosion nightmares*. These nightmares, which occurred every time my basketball team was defeated, were always the same. I would see the ball coming through the ring and the moment it touched the ground, it would explode. During these Sessions, the feeling accompanying the explosions in my dreams is associated with the danger of my existence being crushed and wiped out. Simultaneously, I experience terrible pain. The pain is unbearable and prevents me from letting the Sessions evolve further. I present the same resistance each time I start to revive the intra-uterine rejections of my existence. To sum up:

explosion = experiencing death = fundamental rejection within the uterus = unbearable pain.

The danger of death by explosion is associated with the collaborators-junta who deprive me of the accepting uterus. I would do to them what they had done to me. I would give them a taste of what it feels like to explode, a taste of the symbol of rejection and death.

Answer to question 6 I deny my daughter and wife just as my father denied my mother immediately after my birth, and just as my mother's father had abandoned his wife immediately after his daughter's birth. My daughter has to experience what her grandmother and I had experienced.

Answer to question 7 I abandon politics because, before I return home, I meet and marry a woman who is a good substitute for the previous ideal girl. My political activity, from the obsessional point of view, has run a course between one *good womb* and another.

EXCERPTS FROM AND SUMMARIES OF R3's HISTORY AND SESSIONS

History Female, 23 years' old, married for three years, son six months' old. She complained of anxiety, depression, severe aggressiveness towards her husband, over-emotionality, and vague symptoms from the digestive tract with frequent vomiting and severe periodic headache. Bronchial asthma during childhood.

Session 1 I was cold. I was freezing. The nurse heaped blankets on top on me ... still Siberia. She covered me in a mound of cushions. I felt better. I felt wonderful. I felt as though I was floating on a pool of quicksilver upside down inside a warm cocoon, utterly comfortable, safe, secure. I made little snuffling noises and snuggled deeper into the warm depths. My knees and elbows flexed, my hands came up under my chin. I grew smaller, so did my body and my face. My hands were pulled inwards and I felt that I could not control my muscles. I was completely relaxed. My lids closed. I wanted nothing but to enjoy the supreme comfort in which I found myself. Then I felt as though I were about to be thrown into ice-cold water. I shrank in fear of the contact. I felt constriction round my head, and it seemed as though I were going to hurtle into a chasm of nothingness.

I was terrified. I was born. Then I felt my bottom being slapped. This was followed by a sensation of emptiness, the yawning gap left when something is torn from its roots. My abdominal muscles were sore. It was as though I had just given birth to my son. I was at once a baby, and a mother. I remembered the words which I had felt, and repeated over the years to my mother: "I never asked to be born. I hate you." She had pushed me out of my haven of absolute security, and I was resentful. Yet she was the nearest thing to that security. I clung to her possessively.

To begin with, my mother was my world. I was happy in her presence, her absence made me hysterical. When I was one and a half years old, my brother had an accident and cut his chin. He had to have it stitched. I was so jealous of the attention my mother gave to him that I climbed onto a chair and tried to cut my chin in the same way on the window-sill. I was unsuccessful.

Outside it was raining. There was lightning and hail. I was frightened. I was cold. I jumped into bed with Mummy and luxuriated in the infinite warmth and comfort of her body. I came to like winter. When the weather was chilly I had a good excuse to run to my mother's arms, to bury my head in her breast. Once within that charmed circle, nothing mattered to me, I was safe.

I was hostile to, and jealous of, anything which took my mother's attention away from me. My father, though a shadowy figure, persistently did so. To make matters worse, my mother seemed to be more interested in him than in me. I felt she had betrayed me with my father. Then I decided: if you can't beat'em, join'em.

Like my mother, I paid attention to my father. If she could betray me, I could do the same to her. I began to imitate her as much as possible. I put a handbag on my arm, oranges in the front of my dress, and teetered about precariously, my feet encased in the toes of Mummy's high-heeled shoes. I powdered my face into a ghost-like mask, daubed a gash of lipstick on my mouth, and drew owlish circles round my eyes.

I even played a game with my mother: we pretended our roles were reversed. I played Mummy, and she was my daughter. When I was six, my mother went abroad. I made her promise to bring me a doll which said "Mama". My mother's absence threw me into an anxiety state as usual. The doll symbolized that she was thinking of me and that I was with her, in the shape of a baby-doll. My mother brought the doll finally. When she went out and left me, I comforted myself to some extent by mothering my doll, as if to say: "Don't worry, Mummy is still here." I had become Mummy and the doll was myself.

When I grew up, I wanted to have babies like Mummy. The man I married reminds me of my mother as well as my father, in character and in looks. My desire for security drove me towards a person who resembled the original source of that security; my mother. I could never get back inside my mother's womb, but I could recreate my feeling of safety through identification. First, I identified with my mother, and married a father substitute.

When I became pregnant, I identified, not only with my mother, but also with the baby inside my uterus. I relived, at least in some measure, my feeling of security within the womb. (This explains why, when I returned to the womb under the psychedelic, I also felt like a mother.) While pregnant, I felt that if my baby were a boy, he would be a possible ideal husband-father. If my baby were a girl, I felt she would be myself and my mother.

Session 4 I remember the tension I felt when my parents quarrelled. I felt terrible. The slightest movement brought a tide of nausea and vomit up (though I didn't try to avoid the movements). Pain drilled into my temples and behind my eyeballs, making the world spin alarmingly. It was worth it, though. It made my mother worry about me and give me her attention, at least for a short while. That was what I craved, next to getting back inside her. She sometimes asked me if I would like to "go back into her heart again" and I said: "Yes, yes!"

Frequently, I vomited till I was exhausted. I could keep nothing in my stomach. I got double vision and could not move properly. My body became numb. I seemed to be floating. Objects and people were distant and unreal as though they too were floating in a haze, or seen through some liquid. I was oblivious of my surroundings, safe in a world of my own. (Return to the womb through psychosomatic S & P.)

In winter my mother made me wear a woollen vest because she was certain that, otherwise, I would get a cough. I got a cough anyway. It inevitably developed into severe bronchitis. I could hardly breathe. I used to lie awake making music with my bronchioles, thinking of the inflamed passages, willing the air to pass through, and able only to take in a tiny wheeze of air in shallow gasps of breath. I only felt better when my mother was by my side. I really wanted her to breathe for me again.

My mother had stiff joints and backache. I developed stiff joints whenever I had to perform a task like, for example, sewing, on my own. I would suddenly get unexpected pains in my legs whenever there was a sporting event at school, even though I was a record breaker at normal times. I could not allow myself consistently to do anything well on my own. I did not want to do anything well on my own. It meant that I was increasing the distance between me and my mother, between me and the original source of my security, the womb. I wanted to be dependent in order to simulate, as nearly as possible, the conditions of uterine safety ...

EXCERPTS FROM AND SUMMARIES OF R4's HISTORY AND SESSIONS

History Male, 22 years' old, single, university education. Severe sexual problems affecting his mental and physical health. Severe aggressiveness towards his environment and particularly his mother.

R4's description of his mental condition before the Sessions: My homosexual relationship with X has been going on for about a year now. After each physical encounter with him I feel anxious and very insecure. I've noticed that I also sink into a state of inactivity, confusion and complete inertia. I think that breaking up with A was what drove me to X. (My affair with A was deeply emotional and sexual. It was her decision that we break up. The result was quite a few weeks of depression.)

A's leaving me led me to change tactics. I avoided long affairs and started associating with *corrupt* women (that is, 'easy' women without of course being prostitutes). At the same time I met X and decided to act out the fantasies which have been an integral part of my sexual activity since the day A and I separated. (During the sexual act, in order to reach orgasm, I create an atmosphere which I shall call *corrupt*, depraved; an atmosphere where I have homosexual fantasies. At other times these fantasies assume the form of a whole myth, for instance that the woman I'm making love with is a depraved whore or suchlike.)

I feel very tired and exhausted. I sleep till lunch-time and when I wake up I want to go back to sleep. There are moments when I want to finish with this world once and for all. No goal in life. A feeling of self-destruction rules my life. (I squander my money for no reason, I go out at night, I neglect my studies.) Endless wandering on short and long trips without aim, or rather with the aim of going to bed with as many women as I can. (The only male I go with is X, who is some years younger than me. Men in general don't interest me, nor do I want to strike up the kind of relationship with any of them that I have with X.) I feel unbearable anguish and I cannot stand going on in the same way every day. I have neither courage nor hope. Complete deadening of the intellect. (I think this stagnation came on very slowly, almost without my realizing it.) Refusal to complete a whole lot of projects whose success would be a certainty. (The only thing I've managed to do is to get my university degree with low marks.) I consider the cause of my downfall to be A

who, with her unacceptable desertion, threw me into a vicious circle of misery. With each day that passes I become more and more submerged in intellectual and emotional stagnation. I'm suffocating. I decide to seek psychiatric help.

Session 1   I feel cold. Rapid pulse beat and pain in the jaw. Slight nausea and some dizziness. An unknown sensation begins from the depths of my bowels and spreads to my whole body. These symptoms frighten me. It's as if I'm losing control over my body. This doesn't last long. Suddenly I feel frightened and want to break the whole thing off. I think that I'm going to change after the Session, that I'll no longer be the same. That frightens me very much. The symptoms recede; as they do, I look at the doctor and become startled. His face is all veins, nerves and bones! It's like some hideous illustration in an anatomy book. The doctor tells me that it's an illusion. It doesn't last long. Now my head is empty. Next I want to speak about my relationship with *A*. Simultaneously I want to refer to my homosexual activity. Finally I tell the doctor that I prefer to talk about *A*. (I'm embarrassed to speak to the doctor about *X*.)

I describe my relationship with *A* in detail (I emotionally relive the years we spent together). I note that when I started off with *A*, I was unable to make love to her for three months (I couldn't get an erection). I'd lie down and though I'd feel aroused at first, when I'd try to enter her I'd no longer have an erection. Finally, one evening when I went to visit an uncle of mine, I found the maid of the house there. Nobody else was in the house just then. The maid asked me to make love in a very depraved way. I accepted. That night I succeeded in making love (I ejaculated inside her). The next day I lay with *A* and was able to make love again. From then on I had no problem.

I tell the doctor that when I met *A*, I constantly talked to her about my mother. Now, under the influence of the drug, I'm astonished at how much I insisted on discussing my mother with *A*. I also tell the doctor that I feel a strange fear in front of women. I'm afraid that if I go to bed with them, I won't be able to 'make it'. I consider sex as a duty imposed on me by God knows whom. It is with difficulty that I can find the entrance to the female genitals. This is something which is revealed to me for the first time. I've been with many women and I had never been aware of the fact that a great and strange fear gripped me within.

I realize that when I did it to my uncle's maid, I felt pleasure because I humiliated her. I relive the scene and see the girl in front of me doing whatever I ask her to do to me. She looks *corrupt* and that excites me very much.

The Session continues with events from my childhood which suddenly come to mind and which I relive with great emotional intensity (faces, colours, places, countrysides, houses, all suddenly come up to the surface). I have the feeling that in the midst of all this I'm desperately looking for my mother and can never find her anywhere. She was never really at my side. She was always going out or travelling. She was never at home. I grew up with the household servants and my grandmother. I feel that they give me love but I desperately long for my mother. Nor is my father around during this period (about three to eight year's old). A feeling of great loneliness overcomes me and I begin to sob and ask for my mother. I realize that the anguish I feel in my effort to pinpoint my mother somewhere and the phase I went through when *A* abandoned me are the same.

The Session ends with the following image. I am with my mother in the garden of our house. I'm five years' old and I'm holding her by the hand. Suddenly she leaves me and goes towards a group of friends who are just entering the garden. (As I am vividly reliving this incident, I lift my arm high in mid-air as I did when I was five years' old. At the same time, I feel my body becoming smaller.) The instant my mother lets go my hand to run towards her guests I feel lost and start to cry. I cry as I did then and the doctor urges me to do so without embarrassment. I have the feeling that even when I don't cry, the same anguish of feeling 'lost' dominates me in everyday life as well. A constant feeling of anguish, that is my life. I tell the doctor that I love my mother very much. (This is in contradiction with my everyday feelings where I behave very hostilely towards her and frequently feel that I hate her.) I speak of her very tenderly. It is extraordinary, but I discover that I love her very much and somewhat desperately. I could never have believed that beneath my aggressiveness towards her such a great and desperate love was hidden. I say "desperate" because not once did she realize it nor did she ever spend any time with me. Not once did she caress me nor did she take any interest in her child. My grandmother and the servants were just protectors. Much loneliness in those years. I tell the doctor that I feel I need her just as much even now that I'm no longer five but 22 years' old!

I feel tired. My life seems like a vast loneliness in which I constantly search for my mother. Deception and loneliness! I don't think I knew a thing about myself. I am very satisfied with the Session. It's as if I'm living and thinking in another dimension.

Session 4 I try to analyse the remorse that rules my life. I think: a lifetime of remorse! Love, remorse! *Corruption*, remorse! (Remorse

The Knowledge of the Womb

because of my relationship with *X*; remorse because I'm incapable of forming a unique relationship where I could give all my love. I note that now, while I have been undergoing Sessions, I have formed a relationship with a very intellectual and beautiful blond woman. *A* was also blond and very intellectual.) Remorse then about everything! I feel that whatever I do in life fills me with remorse. I am a tangled ball of thread. I don't know why I do what I do, what its purpose is, what the final aim of my every action or thought is. I believe that there must be some final objective in all this, some point where my life will become worthwhile. I haven't found it. (The drug acts within thirty minutes. I have the usual bodily spasms that I have in every Session as well as the pain in the jaw.)

In the room there is a painting of a classically beautiful blond woman. I look at it. I feel that it radiates purity. I try to define the purity of the portrait. To me this picture definitely expresses the sense of goodness which I've been searching for all my life. There's nothing depraved about it. Nevertheless, I refuse to accept the blond woman it portrays. I say: "I cannot have sex with that woman. Her purity stops me. It's only in *corruption* that I can become aroused."

The doctor asks me what I mean by purity. I show him the portrait again. (As I look at it, a feeling of serenity fills me which, however, is interrupted by anguish and laboured breathing.) I say: "That picture is one great lie!" I shout it vehemently as if I thought it the whole truth of my life and suddenly I discover that it has deceived me, mocked me! I have the impression now that the woman in the painting is mocking me. I'm profoundly convinced that the purity I seek in every woman is a tremendous fraud! (I realize that though I go with *corrupt* women of low intellect, I'm really looking for purity and innocence - rather muddled ideas.)

Suddenly the thought occurs to me that the blond woman in the painting is a very bad woman. When the doctor asks me if only that particular blond is bad, I answer that all blondes are bad. I'm confused. I don't know what to feel in front of the portrait. (I tell the doctor that I soon become indifferent even to the women I keep company with because they don't give me what I want, that which only the blond in the portrait can give me, purity.)

I relive an experience with a blond girlfriend of mine. I had lain down on the bed with her and I had no erection. "To hell with her purity," I tell the doctor. Purity and blond women are associated. Only blondes can love me and yet I have difficulty making love with them. "Pure, blond women," I say to the doctor, "are innocence, the intellect, while depraved women (usually dark-haired) are the flesh which corrupts."

Suddenly, sexual desire for the woman in the portrait takes hold of me. I feel that I want her immensely but that I am impotent. I feel terribly guilty for desiring her in this sexual way. As I'm looking at the portrait I start to cry. The more I look at it, the sadder but also the calmer I feel. Suddenly I discover that the woman in the painting is my mother.

With this realization my body goes into spasms. Spasms in the belly, arms, legs ... Spasms everywhere. I realize that these spasms also occur in my everyday life, though there not so strongly of course. (I am fidgety and jiggle my feet or play with my fingers; even in sleep my body never relaxes.) These spasms are very disagreeable.

So finally the fact is this. All blond women (including *A* and the woman I'm now dating whom I shall call '*M*') are images of my mother. A woman who is *corrupt* isn't my mother (and yet only with such a woman can I feel aroused and fulfil my need for sexual pleasure). I realize that sex with blondes is almost forbidden because it's as if I'm making love with my mother.

Final deep realization: I desperately try to find purity (which I've somehow associated with my mother) and when I do find it, I try to replace it with depravity. I destroy what I desperately seek. (I relive the incident with the blond girlfriend of mine. After we went to bed and I couldn't get aroused, I began to fantasize her as a whore, a woman who goes to bed with many men, who is capable of every perversion and so forth. In this way she ceases to represent my mother and this allows me to have sex. Yet after ejcaulating I felt deep disappointment and loneliness because there was no emotional fulfilment. In some strange way, sexual gratification and emotional fulfilment don't coexist.)

Session 5 I speak about the happiness I've felt in my life. I consider the happy moments to be minimal (even those I believed happy I don't accept as such now). There is something indeterminate and unknown behind happiness which never lets me savour it to the full. I feel the need to shut my mouth and not say a word to the doctor. Anxiety creeps over me and I cannot speak. (I'm afraid that if I do speak, that will lead me onto the revival of unpleasant experiences.) I'm breathing like an asthmatic. Vague fear and anguish.

During the third hour of the Session, I go back to my childhood again where I relive pleasant events (strolls with my nanny and grandmother at the age of four). I consider the years from the age of four until ten happy ones (I am the centre of attention of my grandmother and family friends). When I am ten, my grandmother dies. I am terribly alone. Once more I relive the moments with her but although I feel happy near her, I have the feeling that something doesn't let me complete my happiness. My mother isn't with me. I wander about in that period for about one to two hours, referring in detail to various childhood incidents. Then I return to the present and speak about the women who attract me sexually.

I tell the doctor that I'm attracted to women of low intellect and social class (I associate illiteracy with depravity). On the other hand, intellectuality is associated with purity. Even that fellow X is almost illiterate! M (the girl I'm dating now) is intellectual but I deny her the right to be! When I make love with her, I fantasize that she's illiterate and degenerate. My contradictory attitude and the way I act in life leave me flabbergasted ... I discover that I'm full of contradictions, that I don't see the world as it is, but as I want it to be. There is a force within me that distorts and corrupts everything. It's as if I deny reality, although I have my doubts as to what reality is. Finally, I didn't ever see either A or M as they really were but as I wanted them to be (non-intellectual, *corrupt*, idiotic and so on). In reality the former was a woman of character and a good person, M is intellectual and serene.

Amazed and very sad about my contradictory life I tell the doctor that I was totally ignorant of the motives of my behaviour. I feel remorse for having behaved as I did towards women. The object of the Sessions is to help me rid myself of the anxiety my problems create in me. In actual fact, however, they reveal to me a truth that I was unaware of. And as I'm speaking to the doctor about all this, I start to cry like a baby. I'm a little man who, as he progresses in the Sessions, discovers how emotionally small he is.

A basic realization I made during the Session is that I want every woman I make love with to be completely non-intellectual (because my mother is moderately intellectual) and *corrupt* (my mother is the personification of purity - at least that's what I want to believe). The contradiction is obvious. Every woman I make love to I strive to differentiate from but also to associate with my mother. A feeling of having wasted my life searching for something which I simultaneously deny.

Session 6 I will call this Session the *Session of Light*. I give it this name because the horizon of my inner world began to clear and because this is how I'd like to express the multi-dimensional world which appeared before me. It's as if this Session opened a door onto a vast avenue. A sunbeam penetrated the semi-darkness of my unconscious. At last I was able to see my holy and all-powerful mother more clearly.

As soon as the drug began to act I saw A's and my mother's face on the same plane. I felt deeply that all these years A has been a total substitute for my mother. And then, with that thought, came the light! I stopped having anxiety (the Session had begun with a strong dose of anxiety and dyspnoea). I started to cry and my crying had a cathartic effect on my whole being. I cried because I couldn't believe this total association of the two persons and it was as if I were being cleansed of self-delusions and illusions. My face felt clean and fresh, as if a gentle breeze were brushing against it. I can say with certitude that I had entered another atmosphere, lighter, with more oxygen, a most limpid atmosphere which separated me from things around me and from the doctor (he didn't exist for me).

I had literally slipped out of my body and was dangling in the void - a brand new and indescribably beautiful and free feeling. It was my first contact with the environment without obstacles, without that weight on my shoulders which made me wearily tolerate the world. Now I accepted this world, these surroundings, this furniture, those people walking out in the streets, with my senses unobstructed and my soul free.

As difficult as a person finds it to grasp what the surface of the moon looks like at close range if he's never been there, that's how difficult, and more, it seems to me to describe the feelings from my experiences during the sixth Session. The world I found myself in was a world of new sensations where the subjective element had completely disappeared to be replaced by a brand new identification of the self with its surroundings. Then once again I came face to face with the total association of *A* with my mother. This continued for a long time. A need for my mother grew in me. I wanted to put my arms around her and never let her go. I realized that *A*, the woman I had loved so much, could not in herself give me the unlimited attention and tenderness I craved. For a moment I felt that *A* was a stranger. Who was this woman I had idealized to the point where I demanded the total devotion and love which only one person in the world could give me, my mother!

A is now standing in the corner of the room. I have put her there all of a sudden as if wanting to judge her, to compare her with the other woman, my mother, who is standing diametrically opposite her. Comparison between the two women will prove crushing for *A*. There just is no comparison.

In the hours that elapse, I will destroy once and for all a whole myth. Feelings of anger, sadness, love and hatred (all that I have felt for my mother, for *A*, and the world) will succeed each other for a few minutes. The cause of this dramatic change of feelings is the two women. In the light of this new emotional environment it will take me quite some time before I manage to clarify my position in relation to them. I will go through frantic longing for *A*, for the days when we first met (which I insist on believing ideal). Then my attitude will change. I will look at *A* with the eyes of a stranger. She will cease to mean anything to me; perhaps I shall even feel indifferent towards this 'stranger' who intruded into my life and who rejected me in the end. Then I will reach the point where I can face her exactly as she is, stripped of myth, disrobed, unmasked. I will be able to see her clearly as *A*. Here, at this point, and as all her good deeds, her vain efforts, pass like lightning through my mind, here I will love her. For the first time, a disinterested love is born within me. I don't expect any reciprocation because I have no need of it. I no longer expect her to give me all that my mother gave me. But did my mother really give my anything?

I turn and look at my mother. That woman gave me absolutely nothing. Yet I wanted her to give me both tenderness and boundless acceptance. As an adult I sought the same things from *A* and now from *M*. Neither they nor the other women gave me the excessive devotion I wanted. I turn and look at the portrait of the blond woman on which now appear the faces of my mother, of *A* and *M* as well as all the women I have associated with in my life. For me the blond woman in the portrait is the ideal mother, that is, she has all my mother's characteristics plus all those my mother lacks (meaning that the blond in the picture can give me tenderness).

That is the ideal which, in fact, I will never find: the woman who is my mother idealized. The ideal woman-mother will never say no to me. She will wait for me on the threshold of our home day and night. She will be faithful and mine. She'll forgive all my wayward ways because a mother always forgives her child. Beneath the weight of this infinitely great delusion, I understand now why *A* left me. I always asked for more, and still more. What a ridiculous, what a comic little man I am! Suddenly I feel that I am making love with the ideal woman-mother of the portrait. It is an intercourse complete in every way and an absorption of my body into hers. There are no boundaries between us. We are one.

This ideal woman had appeared clearly to me and I began to laugh loudly (so loudly that even the doctor joined in my laughter). And as I was dangling outside my body, judging my antics, I saw the laughter on my face. It was a horrible contortion of disgust, bitterness and sarcasm. For once in my life I can see and judge without the burden of my blind subjectivity.

Nonetheless, for one moment I want to turn back, to stop this draining discovery. Nostalgia for my past overwhelms me. It's frightening but my old way of life beckons to me not to abandon it. I want to stop this draining discovery of the truth. I see everything, that for so many years constituted my faith, crumbling. I don't want to renounce it. Herein lies the great problem of changing. I'm afraid to exist beyond what I was. But I cannot possibly turn back, I cannot say nothing exists beyond my ridiculous affairs, beyond my wretched acts and the tragic way I behave towards myself and the world. No more can I close the shutters, block out the sun and turn on the electric light. When you manage to face yourself just once, when you can take yourself by the hand and lead yourself to the stage I've arrived at, there is no turning back.

Session 9 Absolute calmness and serenity. Nothing perturbs my mind. No thoughts. No images arise from the past. I don't even want to talk. I feel wonderful, lying on the couch. I remain thus, motionless and mute, for about five hours. When the doctor tries to get me to talk, I refuse to do so very aggressively. He tells me that I'm resisting. I don't accept that. The Session ends exactly as it began, in a state of absolute and utter physical and mental inertia. I feel very rested.

From R4's diary Coming home after the ninth Session, I realize that I really did resist. Generally, I resist in every Session. The form my resistance takes varies from Session to Session. Many times I laugh non-stop or I insist on reliving happy incidents from childhood or I give way to analyses of various events which have nothing to do with my basic problems. During the ninth Session I resisted because I felt that if I gave rein to my memory, I would relive painful events. I realize this. However (and this is strange) as I approach *M* in bed, the same serene feeling which immobilized me on the medical couch for five hours returns. I feel a certain power flowing within me and impelling me towards *M*. We make love and I feel perfectly happy. I didn't fantasize at all. I accepted *M* as she really is. I felt that there were no boundaries between us. I ejaculated without pain. For the first time I feel that for the sexual act to be complete, there must be emotions. Without emotions the act is incomplete. It is as if I accepted my mother totally, as if I made love with my mother.

Session 10 I have lost my whereabouts. My joints ache. I feel a tingling through my whole body. The walls seem to be moving and pressing upon me. A feast of colours fills my visual field. The reality of my surroundings seems like a distant dream which comes and goes through air pockets. I cannot concentrate on the problems which torment me. I am being absorbed by, I'm merging into, the world of the external environment. I feel I'm becoming one with the vase, the chair, the carpet ... I'm suffocating. I feel panicky ... Everything freezes. I don't know what's causing all this. I reach out to touch the doctor. I want to reassure myself of his existence here, of something which suggests human life. My breathing becomes shallow. I'm bathed in sweat. My body is stuck in the foetal position. I can't move it. Multi-coloured images appear before me ... a large forest with thick foliage. A bird appears in the sky (I no longer see the ceiling of the room). The bird comes down and circles over my head. I feel unprotected. The presence of the bird, however, is reassuring. Slowly I am transformed into a nestling. I am the little bird, the baby of the big bird flying above me.

As the minutes go by, this feeling becomes a certainty. My body is covered with down ... Nothing makes me feel human. I want to believe in something and cannot. I'm lost. I'm a piece of meat, a bird. Panic grips me together with a feeling of great loneliness. I raise my eyes towards the sky of this primeval era. I look for the strange, enormous bird. I try to find it ... Slowly I begin to find myself back in the room. I touch my body and recognize it as my own. Next I feel that I am in a nest. I touch my body and feel it covered with slimy down. Around me there is straw. A feeling that I am surrounded by thousands of dangers ... The colours are now green. I can distinguish trees and bushes. This is an endless forest.

At this point I try to get up and fly ... I feel I have wings ... My body is stuck in the foetal position and I can't move it. I fall back onto the couch. Finally I manage to stand on my trembling legs. I tell the doctor that I'm going to fly. I approach the window but the doctor, with a gentle gesture, makes me come back to the present. I fall onto the couch and feel like a bird again. Then I feel pain in my jaw (the same pain that I feel in every Session). I also feel pain where the forceps left scars. I am in great pain and cry. One minute I feel I'm a bird and the next a new-born baby. Somebody is pulling me and hurting me. I see white. I can dimly see white gowns and smell on operating theatre ... I'm being born ... They're pulling me out with the forceps.

Unbearable cold ... much cold. I start to cry in a voice I cannot recognize. It's the voice of a new-born baby ... I try to speak in my own voice but it's as if my vocal cords will produce nothing but a baby's cries. With difficulty I put my fingers to the wounds left by the forceps. I'm in great pain and feel cold ... I'm leaving the warmth in a state of panic. I'm shouting, crying, thrashing about ... I'm covered in saliva and fluids ... I don't want to come out ... But come out of where? Where are they pulling me out from? I can hear the sound of instruments. I'm cold, trembling ... I can smell chloroform. I don't want to come out ... I don't want to be born ... I want to go back. I'm unable to speak. I don't want to move from where I am. I refuse to accept the power exerted upon me by those who are pulling me out.

Suddenly I go back to being a bird. I am on a branch of a tree. I can hear a whole lot of noises but I can't tell where they're coming from. I can see, am almost bombarded with, colours ... Strange and frightening sounds can be heard from the depths of this forest. I can hear the leaves stirring beneath the wind. I've lost all contact with my real self. (In no other Session have I had an experience so intense and so long-lasting.) My surroundings have altered completely and my eyes see nothing by foliage and plains ... I'm not a human being. The doctor is saying something. I don't listen ... I don't pay attention ... I'm lost ... I don't exist.

Slowly everything abates. My mind becomes emptied of colours. Hot sweat streams down my face. My body, my joints are relaxed. I lie down exhausted. (Before, I was either lying down or kneeling or curled up on the couch.) Slowly I return to the present but again I find myself being absorbed by the leather covering of the couch ... I feel that I am leaving my body. It's as if I've broken the boundaries between myself and the matter surrounding me. Everything that stretches out before me, assuredly some god has placed it there with masterly skill. I don't know which god it is ... Anyway, someone has made everything function this way.

I can see before me endless horizons covered with thick vegetation. I feel I'm sitting on the ground. I'm the continuation of the ground, I am part of this ground. No problem affects me. I'm far removed from the ideas of homosexuality, love, mother, father. Everything that I thought I had discovered is only one side of that terrifying past of mine. I'm experiencing an evolution of cataclysmic proportions. I am within everything and I am everything. I hear melodies which harmonize with the colours of this eternal and indestructible nature ... I'm discovering the divine in every particle of matter. I get up from the couch and approach the window. With just this object, this sole proof that I exist apart from nature, I feel I am escaping into the infinity of earth. I am the absolute master of my movements now. I can see the trees in the garden of the clinic clearly. All is perfect, properly arranged, utterly beautiful and still. In the world reigns an awesome equilibrium. I have calmed down. I am happy.

I wouldn't have wanted to die before experiencing this union with the world around me. Now I am almost ready to die ... It is of no consequence because I can feel the eternity of matter. Everything exists, everything in inconceivable harmony. I breathe easily ... I feel blissful. It is a feeling which has nothing to do with joy, nor even with the greatest human happiness. What I feel is beyond any known emotion. It is a state, a perfect state, even beyond sensual pleasure. There is nothing excessive in

---

26 Translator's note: From the ancient Greek, meaning the 'absence of fear'.

this bliss which, in another language, I would call αφοβία.[26] There is no fear, no anxiety or anguish. It is Democritus who used the word αφοβία and said that perfect bliss lies beyond sensual pleasure ... I am beyond heaven and hell. I am motionless and eternal.

Session 13 In the room there is a large mirror. I want to get up from the couch and look at myself in the mirror. As I'm moving towards it, I feel my body undergoing a change. There is a languor in the movements, the steps, in the general 'rhythm' of my body. These languorous movements are the movements of a woman. I look at myself in the mirror but my face is not my own. Gradually I notice that it has assumed female features ... Finally, my mother's face appears in place of my own. The same thing happens with my body. I am, but at the same time I am not, me ... When I look at myself again, I am a woman and that woman is my mother.

For quite some time I stand in front of the mirror looking at this transformation. A feeling of serenity fills me but at the same time this serenity is broken by difficulty in breathing and anxiety. It is that inner anxiety which never leaves me. (The only Session until now in which I've felt absolute happiness and serenity was the tenth, in its last hours.) When the doctor asks me what I feel, I analyse my condition thus: My inability to unite with the woman who is the image of my mother compels me to identify with her.

As I'm describing this need of mine, I see a vulva in front of me. It disgusts me. This disgust at the vulva stops me from penetrating it. I interpret my identification with my mother as being the result of my inability to enter her. Suddenly I feel that I am afraid of the female genitals. Simultaneously, I am suffocating with an unfulfilled love whose object is the possession of the female-maternal body. (At this point, the feeling that I am my mother has become very strong. I touch my body and think I'm touching my mother's body. Even my skin gives off her scent.) This deep identification lasts for about half an hour during which I constantly repeat that I cannot accept the female genitals. The female genitals are my mother's genitals. I cannot possibly accept them. The more the minutes go by, the more I realize that the female genitals arouse great fear in me. (I had never thought that I was so afraid of them, I who have been to bed with so many women.)

Now the vulva has flooded my field of vision (it comes and goes as if seen through a zoom lens). I feel dizzy and start to spin when, in fact, I remain motionless on the couch. An uncontrollable force is hurling me towards the enormous vulva (the whole room has become one enormous vulva). My heart begins to pound and my body breaks into strong muscular spasms. Never before have I felt those spasms so strongly. It's very disagreeable. I'm heading unwillingly for some bottomless pit. The pit is in the vulva. I try to put a stop to this unpleasant situation. In vain. It is the first time since the tenth Session that I cannot control myself (there also, all resistance was futile). I don't want to approach the vulva but at the same time I've almost completely been sucked into it. For a fraction of a second I want to stop falling into it. Everything seems dim and distant ... I'm overcome by spasms. Saliva fills my mouth. I am inside the vulva. I feel awful. (My body assumes the foetal position. I can't move any more. I look at my hands. They are whitish and pink. I can see my nerves and veins through the skin.)

In answer to a question from the doctor I say that I am in the womb and that somebody is punching me in the ribs continually (where I feel the spasms). I'm afraid of the dark. I'm in pain and tossing about. It's my mother who's making these jerking movements and I'm moving with her. A terrible feeling. As if I'm in water and sinking. The spasms don't stop. I tell the doctor that it's horrible in here, that I can't stand this jolting and these spasms which are being imposed on me from without. Suddenly I see the big vulva again. It has now taken the form of electric wires. That is what causes the spasms. It's as if I'm being hit by a low voltage electric current. This goes on for quite a while during which I analyse the feelings of fear and pain over and over again. I mostly repeat the same words and live through the same spasmodic state. I realize that I'm afraid of the female genital organs because they represent the awful situation in the womb and that every contact with the female genitals brings it back. Now I understand why I feel a little pain at orgasm. That pain is the same as the pain I feel now. Orgasm is a state similar to the spasms I experienced in my mother's uterus. The spasms now spread to the abdominal area and the lower back. This lasts for quite a while. Then I calm down and try to analyse the experience from this Session which lasted about six hours.

Thoughts after the 13th Session: Looking at my life, I notice that my emotional state resembles the jerky line on a cardiogram. My whole life has been an agonizing spasm. When I meet a woman, at any place, any time, I feel an irresistible, destructive attraction which paralyzes my intellectual powers and physical resistance. No, it isn't desire but a kind of helpless abandonment to the superior power of her presence in my life. Woman has a destructive effect on my being. Planning contact with her body (before it even happens) creates in my very guts a feeling of pleasurable abandonment to the unattainability of the goal. But even as I'm in the process of gratifying my uncontrollable desire for intercourse with her, this same desire consumes itself in the motions of sexual contact, without any emotional fulfilment. When my penis enters her, I come up against the spasms I experienced in the 13th Session.

All the agony in my life (non-existent sleep or nightmares, fear that I'll be judged negatively by my fellow human beings, constant tension, aggressiveness, nastiness) springs from my inability to find fulfilment in the sexual act. Something just isn't right there. There's something wrong with my whole life. Now I don't dare speak of the sexual freedom I always preached. What I called freedom (to try everything, every perversion, every act) is a desperate attempt, a trick, a game in the dark. This whole process of freedom in sex now takes on the form of a procession advancing towards the centre of the drama. My life seems like an ancient Greek tragedy except that Catharsis never comes. I can see myself imploring God-Mother, a God who has made his decision and can on no account change it. Desolate and shattered within, I drifted from body to body, confusing my reality with that of others. I believed myself to be a proud buck, free to try everything, to act without restraint. The Sessions have cleared up this picture, revealing in its place a hunch-backed cripple, entangled in the nerves of the uterine membrane, dragging himself around some dark point of confusion and disorder, of spasms and sobbing which have dominated and oppressed him since the day of his conception.

I can see clearly what it was that drove me to homosexuality. In the sexual act with a man, I was looking for a woman, although of course I didn't find her. The homosexual act is in essence heterosexual. I think it is an unconscious masquerade. In the active role I put on the mask of the man-father while my passive partner has female characteristics which are determined by passiveness, submissiveness and pain. I am the victimizer and her the victim (in other words, the woman is essentially the man's victim). When I am the passive partner, I wear the mask of my mother. I become my mother and my partner the oppressor-father. And I was led to this kind of sexual contact because the genital organs of a woman reminded me of the spasms and unconsciously caused me pain and fear.

It has been three weeks since the 13th Session. I am sitting in front of the open window of my room breathing in the spring air. I think of all those spring evenings (of every spring in my life) which excited my senses for no definite reason. On such evenings there was always a desire to be alone beside the body of some woman. At the same time there was also the need to run away: to disappear, to flee, to go far away from all these stimuli, these women who sway by in the streets. Suddenly I feel myself being annihilated. Agony and expectancy and emptiness. As I'm sitting there I suddenly feel the spasms and my mouth full of saliva (exactly as in the Session). Not in the least a pleasant situation. I am reliving a past state without the help of a drug. I let myself go for a little, then I get up and change position. With this, the sudden revival of the intra-uterine situation ceases. That night, I sleep peacefully.

Session 14 I repeat to the doctor that at one point I had a good relationship with my mother. When? I realize that when I first met *A*, she herself represented that good relationship. I made love with her without fantasizing. When she abandoned me I entered a period of *bad relations* with the female sex which I now call *bad relations* with my own mother. And now, in this Session, I want to be on good terms with her again. I need to be reconciled with the female genitals, reconciled with my mother, to the situation I lived within her. Indeed, that is why I have never stopped associating with women, even if in a *corrupt* way. Something keeps me near them. That *something* which they promise me kept me from turning exclusively to men. I tell the doctor: "... I'm negotiating. All these years I've been negotiating with my mother. It's as if I'm negotiating with the genitals of all women. I want there to be peace between us."

I relive the days when *A* left me. I'm lying sick on the crumpled sheets of my bed. Sick and lonely. Submerged in anguish and nausea. (My nausea and anxiety are similar to what I felt in the 13th Session when I relived the spasms of my mother's body when I was a foetus.) In front of me now there appears a huge vulva. Horror seizes me at the sight of it. My nausea increases. I cannot bear to look at it. The doctor asks me whose vulva it is. I tell him it's *A*'s. I consider it to be the vulva of a whore. Then I say that it isn't *A*'s vulva but a whore's. *A* has a good vulva in the sense that it isn't repulsive like the one which is now filling my field of vision. I realize that the genital organs of women do not always engender the same feelings in me. Sometimes I accept them and other times I find them repugnant. I say: "... In the first phase of my relationship with *A*, I ejaculated inside her without pain. Our sexual relations were very good. It was a period of *good relations* with my mother (the association between *A* and my mother is total and crystal clear). I was, then, on good terms with *A*'s vulva, with my mother, with my mother's uterus." At this point my body assumes the foetal position again and I feel serene for a minute or two. Then spasms jolt me as they did in the 13th Session.

Then I speak again of all the years I've lived and I feel very bitter. I realize that the pain I feel during ejaculation every time I have intercourse with women is, in fact, the revival of the intra-uterine spasms. I feel as if all these years I've been expecting something to happen. I explain my homosexual activity with *X* as the only way to avoid facing the female genitals and the pain they cause me, it now being clear that the female genitals symbolize life and spasms within the uterus. Clearly, then, the sexual act is nothing less than the return to the intra-uterine world.

An image appears before me. Women dressed in black pass by silently. They give me the feeling that they have been passing by for years and years. They make the same movements. They don't speak. No gestures, no words. I understand that they are bearers of some *message*. They want to communicate something to me. They are bearing my *mother's message*.

The image is so vivid that I think they are in the room with me. Suddenly I ask them: "What news have you brought me?" They don't answer but I understand that they have brought me nothing new. All these women have now assumed the faces of girls and women I had at times been sexually involved with. I relive some of the moments I spent with them. They all bring me the same news: "She doesn't want you. She doesn't accept you!" Their words mean that no matter what I do, I'll always return to the hell of the intra-uterine spasms.

Suddenly they all disappear. A feeling of serenity fills me while at the same time I think with great titillation of a sexual experience I had with one of those girls. She was blond and blue-eyed (like my mother). I relive the act with her. A pleasurable feeling comes over me and I feel my body growing smaller. I remain motionless on the couch for a few minutes in a state of absolute tranquillity. My hands and fingers have a pink hue. I am a new-born baby. Then I feel something like threads and water in my mouth. I have become a foetus, very fragile and very happy. Perfect serenity and warmth surround me. I am in the womb. Serenity within the womb. Suddenly the spasms start anew and then serenity again ... and then spasms. This continues for quite a while. I realize that the serenity with the womb is short-lived but it does exist. I tell the doctor how unhappy I feel that the spasms won't let me feel and exist in total serenity.

After the 14th Session: All my life I have been searching for *innocence*. This *innocence* is a subjective state - the serenity of the accepting womb. That is where I want to return. I return through sex, intellectual work, art, as well as by other means. Everything (actions, thoughts, decisions) is aimed at that serenity. It is, I would say, the goal I have to reach. I realize, however, that the road leading to it is closed. The spasms close it. To reach serenity presupposes surmounting the spasms. That is essential. Nevertheless, spasms and serenity (as I lived the latter in the 14th Session) coexist and disproportionately so. As there were more spasms than serenity, I feel that my body and mind are dominated by them, while the moments of serenity become lost somewhere in my memory.

If I analyse all my acts, I would say that they are *spasmodic acts* which aim at serenity. I make decisions without considering that they may lead to catastrophic results. I am constantly being buffeted about. I always have the impression that something is going to happen to me, something unpleasant. For instance, that I have left the water heater on and the house will catch fire or that even though I have done my job well, someone will assail me and judge me or that when I am in the country where absolute quiet prevails, I think that some explosion will disrupt this tranquillity. I've never had peace of mind. I've always expected some disaster to befall me. There is a deep relationship between the intra-uterine spasms and my everyday behaviour. Every step I take I feel sure they will strike me. (I interpret my lack of self-confidence and my fear as dread of feeling the spasms again.) In the 14th Session I saw myself living like a frightened foetus for 22 years. A feeling that though I am out of the womb, I am in fact stamped by it like a man who is buffeted about and doesn't know what's going to hit him next.

The cause of my behaviour towards women (constantly changing women, seeking their company, conquering and humiliating them or idolizing them) is my hope that one of them will accept me in a state of serenity. The feeling that through the sexual act I would return to the 'good environment' of the womb existed deep inside me (the symbolism is very clear in the 14th Session). Now, through the tremendous experience of the Sessions, I would say that every sexual experience contained a great deal of agony and anticipation (agony because nothing new ever happened or seldom happened, anticipation that some day I would finally ejaculate in a state of serenity).

Outcome of the 14th Session: Two days after the Session I make love with *M* without fantasizing. I feel pleasure during the act and almost no pain during ejaculation.

Excerpt from R4's diary Homosexuality is a perversion but every perversion serves some specific end. Perversion is a necessity. I have become deeply aware of that since the Session ... Nevertheless, my life feels empty. After every ejaculation, whether it was with *X*, whether it be with *corrupt* women or with the help of fantasies, I have felt alone and desolate. The object of this perversion is to avoid the female genitals, that is, to avoid contact with the maternal body. Until the fourth Session I had no idea of the motives which impelled me to orgiastic parties, to those desperate attempts to overcome the unconscious fear my mother aroused in me. The Sessions make me try now to explain the various events in my life and what prompts me to act this way or that way.

My memory, even when I'm not under the influence of the psychedelic, has greatly improved. I'm beginning to remember incidents in my life that I had completely forgotten. Something new is going on within me. I am undergoing an existential change. I cannot say that I am free of the ghosts of my past. I can say, however, that I am changing day by day. Before, the slightest thing would drive me out of my mind; now there is some degree of conscious control. My relations with people around me have changed. My anxiety had decreased. I accept myself more than before. My fantasies, though, have not gone away (perhaps they never will) because their aim is to negate pain. The fantasies are my defence.

I must put down what happened a little while ago and try to analyse it. I had often suggested to *M* that we go to bed with another woman. I wanted to see her make love with a woman. Yes, this too was within the *corrupt* scheme of my ego. There are moments when no powers of realization can restrain this need of mine.

We met *N* at a reception. She was dark-haired (the opposite to *M* who is blond like my mother). The wine we drank brought us closer together and I felt that this woman and I were alike. In her eyes I saw the same self-destructive force. That evening I disregarded the Sessions and my efforts to purge myself of my vices. You don't leave one neighbourhood without knowing how the other one is. Perhaps my ignorance of something better is the reason for this fault in me. I'm not acquainted with anything better to leave what is probably worse but which is my very nature. My nature is pain and spasms which I must avoid. To achieve this I choose the most painless way - *corruption*.

When we undressed, I felt that the atmosphere was not in the least tense. For just one second, reflecting on the detrimental effect such an act might have on *M*, I wanted to stop this new regression of mine. I turned and looked at *N*. She was standing naked in front of the mirror caressing her body. She was caressing herself as if nobody else was there and as if her own body was foreign to her. I realized that this woman was as lonely as I was when I fantasized. (There is loneliness in fantasizing as projections and identifications operate and my ego hardly exists.)

I tried to remember the happy moments of serenity I lived in the womb, that Good and Beautiful feeling of tranquillity and innocence, but the fantasies overwhelmed me. *The Good and the Beautiful*[27] is my mother and I don't want my mother. Suddenly I felt lonely before *N*'s

---

27   Translator's note: τό καλό κάγαθό, in the ancient Greek sense.

body. Lonely even before touching her, even before ejaculating. Finally, the act took place in a whirl where I hardly existed. Each one of the three of us was alone in his or her own world. I participated with all my senses but I didn't feel that I came into contact with anything definite.

In spite of that, I felt pleasure. But while the act lasted, I observed the movements of our bodies. Each body tried to bury itself somewhere, to hide somewhere, to find something. I started off carried away by a mood for great pleasure and I ended up in momentary pleasure. I played a part which, by the time it was all over, I had already rejected. I felt like Heliogabalus, the *corrupt* and depraved emperor of Rome who, having alienated his body in every kind of debauchery, died butchered in the sewers of Rome. After ejaculating, I felt that my life too had ended in the anonymous sewers of my mother's spastic womb. The furniture around me had become ugly. No place could fool me any longer; no peaceful place existed for me. While the caresses last I feel happy because these caresses promise some end, an orgasm that will fulfil me emotionally. But nothing like that happens to me. In actual fact, *corruption* doesn't help me return and ejaculate into complete emotional acceptance; it only helps me approach this goal.

During the sexual act with the two women, I realized that I didn't come into direct contact with my mother. What happened was the following process of identification and projection which I was aware of. When *N* caressed *M*, I identified with *N* and approached *M* as a woman. That is, I became *N*, a woman, and ceased to be myself, a man. The source of my great sexual arousal was *N*, not *M*, and that was because I was now *N* and by extension my mother. In other words, the process was actually a homosexual act on my part as well. I also observed that when *N* caressed me, she assumed a male form and I remained a woman (my mother).

The above emotional interpretations did not occur under an LSD Session.

Session 15 I begin the Session by explaining to the doctor what happened to me with *M* and *N*. I analyse once again the emotions that had ruled me during the three-fold sexual act. I relive the scenes and feel that the whole process gave me pleasure and that the moment of ejaculation was less painful than usual. (The drug is acting potently. I am fully alert emotionally.) After the act I always feel desolate and unfulfilled emotionally. I stress that I don't regret what I did with the two women and that through this act I managed to feel pleasure and not pain, even though I did use identifications. I arrive at the same conclusions as those I wrote in my diary except that during this Session I feel that my ejaculation into

M gave me pleasure. (I didn't feel the usual pain or rather there was pain but it was minimal by comparison.)

I try to analyse the word *corrupt*, the essence of *corruption*. I arrive at a definition. *Corruption* is anything that does not remind me of my mother. (I note that with few exceptions my relationships have been with women of low intellect and low social class. The idea of the difference in class is to put as great a distance as possible between woman and my mother. The fewer points they have in common, the less they are associated.) I clarify the meaning and the essence of *corruption* still further. *Corruption* is the state that promises me the Good. (What happened with the two women was *corruption*, as was what happened with *X*, as are my fantasies. But all these things occur so that I may satisfy a need which aims at the Good and the happiness-serenity of my intra-uterine life.) It's very strange how confused these meanings are within themselves and with each other. My final goal is always the καλόν καγαθόν, *the Good*.

Right now I cannot question the fact that there's less pain in *corruption*. For me, a woman who is *corrupt* is more desirable than a woman of good morals (morality is associated with my mother).

Suddenly I relive the moment I reached orgasm with *M* and I feel I'm leaving the hospital couch and following the path of my sperm which leads me directly into the womb. I realize that the sexual act is a direct return to my mother's womb. I find myself in the midst of spasms and of very brief periods of serenity which is interrupted by the spasms. I would say that my life in the womb was 90% spasms and 10% serenity. The sexual act with a woman - and particularly at the moment of ejaculation - leads me physically and emotionally to the same proportion of spasms and serenity. The sexual act is the trajectory of my sperm on top of which I ride. When sperm enters any woman, I also enter astride it. But I don't enter the specific vagina of the specific woman I'm making love with: I enter my mother's vagina. This realization has an astounding effect on me. It's as if I've suddenly seen the light. I scarcely believe it. I relive this feeling of returning again and again for quite a few minutes during which I have lost all sense of time and place.

The doctor asks me: "Do you always have to go back there? Can't you separate the woman you're making love with from your mother?" I answer that his question makes me feel a strange dizziness and fear. I try to conceive of what would happen if every woman I've been with or will go with didn't represent my mother; if every vulva wasn't the image of her vulva; if, in other words, the form of every vulva didn't symbolize my mother's womb. And while I'm wondering about all this, I suddenly feel very perplexed. It's as if the doctor had asked me a question that was completely unrealistic. It's as if he'd asked me: "Can you become what you're not?" And while I'm feeling the blank that his question created in me, I see a woman at the far end of the horizon. (I have left my body and the room and am in the open air.) This woman represents objective beauty and all that is beautiful. (I am very alert emotionally. My mind is crystal clear. I have the impression that my senses have never functioned so completely, so keenly, so clearly.)

I find it very difficult to describe what is happening to me. The whole question is being faced from a very different angle. To describe it is almost impossible as the experience is subjective. I believe, however, that I have reached the borderline of my own emotional life and that I'm standing on the threshold of another world, another form of life.

I had stopped speaking and sat up on the couch. Before me lay an azure landscape. In the centre of it stood the woman, tall and perfectly proportioned in body and form. She was gazing steadfastly into the distance. She didn't look at me. I told the doctor that this woman represented objective beauty. I felt small and insignificant in front of her. I also felt that though she was beside me and I could see her, thousands of kilometres separated us. There was a time vacuum between us. I wanted to speak to her but I couldn't because I was certain that she wouldn't hear me. This woman had nothing to do with my mother. She wasn't a substitute of hers. A shiver of awe went through me. This woman had none of the emotional characteristics of the human race. She symbolized a free world of which I was emotionally ignorant. Her walk didn't give the impression of *movement* but of *meaning*. Looking at her, I thought that she walked in that sphere of justice, self-sufficiency, goodness and calmness which the ancient Greeks speak of. She was Plato's Idea of *The Good and the Beautiful* - an Idea-Reality.

My need to follow her compelled me to get up from the couch, but with every attempt to do so, a heaviness immobilized me. As if all my human emotions were weighing me down. As if I were afraid to detach myself from them. I didn't speak. I was almost dazzled by her beauty. Later I told the doctor that I tried to follow her, that I wanted to follow her, that I wanted to throw off the burden of my emotions. I said that I'd like to make love with this woman who was not a substitute for my mother. Consciously and for the first time I had, thanks to the Sessions, come face to face with a woman who wasn't my mother.

All Sessions essentially held a revelation. But this one was one of the greatest. In this Session I experienced the following feelings: (a) Return to the womb through my sperm. (b) Separation of woman from mother and the emotional consequences of this. If I make a distinction between woman and mother, where shall I return?

I remained for quite a while in this state of azure where the woman symbolized complete separation from my mother. I saw her walking on without knowing me. (If she had been my mother or a substitute of hers she should have known me.) Everything before me is azure. I can smell, taste, feel. The atmosphere around her is very light and clear. Nevertheless, this world she moves in is foreign to me. I follow her at a distance which is short yet also infinitely long. She shows me the way to a much better world. She tells me: "Cut yourself off from the past and come with me. Begin a new life without the bad memories of the past. Cut the umbilical cord." The world she shows me is something completely independent of my mother. An irrevocable breach with the past. But wasn't it to make this world mine that I began the Sessions? Don't I analyse myself so that I may be free of pain and fear? Yes, but now I can feel how much the centuries weigh upon me, how much emotions stifle me, how frighteningly bound I am to my familiar environment. Even if I follow this woman, in her presence I'll be alone with no way of returning. I feel that I exist only in the past, the given past, meaning my mother and her womb.

All of a sudden I begin to feel afraid. As if I've lost my way. I search for my mother. I want my mother. I compare my mother with this woman. Every comparison proves to be to my mother's detriment. But I want my mother and anything that reminds me of her. For me, my mother's looks are beauty, even if she is a little plump, even if she has a terrible walk, even if she did torture me in her belly and fill my life with pain ... I am ready to renounce the stranger's invitation, ready to curl up again in the spasms of my intra-uterine world. My life is agony and spasms. Nothing more.

And yet I try to follow the stranger again. I feel her body next to mine. I want to make love with her but I don't feel in the least bit aroused. Everything about the touch of her is cold - just the way you feel when you touch an ancient Greek statue. Suddenly I decide to ejaculate inside her. Everything is cold. It's as if my body doesn't exist, as if it has identified with my sperm which passes through her body and falls, solidifies (I feel that I've become cubes of crystal) and falls (I fall) from the other side of her body into chaos ... With a woman who is not my mother there can be no return. Return must necessarily be to none other than the womb I knew and the memory of which I have retained. Never mind if it's painful. It's enough that some place exists, the only place I can return to.

I move back in time to my mother's rooms. A well-known environment which oppresses me but which simultaneously spells security for me. The furniture which fills her house begins to gleam like small yellow lights. A colour both warm and sick which expands on my visual field, replacing the free, azure horizon and blotting out the strange woman. The glimmer of the yellow lights imposes itself upon me. The stronger the lights shine the more sorrow grows within me. I begin to cry without knowing why, I feel very sad. Suddenly I feel that I'm a traitor. Yes, I'd wanted to betray my mother and her world. I wanted to betray myself. I feel sad that even the thought of following the stranger passed through my mind! It's ridiculous but that's how it is.

I relive the spasms again and curl up on the couch like a foetus. I accept them though with pain, yet at the same time I need them. I cannot live without them. Simultaneously, however, I want to stop them, I want to change my way of life, to be free of them. I toss from side to side full of anxiety. I'm astounded at this tragi-comic realization. What is happening is so contradictory, so illogical! Then I decide that I will refuse to continue being the victim of the spasms. I've been out of the womb for so many years - this whole story of returning must be a fantasy. I can deny my past! I must do it! I must try!

The spasms come periodically after a short respite of absolute immobility and serenity. I make a conscious decision to neutralize these attacks. I cannot check the first wave of spasms. Nor the second. For a moment there, while I'm lying motionless expecting fresh attacks, I try to tell my body to refuse to move. For a fraction of a second I refuse to feel an attack which is on the verge of shaking my body. I succeed but immediately afterwards waves of spasms rack my whole body. I cannot stop them or at least not alone. I stop resisting and let myself go. It is impossible to stop the spasms. I feel like a child's toy which you wind up: now it's still, now it claps its hands and stamps its feet. I start to cry as the azure stranger appears on the horizon again. I cry because I cannot change, because I'm losing the beauty and serenity, the freedom beyond my total dependence on my mother's body, forever. I don't think I have ever cried with such despair. Gradually everything subsides. I will never make *The Good and the Beautiful* my own, but I know it exists.

Session 17 The Session begins and I am deeply conscious of the fact that it's impossible for me to smash the intra-uterine world. The image which keeps passing before my eyes is that of a small white dot-cannonball (myself) which traverses the dark world of spasms, determined to smash the inner shell of the egg-womb and to emerge into the light. (Light symbolizes breaking the chains which keep me immobilized and forever dragging myself along in the same emotional ratio of anxiety to serenity.)

This white mini-cannonball (myself) sets off with force and conviction on its outward trajectory, towards the liberation of my ego from my mother's ego. (Conviction is created by a new love affair or professional plans which give me hope, or finally by any act which promises me a better tomorrow ...) The cannonball passes through all the atmospheres and states of spasms (*corruption*, homosexuality, half-finished jobs, a life wasted by anguish ...) and disintegrates on the inner surface of the egg without ever piercing it and getting out.

More deeply still, I feel in this Session that my personality is essentially that of my mother's. All my life I have tried in one way or another to create an ego of my own, but with no success. Of course, I have my own physical being but at bottom this being functions with my mother's emotions. I see her as a block of stone sitting on me, dominating me. I am literally crushed beneath her vulva. (I have also experienced these feelings in previous Sessions, though not as intensely as I'm experiencing them now.) I see that my perpetual fatigue is my mother's fatigue. (She is always complaining of being ill and tired without there really being anything the matter with her. The same with me - always tired, always sick. A mental illness binds us. My being and hers are almost the same thing.)

The more the Session progresses the more I can feel my physical and emotional dependence on her. As if the umbilical cord has not been cut. Within me there is an uncontrollable force that drives me to this or that act, this movement or that decision. I realize that this force is very powerful and emanates from the body, from the womb of my mother. I am an ant trapped in an inverted glass. I can feel it and I have difficulty breathing. Must I then live in this trap forever? I want to act for myself and yet I act for her. Unbelievable. These Sessions are a bright sunbeam which illuminates the darkness of my ignorance. Never before have I correlated things so 'different' from one another as in these Sessions. It's as if my mind is being liberated and my senses awakened all at once.

Next I speak of the necessity of *corruption*. It is the only way I can overcome the spasms. Whatever it is that can take me closer to my goal, that is what I'll pursue. I consider the entire sexual act as a way of returning to the womb (regardless of whether the method is called heterosexuality or homosexuality, *corruption* or *the Good*). I ask the doctor: "Is it not tragic that a person who fears the terrible vulva of his mother becomes the vulva himself solely because his final goal is union with his mother's body?" It's laughable to speak of morality when there's so much pain ... I have undergone a series of Sessions. I've relived my life since the time of conception. I've felt pain again and again and again ... There have been periods in my life where I've abstained from all sexual contact for weeks

... In despair I either held myself back or I threw myself into destruction and the agonized quest for *the return* ... And now, I can definitely say that in the name of *that return* I'll always be ready to try anything. There is always hope, no matter how many disappointments I suffer, because hope is interwoven with my need to return to that place, that original place - the womb - or even beyond it ... till I find serenity, absolute and eternal ... Yes, death is perhaps the final return ...

Session 18 The Session begins with fear. I feel very afraid and want to be near my mother. I'm a broken man who wants to be at his mother's side. Deep love for this woman begins to grow within me. Wherever I go I'll need her, tremendously. She has given me some moments of happiness. I want to go to her and become one with her, to get inside her. I feel that my body is exactly like her body and that her agonies are my agonies. How can I explain it? It would be inadequate to say that I am an extension of her body, indissolubly bound to her being. My mother and I are one and the same. An enormous problem, as in this total identification there is both security and insecurity.

A strong feeling takes hold of me. As if I must steer my life to some goal. I want to reach that goal and there to prostrate myself before my mother and weep at her feet. That's the point I want to reach: to kneel down and weep before my great mother. (I can see her clearly in front of me, imposing and great, ready to accept my tears. This image is followed by feelings of my own insignificance and adoration for her.) Like a child I want to go to her side and weep. I want to weep out of happiness, complete happiness which she will give me. That's how I want to die. I want to die beside her. I cannot possibly imagine myself dying far from her. I want her to be the one to close my eyes. (I had always said to *M* that I wanted her to close my eyes when I died but in fact it is my mother I see doing this.)

I feel that I want to see my mother with a great deal of love. I should already have done that. I should already have gone to her, fallen before her and told her: "I've come at last! At last I've seen you with love!" These are the words I want to say to her. "Mother, I want you," and then she ... she would take me in her arms where all pain would disappear. It's enough that she'll be at my side and she'll give me strength, strength to exist, strength to breathe! "I am a part of you! I am a state of happiness!" In other words, with one and only one simple word, with just one sentence: "Mother, I want to be with you!" Can one utter simpler words than that?

Now I have the feeling that my mother is good and that I too am good. I feel that her goodness is a prerequisite for mine. The more goodness

The Knowledge of the Womb

she gives me or has given me, the better I have become. I want to tell her that it's not worth our quarrelling with each other, it's not worth ruining our lives telling each other off. It's not worth our crying and shouting because whatever I do in my life I do for her; even what I'm writing now I'm writing for her.

At this point this intense love, this belief that my mother gives me much love and acceptance, diminishes. Essentially, I realize that what I'm looking for is to return through the sexual act to a womb which would give me more serenity than what it actually gave me. I realize that since the beginning of the Session I've been desperately revolving around my mother's *goodness* because that's the only thing that interests me. I deliberately forgot the percentage of anxiety.

Now I can see the members of my family one by one and I feel proud to be descended from people of intellect. I love my father because my father is strength and strength is security. I often think that if my father dies, I won't be able to live. Now, under the influence of the drug, I see both myself and my father as beings that move about in space, that come and go without having any control over their length of stay on Earth. I feel that around me many things are moving about and that if you remove one thing, another will remain. If my father departs life, I will remain. If I go, he or my child will remain. (Suddenly I want to have a child - a very strong feeling.) Then again I suppose that if my father dies, I'll remain alone. A power impels me to unite with him, to unite with all my ancestors. In actual fact I do feel united with them. I see myself with my father and mother around the fire. I feel that I am settled. Settled? But what can being settled be? You've settled down, they tell you, congratulations! But where? You've made a home, you've done your job well, you've succeeded socially. You're settled!! But no. That's not how people become settled or at least that's how they think of themselves as being settled. Actually, there are a great many things which are never settled.

Suddenly I raise my voice and shout to the doctor: "Listen! I can reach a place which is far more settled that the one I think of as being settled ... and that place is somewhere where I'll feel completely secure. It will be a place that is noiseless and silent and serene. It will be my mother's womb, not as I experienced it but as I wanted or ought to have experienced it. And if this had really existed, then I too would be able to find a similar place in the world and settle down but that's out of the question."

And again my mother appears before me in full, as if she is three metres away from me. I feel myself becoming sexually aroused at the sight of her. Really, I love women just as I love my mother. Her power is my whole being. And she's never known her power. She doesn't know how much power she has over me. She and I are eternal.

Again an image where my father and mother are bending over me. I feel I'm a baby in a cradle. All three of us have something which unites us in eternity, as if we are tied to each other by invisible threads. Behind us is a long line of ancestors. I feel that I am carrying this line within me and that it weighs me down and gladdens me simultaneously. I cannot visualize myself cut off from it.

The line becomes lost in time. The first persons in this long line are my parents, then my grandparents, then my great-grandparents and still one generation beyond them (I know their faces from photographs and portraits). Then the line continues with unknown people who become more and more distant. I do not know them by sight but I know them emotionally. All of them have passed on to me messages and various other things which I cannot make out clearly and which are something like hopes and pain and joy altogether. They tell me: "We have thought but we cannot be the only ones who do the thinking. You too must think for us. Even if you want to, you cannot forget that we existed before you did. Since you were born, you too have an obligation to think." My God, before me there appears a large main avenue where people move about in different periods of time. The avenue of the human species ad infinitum. And I am there with them and I must do something - definitely I must. Action! Action! I can't avoid movement and action in this life.

I can see the people wearing masks and pretending that nothing that has occurred during all these centuries interests them. Most of these people are a facade. They give me the impression that they have deliberately blindfolded themselves. But beyond the facade and our antics, fate certainly exists.

Now I feel afraid. I feel very afraid, alone as I am on the avenue. I try to be united as I was a short while ago with my mother and father. Nothing. Anguish and great fear grip me. Something exploding within me is making me afraid. The spasms begin and there's water in my mouth. My arms become stiff and my body starts moving into the foetal position again. No! Not again ... I don't want to. I'm resisting greatly, dispelling these symptoms. I just manage to stop myself from vomiting. I want to get away. I try to think of something else ...

The spasms continue, as do the sick feeling and dyspnoea, but in front of me now I see ancient Thebes. Yes, Aeschylus' "Seven against Thebes" comes to mind. Eteocles is standing at the seventh gate waiting for his brother, to kill him in defence of his city, his security. He cries: "now the gods have renounced me!" Which gods? Now the gods have renounced me. I cry out too and begin to weep. I feel very afraid. There is no one beside me. Yet Thebes is mine and I must defend it. I mustn't let my brother take it from me. Closed up inside Thebes, the people are weeping and wailing (I weep too). Thebes is in turmoil and spasms rack my body again. Thebes is the womb and I'm in the womb again and suffering and yet I don't want to live without it, cannot live without it. Inside Thebes there is great agony, outside it loneliness and fear. Fear within and without. That's where I was born, that's where I'll end up. This thought fixes itself in my mind. My legs and arms are trembling. I'm surrounded by people who point at me and say: "Here is the writhing foetus! Here the homosexual!" A sudden feeling that I am my mother. No! I don't want to be ... I'm not my mother. To be homosexual means to have my mother's body.

I feel myself being absorbed by my gigantic mother who is crushing me. I feel like a foetus and a woman and a man all at the same time, the man trying to exist independently with his own attributes and not being able to do so because he is being assimilated into his mother. I'm tired of trying to detach my material and mental being from hers. That woman has been destroying me for years. This city of Thebes is stifling me. I want to get out and get away, to cross over ... Where? I want to get away from the spasms and the blood that covers my eyes. I want to cut away from the past, to be free, to escape ... to die! I try to find my mother, to find the path that will lead me back to her. Death.

I saw an image of a formless mass of flesh, blood and fluids. I saw my death somewhere in the future. A death identical to my intra-uterine life and my birth. I saw my body being abandoned in the vortex and the dust of an uncontrollable gallop towards the, to me, absolutely forbidden beauty of serenity. Speechless, I saw my body growing old, small, slowly reaching its end ... And there, in a landscape of sand and garbage, it spewed out its last breath among the spasms, the turmoil and dizziness it had once felt in its mother's womb. I could not tell whether the death that appeared before me was the intra-uterine state I had experienced or an inevitable re-enactment of this. Nevertheless, speechless and terrified, I saw the past repeating itself in the future. I saw a man, his hands thrown up in despair, running ... running and throwing behind him his useless clothes, his suitcases, his furniture, his possessions, his intellectual works, all his useless culture ... running with the desperation of a condemned man, knowing that at some moment his legs would give, his arms would fall down feebly, and his eyes would sing into a primeval, fearful darkness.

The image lasted for quite a few minutes and it gave me the impression of an irrevocable decision. Twice in my life I have escaped death in car accidents. I don't know why I write this ... "a mass of flesh, blood and fluids in the garbage."

Session 19 (The Father) My effort to make this written record of my autopsychognosia sessions would be incomplete if I didn't mention the *Session of the Father*. This Session clarified for me the symbolism of the homosexual act, what my father symbolizes in this act, the role of my identification with my mother, and more generally I lived the terrible oppression I felt subjected to by my father.

I begin the Session by describing to the doctor how inhibited I feel in my father's presence. It's impossible for me to feel free, to express myself, and as a rule I disappear whenever I catch sight of him. As the Session progresses I remember events from my childhood and adolescence. My refusal to go to school, to do whatever my father tells me to do is all-embracing. I get my education grudgingly, I do athletics reluctantly, but I finally realize that there were many things in my life that I didn't do for the simple reason that my father wanted me to do them. I look upon him as an adversary, the adversary and obstacle to my great desire to be alone with my mother. The father is at the mother's side and that prevents the son from being the one who monopolizes her love and attention. I see and feel him as a lord seated on his chair, dominating everything and making everyone obey his own wishes whether they want to or not. I feel an urgent need and desire to take him down from his pedestal! I want to take his place, I want it to be me who dominates, me who possesses my mother, me who gives orders.

This realization is astonishing as until then I'd thought that whatever decision I made in my life I made it because I wanted to and for no other reason. Now I see that my actions are the result of a command (positive or negative). My father wants me to become such-and-such? No! I'll become exactly the opposite, even if in my soul I crave to become what he too wants. Very irrational.

I realize that the great love I feel for him is basically the need to become him and be with my mother. By loving my father I satisfy two emotions. First, through imitating him completely I become him and get close to my mother. Second, my love derives from a need for the protection he gives me. I love him because he protects me.

At a certain moment in the Session I stop being myself and become him. I see that my general behaviour in life is to imitate him in every respect, for instance liking the colours he likes, dressing as he does, becoming learned like him ... becoming his very image! I notice that I've succeeded up to a point ... Everybody says that I resemble him ... But I feel that I will never reach him! I cannot reach him.

At this point I stop interpreting my feelings towards my father and start to tremble. I'm very cold. The doctor brings me a blanket and covers me ... Suddenly I'm transported to a place I cannot recognize ... It's in the open air ... It's cold ... I'm dressed in rags ... An enormous eye appears before me. It is a big, clear, cold eye that looks at me condescendingly. I still feel very cold. It's as if the eye is telling me: "You will never attain my wisdom ... No matter how much you try, you will never reach me!" I drag myself along in front of this eye. I'm a ragamuffin, a slave. I feel like a slave in every sense of the word. Beside me are other slaves. I do not know them. All of us (a line of ragged slaves) are in front of a house which looks like an ancient Greek structure. Inside the house, behind a window, the eye looks at me ... Bit by bit the eye becomes part of a face which I begin to see clearly. It is the face of an ancient Greek.[28] The ancient Greek looks at us ... mocks us. We are all slaves before him, unworthy in the presence of his greatness. We are on the march. We have stopped in front of his house but they will certainly take us from here and lead us far away ... to places fit for slaves to live in.

I feel sorrow for myself and love for the Eye. I turn and look at the ancient Greek. Silently, I ask for his help. His answer is a cold look, like a thunderbolt ... He is not bad but he is cognizant of our worthlessness ... We are not worthy of being helped. He doesn't hate us; he simply renounces us. He says: "Years will pass, centuries, and you will still be where you are, wretched creature!" He says it somewhat bitterly, not nastily. This man seems to be beyond all emotion. He is a superhuman full of futile compassion.

This image occupies me for about an hour. I describe my feelings to the doctor. I describe the ancient Greek and try to see what he symbolizes. My first impression is that I'm living in another era, thousands of years ago. My second impression is that the Eye and the ancient Greek are my father. He has my father's gentleness, his air, and he is the symbol of strength and wisdom which I'll never be able to reach! I realize that in everyday life, without ever having been aware of it, I've always felt like by father's slave and humble servant. This is a purely subjective feeling because my father has never behaved in an authoritarian manner towards me. ... He has always been kind, affable, affectionate and helpful towards me. But just the fact that he is my father is enough for me, his child, to feel

---

[28] R4's note: The bronze statue of Poseidon in the Archaeological Museum of Athens, Greece.

like and inferior being. I feel I cannot possibly reach my father. My father oppresses me in my thinking, my life, my decisions. I try to refuse to do what he tells me to do, but that doesn't save me. I am under his power. My obstinacy, my refusals, my aggressiveness towards him only make me even more of a clown! In front of him I am a clown.

At this point I feel the spasms beginning. I see my body in pain and covered in rags. I'm full of inferiority complexes. Whatever I go to do is a failure in advance. I don't complete anything in my everyday life. I'm a clown, a ragamuffin and destitute beggar in front of my father. (All these feelings are completely unknown to me till that moment. In fact, I had always thought that I had my own personality. Now I compare it to my father's and I see that I am a zero. His position, his power prevent me from believing that I too can become something.)

The Session continues with interpretations. Now and then I relive the sensation for the Eye. I have completed the picture at last. The son and the father. The two adversaries. Object and cause of the struggle: the mother. The father possesses the mother thus preventing the son from approaching her. The final aim of my love for my father is to conquer my mother. I detect erotic and sensual elements in my love for my father.

At this point (third hour of the Session) I begin describing the homosexual act to the doctor. Everything becomes clear. My body grows thinner and becomes my mother's body. In the passive role I am my mother and the active partner is my father. Weakness and strength! The symbolism of the active partner is definitely clear. The active partner is my strong father, my protective, hateful, beloved father ... I try to analyse what exactly happens at the moment of orgasm. Is my ejaculation a return to the womb or is my entire self the womb which reaches auto-orgasm? I realize that it is the latter. Identifying with my mother makes me function like my mother, like a woman. My sperm goes nowhere. It returns to my own body. I feel base and humiliated. The humiliation of my person is what the passive part in the homosexual act is. God, how humiliated I feel! I am my mother! I'm humiliated like my mother! The female is always an object of humiliation. I'm convinced of that. The active partner is ultimately hateful because he is a power that imposes itself upon me. I do not accept this power. I reject the imposition of power on me as much as I may seek it.

And yet, the purpose of the homosexual act is for me to feel less pain. By becoming my mother (in the passive role) I avoid entering the womb - my orgasm is my mother's orgasm. In the active role I am my strong, powerful father and the passive partner is my mother ... At bottom the act is a heterosexual fantasy.

Fear In every Session I was overcome by anxiety. I felt afraid. It's certain that the fear inhibited me. It began with a feeling of emptiness inside me; anguish whose cause I was ignorant of in the beginning but which, as the Sessions progressed, began to become clear, finally culminating in the fear and agony of the intra-uterine spasms. I was afraid to relive the disagreeable situation of the spasms (electrodes) which literally shook me. In the 13th, 14th and 15th Sessions I relived the womb with about the same intensity. At certain time, however, the spasms were fewer. But even when I knew the cause of my fear, that didn't prevent me from feeling fear and emptiness each time a Session began. At the same time I detected the same quality of fear in my everyday life. I'm afraid of the colour red, I'm afraid of blood in general. It arouses fear in me and a nauseous feeling whose cause I cannot explain completely on the basis of the quality of anxiety I felt in the Sessions and particularly during the moments I relived the jolting of the spasms. Perhaps this nausea, this anguish which sometimes reaches extreme anxiety and which is provoked by certain external stimuli (mostly unknown) does not have the same cause, that is, it is not due to the spasms.

Thoughts on the quality of fear: (a) I'm afraid of whatever causes me pain, and by that I mean emotional and physical pain. I don't know precisely if the neutralization of physical pain automatically leads to the erasure of emotional pain. Physical pain, of course, is a kind of memory of pain, but its intensity is a fact. The spasms of my intra-uterine life - and this is something I feel deeply - have worn my body out to such an extent that there are moments where I feel completely listless and this in turn brings about total mental torpor. The physical fatigue that I feel has a direct effect on my mental state (feeling that I have been beaten up and harassed immeasurably and that I can barely drag myself around even if I sleep fourteen hours a day). (b) If neutralizing the memory of physical pain (neutralizing the spasms) results in the erasure of mental agony, then I'm afraid I'm left with few hopes or at least with fewer possibilities of becoming someone other than the person who was born. (It's a question of fighting the past not only with knowledge but with will. I don't know, however, if there is any margin for will in a suffering body and equally suffering mind.) (c) Result of the Sessions: I can control my everyday fear more easily. I consider this result fundamental. In some cases, however, any attempt at control is a failure. The intensity of the fear and anxiety is such that it nullifies all thought of control.

EXCERPTS FROM AND SUMMARIES OF R5's HISTORY AND SESSIONS

History Male, 21 years' old, single, student.

When I was four years' old I would get an erection and feel a strange excitement whenever I looked at photographs of half-naked men who had extremely well-developed muscles.

Between the ages of seven and thirteen I played girls' games with little girls. I avoided boys' games. I never played 'cops and robbers' or 'cowboys'. I loathed quarrels and fisticuffs with other little boys. I ignored the world of boys. I liked to comb the hair of my little girlfriends' dolls. During that period I met G. She immediately became the companion of my games and holidays. We played at theatre and I usually took female parts. I was sure that I would marry her when we grew up, but I wasn't sexually attracted to her in the least.

Also during this period, a picture of a Red Indian in a story book made a deep impression on me. I drew a wound on this man's chest with a red pencil. I was certain that he didn't suffer because he was very strong. The thought that he didn't suffer made me feel a strange excitement.

Towards the end of this period, I identified with a female singer. I lost no opportunity to imitate the way she sang and danced. To me she was a goddess; I adored her but she didn't excite me sexually.

I was a good pupil. I had some good friends. Nobody criticized me at school. Altogether, I was very happy with the atmosphere there.

When I turned thirteen, I changed school. Disaster. The atmosphere there was torture. Because I ignored the world of boys I became a scapegoat. I felt clumsy and stupid. Gymnastics and sport terrified me. I had but one friend with whom I shared the same intellectual interests. All the others looked upon me with scorn.

At the age of 13 I dared to open a sports magazine for the first time. Its pages were full of Mr. Universe photographs. I trembled with emotion and a strange excitement which this time was clearly sexual; I had an erection. A few days later I saw a Negro on television displaying his strong muscles. I was alone. I had an erection. That evening I discovered masturbation.

Gradually I overcame my embarrassment and started buying bodytraining magazines whose photographs of super-athletes gave me my most pleasurable moments. I began to follow men I saw in the street who impressed me, but I would never dare address them. During that period I started to feel ashamed of my homosexual tendencies. Other boys, who made me realize that I was not like them, made me feel this. One day, for no reason apparent to me, a classmate hurled the word 'faggot' at me. After that I felt that my every movement drew mocking looks from men.

The shame and fear which those around me made me feel did not prevent me from identifying with another female singer who became my new idol and the model I frequently tried to imitate, while dressed as a woman.

The emotional-intellectual interpretation R5 gave during the Sessions to this behaviour: "By imitating another person, I took on their personality. The whole process helped me eliminate my own insignificant personality and all my unsolved problems. When I played the part of the female singer I had the distinct impression and firm conviction that everybody around me loved and admired me. In other words, this was a situation which was diametrically opposite to the situation I faced in everyday life where people gave me mocking looks and rejected me. I felt (and still feel) the need to be admired because only thus do I not feel like a piece of rubbish, a nothing."

From my mid-teens, I began to feel that masturbation was not fulfilling enough. I began to feel the need for sexual relations but I was not optimistic about finding a sexual partner. I started projecting manly looks onto some of my classmates. Perhaps they realized it and they hate me because I was a homosexual.

When I turned 19, I enrolled in a foreign university. My first months there were very unpleasant. I felt completely disoriented. My fellow students were withdrawn and cold. Much loneliness. I decided to write to a homosexual club. The next day I was visited by a blatantly homosexual man. He told me that he wanted to get acquainted with a young man. He complimented me on my good looks and asked me if I liked him. Though he hadn't impressed me, I agreed to meet him the following evening.

We did meet and after dinner he accompanied me to my apartment. I felt ill at ease and was silent. He lay down on the bed and suggested I lie beside him, which I did. He started kissing me on the mouth and hugging me. I felt nothing in particular, or rather I did feel an unpleasant sensation when his tongue touched my lips. He asked me if I loved him. I realized that I had to do something. I decided to become more passionate. I entwined my legs with his and embraced him. I felt very aroused and came very close to ejaculating, but finally I did not.

The next evening we met at his place. As we were sitting on the couch he started to kiss me. He asked me if I wanted to make love. I said "yes".

He asked me if I knew exactly what was in store for me. I panicked. I lost all desire for sex. And yet, we went to bed. Disaster. I had no erection. I was a lifeless body. He was aroused. He kissed me everywhere. He felated me. He told me I was very handsome. He penetrated me. I didn't feel much pain. I told myself that I had gone too far and that it was useless to continue this relationship which I had known from the beginning didn't interest me. I told him I felt inhibited and that I wanted us to stop making love.

It did me good to speak with him. At last I was speaking about my problems to someone who listened and answered. I saw him for a third time. I told him that I had decided to see a psychiatrist. He advised me to waste no time beginning therapy because if I continued my homosexual activity I would never be able to stop it. I asked him what precautions I should take as a homosexual. He told me that I should have my blood tested for syphilis every three months. Instantly I felt that I had already caught syphilis because I felt acute itchiness in my anus.

During that period various obsessional ideas developed which greatly tormented me. Finally, I decided to stop my studies and go to Cairo for autopsychognosia sessions.

Sessions 1 - 4   The main characteristic of the first four Sessions is that R5 does not allow them to evolve. He realizes that the cause of his resistance is his unconscious effort to avoid reliving traumatic experiences. Gradually he succeeds in diminishing his resistance.

Session 5   I feel that the dimensions of my body have diminished amazingly. I'm closed up in a dark, narrow place. My body, arms and legs are curled up. An unpleasant sensation of heat. I'm sweating. My arms are going numb. The muscles in my left thigh are contracting. My breathing is becoming heavy, laboured and spasmodic. I feel as if I'm being strangled. I feel something powerful pressing on me, pushing me out. I try to resist this power by contracting my body. A desperate, futile struggle. I feel I am being pulled upwards; I'm suffocating. I'm being annihilated in the most horrible way. This is death. (R5 considers the above experience to be the rejection of expulsion-birth.)

Session 7   R5 describes his sexual activity, something which he did not have the courage to do before this Session.
I isolate myself in a room.   Stereotyped fantasies.   On the scene appears a very heavily built man with extremely well-developed muscles. He is the typical Mr. Universe or Superman. He is my protector. His main

characteristics: all-powerful, terribly violent, brutish, no trace of intellect. An essential feature of the fantasy: this all-powerful man displays his strength to me by performing extraordinary feats; for instance, he lifts cars with his bare hands, he neutralizes hordes of enemies who want to ill-treat me. Frequently, I fantasize him torturing in the most horrible way someone whom he finally strangles, squeezing the victim's chest and neck with his arms. When the fantasy begins I start masturbating. The more violent my protector becomes towards his victim or the more remarkable feats he performs with his powerful muscles, the more excited I become. I reach orgasm the moment the victim is about to die.

Since I was 19, this sexual activity has alternated with homosexual activity which is characterized by my inability to reach orgasm. That is, despite my strong sexual arousal, just as orgasm is approaching I am overcome by terror which instantly neutralizes erection and all sexual desire. I assume the foetal position, my breathing becomes spasmodic, I moan, and feel just as I feel in the Sessions when I relive the womb rejection (see Session 5).

Session 11 I'm in another sphere of existence. Everything is transparent. I'm floating. Very relaxed. A sleepiness sleep. Wonderfully relaxed. Everything is like a weightless cloud. My limbs and my torso are extended and relaxed. I'm floating. I am in a wave, in the curve of a wave. I'm a soft mass. No defences. I feel wonderful. Where am I? I don't exactly know where I am. I am beyond this world. I feel very free. I'm flying over the ocean like a bird. I feel I have wings. I open my arms like a bird in flight; I laugh. I am somewhere totally different to usual. I feel I am a part of a cluster of luminous rays, in the shape of a tunnel. Blissful state.

Lethargic state. Void. I'm a flexible mass. I could remain like this for hours, floating between two sleeps. State of oblivion. Forgetting yourself, your passions, life's sufferings. Just opening your eyes is painful. I see the damn light, the damn lamp, the damn room, damn reality, the damn world. It's much better with your eyes closed. State of drowsiness. I have no desire to talk ...

... Again I feel I'm in water. I'm swimming. I am submerged in the deepest sleep but it is a sleep in which I retain full consciousness of my existence. How terrible you feel when you open your eyes! It's just like when I wake up in the morning curled up in the foetal position, the rejecting foetal position; all my bodily functions are out of order. I close my eyes. It's fantastic to feel that here there is only you and the whole world is over there. People are damn egoists. They care only for their own happiness and pleasure. They close their eyes to the next person's suffering. How wonderful to be far away from the world. I want to be far away from filthy reality. (R5 considers the subjective state described above to be the revival of his intra-uterine acceptance.)

... Once more I'm in a state of bliss. Now an unpleasant sensation of heat and so on (as described in Session 5), I feel my heavenly bliss is in danger of ending. I struggle desperately not to get out. Unbearable pain. Death ...

The trauma caused by the rejecting womb predetermines the nature of my sexual activity. Orgasm with a real and not imaginary partner, instead of leading me directly to the accepting womb, reactivates the process of the rejecting womb-mother-woman. This process is truly unbearable. It leads to a horrible, tortured death. I refuse to live through this kind of death and I irrevocably decide to do away with women forever. The heterosexual act annihilates my being. It is death.

I feel that just as the process of the rejecting womb marks the end of intra-uterine life, so orgasm marks the end of the sexual act. For me, the following formula holds true:

The sexual act with a partner could lead me to bliss	→	Accepting womb (intra-uterine life)
The sexual act terminates in orgasm - death - unbearable situation.	→	Intra-uterine life terminates with womb rejection - death - unbearable situation.

The need to return to the womb obliges me, since I have done away with women, to turn to men; but male partners also unconsciously symbolize the rejecting womb. Thus, the only way for me to revive the accepting womb is to isolate myself, go into my fantasies (see Session 7) and masturbate. The all-powerful man of my fantasies has the same power as the all-powerful womb-mother. However, whereas the womb tortures me, the all-powerful man protects me and tortures someone else in my place, someone who finally suffers what the womb has in store for me - the torture of suffocation. So, since someone else almost dies instead of me, I can have an orgasm, I can return to the womb.

This violent, criminal fantasy gives rise to a feeling of guilt-persecution combined with obsessional acts and ideas which contain strong sadistic and masochistic elements.

I become terror-stricken at the thought that I leave traces of my identity around. Sperm on my clothes. A woman's pregnancy from my sperm. The thought of procreation instantly makes me feel that the foetus is first of all unwanted, that it has been conceived by mistake and is something that must be eliminated. I feel as if I am the one who is going to be pregnant with the frightful foetus. Since my sexual activity doesn't lead to catastrophic pregnancy, it leads to disease which results in death through decomposition.

I have always been afraid of illness. Every time I fell ill I would exaggerate my illness out of a desire for self-destruction (masochistic element). I am pessimistic about my health and this has an adverse effect on my everyday activity. At the same time, I feel the need to be loved and admired. I say I am ugly in order to be reassured to the contrary, as that will make me feel accepted.

Session 14 I have made a peace pact with myself:

Article 1: Refuse to have sexual contact with any woman.
Article 2: Refuse to submit to any person or environmental condition that tries to impose its authority on me.
Article 3: Do the opposite of what I am told, ordered or expected to do.

My policy towards all authority - resisting and not submitting to it - makes me feel different. Though I am weak, I become strong. By being homosexual I am different to what they want me to be, therefore I am strong ...

There is a striking contrast between the blissful feeling of the accepting womb and the feeling that I'm a nothing which arises when the womb rejects me. The womb rejects me because I have no worth.

Session 17 The penis attracts and disgusts me simultaneously. The penis is often a feature of my fantasies. I put gigantic genitals on Mr. Universe photographs. In my homosexual activity I prefer not to see my partner's penis. I ask him to undress under the bedcovers. A man with an erection is repulsive to me. An erect penis reminds me of the time I saw my father naked in the bathroom. I look for images radically different to those I retain of my father. I repress and forget anything which reactivates revolting memories of my father, anything which symbolizes the sexual act, because only in this way can I function and make love as long as I can't avoid seeing my partner's penis which repulses me.

If a woman's legs are close together, the vulva does not disgust or shock me particularly. But if the legs are wide apart, the sight of the labia is repugnant to me.

How they differ:

VULVA	PENIS	MALE ANUS
It is slimy. It is invisible → unknown → dangerous. When you enter it you are in direct contact with the womb → danger of a child being born → catastrophe.	It is visible → something known. It is not dangerous because it does not give birth to babies.	It is invisible but not dangerous because it does not give birth to babies.

The negative aspects of the womb: terror of my being reproduced. The female genitals are disgusting. The terror and disgust rob me of all desire for intercourse with a woman.

When I am in bed with a man, the first thing I feel is the need to sleep - total escape. At the same time, I feel fine, as if I'm in the accepting womb. I feel protected in my partner's arms; I want to sleep and not to bother about the sexual act, even if I have an erection. This is because I refuse to be active. I want to be passive. I want to abandon myself to my partner's desires. I envy women because they can pretend to be excited and to have orgasm. If I don't have an erection, I can't pretend to have one. It's a terrible thing that I cannot reach orgasm in my homosexual activity. I feel stupid in front of my partner. I believe that he will think me a paltry sexual partner. If I didn't have a penis, I could easily pretend to feel pleasure and so I would deceive my partner-adversary. I place great importance upon my partner's opinion and feelings. We must reach orgasm together. I feel that my partner gets upset when I don't reach orgasm ...

My sexual partner symbolizes someone very important ... Who? Someone to whom I must give pleasure. I forget my own pleasure for the sake of his; everything for him. If he doesn't reach orgasm I feel sad. It does not matter that I don't have an orgasm. I'm happy when I give someone pleasure; it's as if I'm feeling it. I play an entirely passive role, almost like a married woman who must satisfy her husband. It's like a duty. And so I seek intercourse without wanting it.

My passiveness and my lack of desire for intercourse symbolizes denial of my sex ... I remember that when I made love with D, I curled up like a foetus the moment I felt orgasm approaching. It was an endeavour to protect my genitals and avoid ejaculating.

I come back to my subject: Who does the sexual partner I must satisfy symbolize, and what does the simultaneous endeavour to protect my genitals symbolize? ... My mother? ... In the womb I am passive, my mother all-powerful. She does whatever she likes with my body, she makes me suffer ... I don't exactly understand what's going on between my mother and me but I find it even more difficult to understand the nature of my relationship with my father ... (with hostility) I have no intention of satisfying my father or of arousing sexual desire in him ... But why does my father's phallus shock me? A man's penis is not 'very beautiful'; it reminds me of my father's penis.

My father's personality repulses me ... I imagine my father making love with my mother and reproducing me with his penis, symbol of my suffering ... I don't want to identify with my father or give him sexual gratification. On the contrary, I want to take revenge on him. But why? He pushed me towards women. He showed them to me as sex objects when the very idea of sexual contact with a woman terrified me. My father had an inordinate heterosexual bias which made him associate everything with women. He was unfaithful to my mother. Each time he pointed a woman out to me, it was as if he was trying to show me someone other than my mother; it was as if he was being unfaithful to my mother ... I reject anything that reminds me of my father ... and yet my various sexual partners symbolize him. I get revenge on him with my homosexual activity yet simultaneously I find him again in the men I go with.

... I associate my partner with my mother. In my partner's presence my personality is obliterated, just as it is with my mother; to her I deny my own pleasure. With any other woman it's even worse. I have to prove to her that I'm a marvellous lover, the perfect lover, and that's impossible. I can't even get an erection for that woman who devours male genital organs, that crocodile-woman who lies in wait for her prey, to gulp it down ...

My partner is the one who has the active role. Why do I associate him with my mother? He throws me back into the womb as if I'm a caterpillar, a half-dead zombie in front of my mother, and she denies me my existence, my dominance, which would enable me to be active. Is my mother's role an active one? My mother's dominance is linked to the fact that I must satisfy someone who symbolizes my mother, and her authority is asserted by the fact that she makes me do something for her pleasure at the expense of mine ...

Women symbolize dominance and castration. My sexual partners are not dominating women, but they have the active role and contact with them makes me feel sexual arousal which alternates with frigidity because to be penetrated is painful. Rubbing against a man when we are face to face excites me. When I am in the passive position with the man behind me I feel excited, I like being penetrated, but I feel pain and I'm not relaxed; I feel tense and that, finally, makes me feel rejected ...

In a heterosexual fantasy I play the part of the woman and feel extremely excited. The thought of going to bed with an exclusively heterosexual man excites me because then, in the fantasy, I am truly the woman ... Does this woman symbolize my mother? I don't think so because I am sensual whereas my mother is cold ...

... At the moment I feel muscular contractions in my whole body ... I curl up ... The contractions make me take the foetal position ... My breathing becomes loud and spasmodic ... I cry helplessly ... I tried to resist in every way I could but I got nowhere. A foreign will imposed itself on me. A vain, futile struggle, ludicrous revenge. Everything I do is ludicrous and futile. Now I'm laughing and my laughter reminds me of 'B'; I identify with him. I often identify with others because I don't have a personality of my own. I have an identity problem (laughter). I need to find a personality in art, in homosexuality, where everyone has the same religion and where everyone feels more secure ...

... In intellectual matters I try to share my partner's opinion. I don't contradict him because I want to be on good terms with him ...

You cannot have clear ideas about something unless you have experienced it and know what you're talking about. However, from the psychological point of view, I reject erroneous interpretations. I analyse people as I analyse myself.

Whenever I make someone's acquaintance, I feel the need to express everything immediately, to say in just a few seconds, if such a thing were possible, that I am a homosexual, that I'm undergoing autopsychognosia, that I have been living in Egypt and so forth. I feel the need to display extraordinary knowledge and attributes, to tell of sensational experiences I have had which will give some worth to my insignificant being. I want to impress, to charm within the space of ten minutes by saying who I am, what I can do, what I have experienced. After this exhibition, I become despondent. I want others to admire me because I feel worthless before the womb-dominator ...

I wonder if I project my worthlessness when I compare myself to others? I don't think so. Comparison consoles me rather. The others are worse than I am - as a rule homosexual circles are degenerate and sordid.

On two different occasions I went home with fellows who looked like criminals. I regretted it. Both were coarse. I realized that what I need is a lot of tenderness and affection.

One day I bought a black leather jacket. I thought that by wearing it I could act the man. Every time I look at myself in the black leather jacket I realize that I look like a baby and that irritates me. I want to be a man. I've moved about in almost all homosexual circles, I've tried everything, but I haven't met anyone worth having a close relationship with. Furthermore, I'm afraid of being a disappointment because I can't reach orgasm and I'm also afraid that my partner will disappoint me. I'm sick and tired of always taking the wrong path. Playing roles that aren't your own is no help whatsoever. I move in orbits which are diametrically opposed: sadism and pacifism. In the former I feel pleasure when I see the pain of someone who is being tortured; in the latter I seek human warmth and tenderness ...

The image of the ideal man, now after 16 Sessions, is not a fixed one; but the basic element of the ideal image that I had when I was four years' old remains unchanged; the 'protective man' who will protect me on his own initiative because I can never be the one to make the first move. Thus it's impossible for me to approach a woman because I can never take the initiative and women expect men to make the first move. And if I happen to come across a woman who takes the first step, then terror grips me. At parties I have no difficulty approaching a girl and flirting with her but I feel no sexual excitement. I'm afraid that if we end up alone in bed, she'll have a soft penis in her hands. The anxiety of being impotent haunts me constantly ...

Fantasy: I'm making love with *G*. (*G* is the girl he has known since childhood; they grew up together like brother and sister.) In the beginning everything goes well, but soon I feel my penis growing smaller in her vagina. My penis slips out, ridiculous, looking like a caterpillar ...

When I am with a man I don't reach orgasm but at least I have an erection. During the homosexual act I feel tense, I analyse everything, I fantasize, I feel anxious. I feel the need to justify myself. I tell my partner: "You know, I have strange reactions. You excite me sexually and at the same time I feel frigid. In the end I can't ejaculate and I panic."

I dream of my passiveness being satisfied by a partner who is sensitive, affectionate, refined. Yet when I masturbate when I am by myself, tenderness doesn't enter into it: the brutal element alone dominates my fantasies (see Session 7).

Fantasy during the homosexual act:

ME	MAN
passive	active
woman	very manly
victim submissive to the man	exhibitionist-brute-executioner

Penetration of the anus is a bestial act with no feeling.

Fantasy during masturbation:

I ← am protected by ← Spectator. I approve of the victim's suffering and derive pleasure from it.	E X E C U T I O N E R → tortures Emotionless. He displays his strength and inhumanity.	→VICTIM Always a worthless man who has been denied the right to exist.

    The executioner is the base of this edifice and he unites my ego with the victim. Although I am the same person as the victim, I have nothing to do with him; that is, I separate the ego which feels pleasure from the ego whose right to exist is denied. In this fantasy I achieve a kind of catharsis-liberation as immediately after my ejaculation-pleasure the executioner ceases to be an executioner, because I no longer need him: inhumanity kills inhuman vengeance ...

    I'm afraid of venereal disease. It's an ideal excuse for me not to have sex as sex makes me an easy target for attack. When I am afraid that I'll be attacked, darkness overwhelms me, I don't want to live, I want to escape, I want to die in an endless sleep, I want to forget everything, I want to repress everything; I am nothing. I have no complexes about my homosexuality. It doesn't constitute a moral problem for me; on the contrary, I feel proud that through my homosexuality I can get revenge on my father. I'd be happy if I could reach orgasm through my homosexual activity. Unfortunately, though I don't, and so my so-called revenge is non-existent. But the most important thing is that I don't know how to get revenge. When I start a fight I soon become exhausted, I become castrated, I very quickly let myself be dominated by the other person. When I was small, I would hit back when someone hit me because I wanted to stop him from continuing ...

The Knowledge of the Womb

My obsessional acts and ideas exhaust me mentally. The worst obsessional idea is my fear of transmitting venereal disease to a sexual partner. When I had a fungus infection I felt the need to confess it to each of the partners I had at the time. I felt terribly guilty at the thought that I could probably ruin my partner with the venereal disease I'd transmit to him. If my partner transmitted V.D. to me, it wouldn't be so terrible because I'm used to being half dead ...

I often feel my voice is ridiculous, especially when I am speaking to the doctor. Before telling him something specific, I feel that it is extremely interesting; but the moment I say it, it loses the value I thought it had. I think that even the atom bomb itself would be reduced to a grain of sand. That is because the doctor castrates me like my mother and father who paid no attention when I told them of the adventures I had on my various trips ... When I get angry I feel like an insignificant little woman. Sometimes I become irritated and I shout and desperately try to get something I want, and as soon as I feel that I'm going to win I immediately lay down my arms and agree to do whatever is asked of me. I subsequently submit completely and hold my tongue; this way I feel I am atoning for my irritability and shouting ...

I dream that I am making love with G. At first it is beautiful, warm, my erect penis penetrates deeply into her vagina. But shortly before I reach orgasm, my erection is no more and my penis comes out of the vagina impotent, looking like a caterpillar. That is the reason why I have no desire or intention of making love with a woman. I know in advance that as soon as I approach orgasm my penis will make me look ridiculous. How embarrassing. How depressing. Knowing in advance what the end will be, I neither want to begin nor even get excited. The penis coming out of the woman's vagina soft is something terribly depressing ...

What does the partner symbolize? To begin with, I reject my father's authority over me. I refuse to let my sexual partner reactivate the memory of my father but I see my father in everything that my partner has as a man. The way I am aggressive towards my father in everyday life shows me that I can neutralize him; for instance I ignore his existence, his teachings and exhortations for me to have heterosexual activity. Yet I feel that trying to neutralize him in this way is ridiculous and that causes me permanent emotional conflict. If this mask of aggressiveness is taken away from me I will have nothing. I'm a mixture of absolute passiveness and explosive energy. I have a lot of energy in me which I passionately expend on dancing and singing. If my passion for singing and dancing and my need for revenge are taken away from me, I'll be left with nothing ... My thirst for revenge gives me some worth which covers up the feeling that I am a nothing. But I have no stamina, my strength is frail. I often regret what I have done ...

At the moment I feel I'm floating face down, not in the foetal position which means rejection by the womb. I'm trying to avoid being ousted by the womb. I can see horrible, monstrous creatures which threaten and terrify me with their ugliness. Everything around me is grey and frozen. I can see haunted castles. I see a dim sun that barely gives out heat. There are ants all around me. I see people with their legs apart, huge mouths dripping blood. I start to cry. I'm reliving my birth ... My breathing becomes rapid and loud ... I'm sobbing with despair ... I'm groaning with anger and my cries express all the strength with which I'm trying to hang on and not go out of the womb ... I feel I'm being strangled ... Finally I feel myself being expelled and I'm overcome by spasmodic coughing ...

I wonder why I exist? All sorts of things degrade me: my persecution complexes, my obsessional ideas. My obsessional acts are performed in a way that debases me, that lowers me to the level of an idiot. My obsessions hound me constantly and lead me to self-negation, to self-destruction by a power which isn't mine but which is inside me, a power that belittles me, that points out my incapacity to me, that reduces me to tatters, that shows me I'm nothing. This power within me functions like another consciousness which makes me see everything around me with gloom, which robs me of all energy, which makes me passive. I don't want to live because I don't know how to live. I search desperately for something to fill in the blank spaces.

The exhibition of my limp penis is a form of belittlement because it points out my impotence; it's as if I'm showing my mother that I'm a nothing. For the past two years I have been drawing away from my mother and I feel sad that she suffers because I'm far away from her. I always tried to do what would please her. I would have been prepared to become a little baby, the consequence of which would have been submission to her domination. When she came to Cairo for a few days, her presence oppressed me. She criticized whatever I did, just like before; even the fact that I smoke now and then. I can see her: hard, withdrawn, sometimes nasty, implacable. Tears roll down from my eyes. I want her tenderness and she gives it to me beneath the unbearable burden of her castrating domination. If I go back to her, I'll go back to what I was; her satellite ...

At the moment I feel that my father is soft, tender and passive in comparison to the dominant figure of my mother. My father is hypersensitive, a trifle would make him cry. I feel him as being very vulnerable. He has great abilities which he inhibits ...

Why do I feel the need to say that I'm a homosexual? Maybe I'm not a homosexual? To belittle myself perhaps? No, on the contrary, I'm proud of it. I have no moral problems. I'm not ashamed. I feel proud that I'm not like everybody else. Homosexuality gives me worth.

I can see the following image: my mother and father are making love. My mother looks gigantic and she's penetrating my microscopic father. My mother is the active one here.

From the physical point of view my homosexual activity still has its problems. I have a soft penis even with a male sexual partner because at the moment of ejaculation my sexual partner 'becomes' the womb, a symbolism which makes me want to cry, which makes me suffer, which makes me suffocate, which takes me close to death. So I avoid ejaculating and instead I have fantasies of a passive nature which give me pleasure.

Can I get rid of my fantasies? For the time being I am altering them, trying to make them less inhuman. In my fantasies I prefer to have someone else tortured rather than myself. This fantasy excites me and that's why my old fantasies have continued till now, even though I no longer accept them ...

In love I demand exclusiveness. I am totally dependent on my sexual partner just as I was totally dependent on my mother ... My love affair with B did me harm. I must build on what has remained. I'm tired of always being deceived. I need security and clear ideas about my life and about love. For the moment my ideas keep changing every day.

R5's conclusions after Session 17: For me, the mother-woman is the big mouth which devours-castrates male genital organs. I want a mother-proctector who will not be a mother-castrator. The woman who devours the male genitals arouses the fear that my penis will be soft, not erect. When I think of the possibility of my having a relationship with a woman, the image of the soft penis comes immediately to mind. How depressing. The woman wants to destroy my sexual capability and so she demolishes me. My penis must be soft. My penis must be incapable of procreating.

Session 19 Once again I'm certain that the doctor has cheated me. He gave me an injection of distilled water instead of LSD. He wants to see the reactions I'll have as a result of auto-suggestion. He's trying to deceive me. Everyone tries to deceive me ...

I'm certain in the sexual act that something isn't right. I feel that certain conditions are necessary for it to evolve satisfactorily; for instance, I have to remove my belt beforehand or else it'll go wrong. Just one small detail is enough to spoil everything. I want everything to be perfect and yet everything is imperfect. I want everything to be in impeccable order and yet everything is in confusion ...

Waking up in the morning is torture. I have no desire to get out of bed. I feel that this resistance symbolizes my resistance to leaving the womb. My mouth is dry. There is a taste of death in my mouth. I feel horrified when I see old people: they look like death. My head feels heavy. I don't want to speak. I'm resisting. The same in everyday life: resistance to everything. Nothing in life is worth anything. Everything leads to a nothing. Failure in everything. The Session will fail. What use is any effort I make? Intellectually, I come to the conclusion that I'm no worse than a lot of other people, but that doesn't help me because emotionally I feel I'm worth nothing.

The doctor subjects me to Sessions out of charity. I often wonder what the purpose of the Sessions is, as long as I'm worthless. As if I don't want to know the cause of my suffering. I'm sure everyone is deceiving me. The doctor is deceiving me. Since he gave me an injection of water instead of LSD, why should I ejaculate? (Here R5 immediately corrects his slip of the tongue and says:) Why should I gesticulate when I speak? I don't want to be deceived and above all I don't want to play their game. I'm the victim of a preposterous farce.

When I gesticulate I make myself look ridiculous. I give satisfaction to those who make fun of me. They expect something of me. I feel exhausted. I want to destroy everything around me. This is the night of the night within the night. My mouth is dry. I have no desire to talk. I feel extremely tired. I feel nothing. I'd like to howl but there is nothing. I am nothing within nothing. I'm saying nothing. The tape recorder is recording nothing. I'm not something essential in life. I think that the doctor is smiling ironically. I'm not an interesting type of person because I'm a nothing. What use is the Session? I know nothing. It's awful. You're expecting something. You and the tape recorder are expecting to see me being tortured, to hear me groaning. Stop that tape recorder. It's a pit full of lies. It wants bloody crimes, it want violence, it wants sex, it wants violence and blood. It's waiting to hear me being tortured. No, I'm not going to satisfy such a vile desire. Does what I'm saying interest you? Well then, I'll say nothing. I am nothing so that I won't be what you want me to be.

(Pointing to the speaker on the tape recorder) I'm not going to put my thing in that machine: it'll cut it to pieces. It's a diabolical machine. It gets into your thing (penis) and there's nothing left. The diabolical machine is lying in wait for my thing. Take that machine away from me. (The doctor removes the tape recorder.) I'm safer that way. The diabolical

The Knowledge of the Womb

machine has the taste of death. (R5 sees the speaker as a round opening with teeth; he feels these are dangerous female genital organs.) ...

It annoys me to know that something is expected of me. I feel I must be active and productive. I feel that everything must be done perfectly. When I wake up in the morning panic grips me at the thought that I've lost time. Loss of time symbolizes something which is not perfect. Every morning they want me to suffer. Every second makes demands on me: do this, do that ... My whole body has to obey the order. My mind too. It's awful because neither my mind nor my body can obey. Every second I have to do something to prove that I'm worth something and that is impossible. I want to feel calm and yet I'm caught in the grip of obsessional acts and ideas. I'm expected to be perfect and I feel that I can never live up to what is expected of me ...

Session 20 ... I can see spiders. Hideous and horrible monsters. I can't stand it any more. I can't stand it any more (repeated many times) ... This body isn't mine. I don't like this body. I don't like the everyday sensation of this body. It's badly proportioned. It's always my father's body. It's ugly. My body resembles a woman's body: narrow shoulders, broad pelvis, slightly rounded belly. When I am dressed, I can charm people with my face and well-groomed attire. Naked, I'm afraid of being rejected. I need to be wanted not only by men but also by women ...

... I'm fed up with everything, everything, everything! Every day I relive the sensation of being strangled. When I think of sex with a woman as being the expression of an effort to return to a state of 'normality' and peace, I feel the need to cry like a baby. What a horrible, what a sordid life! It's your fault (speaking to himself), you should have returned to your mother, to your womb, to woman, because that is really the only true way. I weep for my sordid life and my suffering but I cannot return to the true road: it passes through unbearable pain. I don't want to find myself back in a state of oppression where I'm dominated completely. I don't want to feel that I'm losing my body. Homosexuality is less pain ... When I reach orgasm through fantasizing and masturbating, I cry. It is the moment in which I lose all control over my body ...

R5's description of his first heterosexual experience I had expressed all my sensuality in an oriental dance, my body close to the body of a woman I was dancing with, when I suddenly felt that dancing was perhaps the only way I could function sensually with a woman. At the same time, I felt protected because I was dressed and sure of myself because I like dancing. At the end of the evening the woman I had been dancing with

111

approached me and told me that she wanted to see me again. Because I am a weak person, I never say no to anyone and I cannot tell someone: "I don't want to see you again." Furthermore, I cannot lie and so I gave her my phone number. Because I wanted - but at the same time I didn't want - to see her again, I invited her to a party I was giving, thinking that I could easily avoid her by mingling her in with the other guests. Before the party I had masturbated with my usual fantasies to avoid any possible sexual desire for her.

The party has begun. It is late and she still hasn't come. I'm a little disappointed because I like being found attractive and I really want to be attractive even to this female admirer because I feel that she truly does admire me. She arrives late. I play it cool. I don't pay her particular attention and I talk with everybody. Yet I feel her eyes on me. She holds the microphone for me as I sing and I truly lose all my inhibitions singing. We dance and talk. She quickly confesses her sexual life to me. She had had a relationship with a homosexual who had never had another woman. She explains her love for him: she had become disappointed with the behaviour of many men and so she appreciated the finesse, the tenderness and sensitivity of homosexuals. I listen to her carefully and feel that she understands me. She tells me her thoughts on me: I have not yet decided whether to be homosexual or heterosexual and am still searching for my true nature.

I confirm that and confess my tremendous problem: I never know what I want. I cannot want and I cannot not want. I can't say no and I can't say yes. As far as my partners are concerned, I never know if I really want a sexual relationship with them or not. At bottom I do feel the desire for it but I never want it because I always feel afraid. I look at her and reflect that she isn't very pretty but she seems to understand my problem; she is sweet, she has had experience with homosexuals and she seems to want me. Then why not go to bed with her? I'm prepared to do the maddest thing I've ever done in my life. If I don't do it today, I'll never do it. I must take advantage of this opportunity, look upon it as an experience, even a test that, for better or worse, I must go through. I tell her what I want and also that I've never been to bed with a woman. She seems astonished. She confesses that this makes it difficult for her but in spite of that she wants me. Her face reflects fear, sadness and doubt. Both of us, in fact, are afraid. She confides to me her permanent fear of becoming pregnant because she doesn't always take the pill. That throws me off balance but she assures me that she is prepared to take the risk. This possibility brings me face to face with one of my worst phobias - that of pregnancy and childbirth - and so I tell her that she can easily refuse and I confide in her

The Knowledge of the Womb

my own great fear on this matter. But then, everything terrifies me, so I close my eyes and she is ready to spend the night with me.

First I kiss her, though without much pleasure. Her mouth is small and fine and I'm not used to that. Then she undresses and I caress and kiss her. How different this is to being with a man. I'm used to large male hands and now I'm holding small hands. When I lie on top of her I'm afraid I may hurt her because she feels fragile to me and that inhibits me, it makes me falter all the more. At first I don't want to take off my underpants. I don't feel at all aroused and it would be like admitting that I am impotent. She puts my finger in her vagina. It is a terrible sensation which really revolts me but I say nothing. It is slimy, warm and moist and it reactivates all my phobias. It is like a jellyfish and while I had never previously touched female genitals, it is as if I had known this feeling of revulsion before ... The vagina secretes a fluid like sperm, with the same smell and that amazes me. I don't like the consistency of these fluids nor this smell. I really feel no arousal at all. This is total castration ...

We speak about *X* and that pleases me. I'm speaking about men and that excites me. Sometimes I find myself in a passive position, as if I'm expecting her to behave like a man. She begins to masturbate me and I feel aroused. I'm suffering, I feel pain in the genitals as if they are bleeding and I start to cry. The more I suffer, the more she masturbates me and the more I want to cry. I control myself a little but this must be terrible for her. The pain comes from excitation: it is just like the way I feel when I'm about to ejaculate with a man. I tell her to go on masturbating me because, even though I'm suffering, at least I feel something and that's better than nothing.

I take her in my arms, I hold her, I squeeze her, I lift her. We are sitting facing each other in each other's arms but I have no desire to kiss her, I don't feel like it. I feel very active and dominant at this stage. She wants me to penetrate her but I can't conceive of it without a real erection and I don't do it. She puts her finger into my anus and that surprises me but I like it well enough. Then we fall asleep. At first I feel like a small baby curled up like a foetus and in need of protection. I'd like a man to be squeezing me in his arms at this moment. Her presence cannot satisfy me. She keeps reaching for me and I don't want to any more.

In the morning I'm glad when she leaves because I don't want her body any more. She was a very nice girl. I couldn't have asked for more understanding for my first time. I don't want to begin again in the immediate future but I didn't feel terribly traumatized because she was gentle and refined. The thought of pregnancy and childbirth could have made me feel very afraid; although I did not ejaculate, it seems to me that if I had given one drop of my sperm, it would have been like giving a drop of my blood.

EXCERPTS FROM AND SUMMARIES OF R6's HISTORY AND SESSIONS

History   Female, 20 years' old, single, no profession. Before beginning the Sessions, R6 had said the following about her mental state : "Ever since I was a small child I have felt like a frightened animal. I'm afraid of everyone and everything. I can't find understanding or support anywhere. I'm full of guilt feelings. I punish and torture myself because of these feelings. I live a life full of anxiety. I feel so alone. A life full of insecurity where everything, even the simplest thing, terrifies me and often causes me extreme shame.

"Until I was fourteen, I tried to hide my agony from my family until one day I could contain myself no longer ... A social worker referred me to a psychologist. In his person I sought the security and affection I needed so much. Unfortunately I had only 2 - 3 appointments with him and then nothing. Again I felt lost ... Five terrible years of suffering passed ... I visited the same psychologist again. He considered that I should see a psychiatrist and he recommended Dr. Kafkalides to me. And again I sought in the doctor the security I lacked. With him I found understanding. I felt I could trust him. But I wanted - in fact, I very much needed - to be completely dependent on him. I wanted him to love me as if I were his child. I wanted him to love me above all else. Naturally this desire of mine tormented me very much psychologically. It was in this state of mind that I decided to begin autopsychognosia sessions."

Session 2   At the moment I feel I've taken on the appearance of the nymphomaniac[29] ... Now I feel as if I've taken on the fierce appearance of my mother ... I want to become a foetus. What should I do? (The doctor recommends that she assume the foetal position. She does.) Again I've take on the appearance of the nymphomaniac ... again the appearance of my mother. I'm afraid of her. She'll tear me to pieces. Now I can see Christ ... I don't feel relaxed in this position (the foetal position). I'm afraid to return to the womb ... I can see red circles ... I'm afraid to return to the past. I feel very small and I feel aggressive. I felt as if I was entering something and I became frightened. I could see circles. I would have felt

---

[29]   Doctor's note: R6 is referring to a neighbour of hers who was considered a nymphomaniac.

closed in and I wouldn't have been able to escape. I repress that feeling because I'm afraid. I feel shut in and I become a skeleton. It's unpleasant and I don't want to feel like that. I feel small. (R6 stammers) ... I feel that something is covering me. I feel I'm an object of contempt. I can feel only my little head. I feel closed in and as if they're choking me. (At this point R6 puts her hands around her throat and squeezes it.)

It's as if I've taken on the appearance of my little niece. I see light and then darkness again. I feel that there's something I can't escape from. It's as if they control me ... They do whatever they like. "They" are my parents and more generally Nature. It's as if I've been tied by the legs. I can feel only half my body. I feel that something inevitable is going to happen ... I can't stand it ... I feel as if they're choking me. I'm a baby. I feel naked. I fell aggressive towards everyone! Perhaps I'm in the womb ... but I'm afraid ... very afraid. I feel that maybe I'll die. I feel I'm choking., There's something on my head, like strong pressure - like the pressure I feel in my sleep which wakes me up. As if I'm dying. I didn't want to go into that place. I didn't want my conception to take place. I feel as if I'm being punished because I was conceived, and I can't escape. I want to get out but I can't. My vile mother has closed me inside her womb. She didn't want to have me with my father. For nine months that's how I felt ... as if I was choking ... as if my parents are punishing me. As if they want to kill me because I'm a girl, a lousy female. I can't bear feeling choked! As if I was born and my father is choking me ... I feel I'm also vile because I'm a girl. I can't stand being closed in. (sobbing) ...

... I still feel that I'm in the womb as if ... as if I don't believe all those things ... I felt that after their sexual act I entered the womb and afterwards I was born. That's what was inevitable. Now I await my fate! I feel I'm choking, as if I knew they didn't want me and that's why I feel I'm choking. The cramped place I was afraid of is perhaps due to that. As if I'm going to be choked to death ... My parents are choking me. I'm afraid that I'll die. My legs don't feel free. At times it's as if something gets into my throat, but I don't know what it is. I feel that I'm an object of contempt. It's as if I've come out of the womb ... but it's as if I'm ashamed that I'll be seen! Sometimes I see darkness and other times half-light ... now only darkness! As if a dead child comes out ... a dead child after nine months of agony in the womb. As if the nymphomaniac is being punished by being forbidden to have sex.

(to the doctor) Feeling as I do like a foetus and grown up, I'm looking at a part of your body that I shouldn't be looking at and I take on the appearance of the nymphomaniac. I feel that people are telling me that I'm being punished just as a nymphomaniac is punished when she can't be

The Knowledge of the Womb

gratified sexually. My parents' sexual act isn't pure and that's why I feel scorned, humiliated ... When I come out of the womb, I feel that the sexual act is forbidden me because I'd been rejected by my parents etc. ... As if I come out of the womb of a nymphomaniac who is forbidden to have sex. I feel that everyone around me feels contempt for me. I feel defenceless and within me I wonder when I too will get my revenge by being aggressive towards everyone. I feel I'm out of the womb ... I'm vile ... I'm not pure. I'm an object of scorn ... I feel insecure because I don't feel pure. Everyone despises me ... I feel that I deserve to be despised because I'm not pure ... That's why I feel ashamed in front of people. As if I come out of an oven! (At this point R6 refers to an excursion she had been on, during which she visited a brick factory. She goes on to say:) At the brick factory I was scared they'd put me into the oven. (Here she explains that the oven of the brick factory symbolized her mother's womb.)

I can't face small children because maybe the affection I'll give them won't be pure. I feel that small children despise me because I'm not pure! I feel like a foetus and I can see my little niece scorning me and I say to her: "You want affection but I'm not going to give it to you!"

I reject the sexual act because through sex I'll return to the womb and I'll be terribly tortured all over again.[30]

Session 14 When I saw my mother pregnant - I felt I was in her belly - and she was hitting me furiously, I realized that she wanted to remove me from her body and I felt afraid because everyone was against me and at the same time I felt very weak. I don't want to see phallic symbols (such as candles which are on the doctor's desk, the knife which is illustrated in a painting in the room). They cause me pain because I associate them with the male genital organs. In the place of the man's genital organs I'd like there to be a hole just so that they could urinate, but without a hymen. I'd also like men to keep company with members of their own sex but without them having sexual relations amongst themselves. As men won't have genital organs, they won't have sexual desire or relations, neither amongst themselves nor with women. A fat man without a sexual organ comes into my mind. This man comes from the past. There's something primitive in his appearance. He says to me: "What can I do with you now that you've cut my genital organ?" His voice expresses sarcasm and punishment. Actually, he doesn't really care about not having a penis because he's old

---

[30] Doctor's note: Symbolism of sex for R6.

and anyway, even if he had a sexual organ, he wouldn't be able to have sexual relations because of his age.

I can see the image very clearly before me. This man, wrapped in a tunic, was having a discussion with someone and he said: "Forget her. Do you think I'm going to be concerned with that brat of mine now?" I felt he was rejecting me and I removed his genital organs to punish him. Let him feel as I felt in my mother's womb. That man was my father. For him, it's as if I don't exist.

Every movement I make I connect it with sex and into my mind comes the image of Christ with a crown of thorns crucified on the cross. I resemble him - I'm pale and thin just like him. We don't care that people pay us no attention, sick and pale as we are. We want them to despise us!

Suddenly the images disappear and a small monkey appears before me. This little monkey scorns me, even the monkey scorns me. Now I feel I'm becoming a big monkey, ready to tear the little one to pieces.[31]

I now see the doctor as my father. He's taken on the appearance of my father. He is a liberated man, meaning he doesn't have any problems. Beside him stands a woman who has my mother's features. Both of them are looking up at the ceiling where there's a hole from which water is running. Suddenly I feel very ugly in the face, as if I don't have a face. My face is different to other people's. My father and mother want to leave, as if something is threatening them. It's the hole that's threatening them. The man leaves and abandons his wife, my mother. The woman is trapped! She's caught and she can't escape. Oh! What a mean person that man is. Why did he go away and leave her? He wanted to throw off his past and he left. He didn't want me ... Something is pressing on me ... it's choking me ... They're trying to get me out ... They don't want me ... But when I come out, so will that man! But that's impossible.,

In front of me now is the local garbage truck collecting the rubbish. When I come out I'll be a bit of rubbish, while he (the man above) will be a man. I won't exist, but he will. No! No! That can't be. Why do I feel so discarded? That's how I always feel. I can't bear to continue this scene. I feel very afraid and anxious ...

I can see a fat old woman who comes from the past. A very bad woman. She's holding a broom and she's sweeping the rubbish which is me. I'm certain that this woman is an ancestor of mine. I feel I'm lying

---

[31] R6's note: I feel like this because I want to defend myself against the small monkey and the only way I can do that is by becoming big and fat like my father so that I can tear it to pieces.

The Knowledge of the Womb

in the mud of a tortured past and that they're treading on me. Everyone is against me and they're crushing me and treading on me and I'm in the mud, a piece of rubbish.

Now I can see a clothes line in the yard of my house full of trousers. They're my brothers' clothes. So many babies and they're all boys! What did she want them for? What can my mother do with so many boys? Why did I also come along? What can I do with boys? I can see my face as being very ugly, as if I don't have a face. Why should I also be amongst all those men? What was I after? I feel like a nymphomaniac.32

I feel that none of those men want me amongst them. I want to cut that clothes line with the trousers! I just don't want to see anything! I'm the only woman amongst my brothers. Like a pig, that's how I feel. I can see a black crow which wants to snatch something. I'm the black crow. I want to grab at happiness and I become a bird to do it. But nothing happens. What was I doing in the house seeing that my mother was there! Isn't one woman enough? Besides, my mother wanted to be the only woman around.

I see an opening in front of me ... They want to get me out. I shouldn't exist! I shouldn't exist! Since I don't have a body, why should I exist? Is it my fault? ... my fault that I was conceived? She didn't want me.

Now I feel like a fish. That fish lives in the water but it feels very cold ... The water's very cold, freezing. So I can't even live as a fish because I'm a human being. I'm thinking once again of the original hole in the ceiling with water running from it. I feel like urinating. Water is running out of the hole again and together with the water comes me ... a piece of rubbish. When I'm far away from people, my life will be better. But I must learn to live with them ...But how? How, seeing that they reject me? That's my big problem. My father sees me as a piece of rubbish. Since I'm rubbish, it means that I don't exist. How then can I live with people? Will I feel that I am something? Now I can see my father staring into my mother's womb where I am. Why are you looking at me in the womb? You should be ashamed of yourself! To me he feels like a guard waiting for the moment when he can take me out and torture me. I say to him: "I won't come out. I'm not allowed to come out. I don't have the strength." But that doesn't concern him because he is himself. Everyone looks out for himself. I can't see ... I can't see myself as existing ... I see knives,

---

32 R6's note: In previous Sessions I have also felt like a nymphomaniac. For me a nymphomaniac is a woman who has many sexual relationships in her effort to find security. She wants to enter the womb to find security. But the womb always rejects her and so she never finds what she's looking for.

leaves ... but I don't see myself as existing. Nor do I see my mother. That's how discarded I am, then. I feel like that wherever I am, all the time.

The womb is something unclean. It contains folds, pieces of glass ... When someone enters the womb, that's it! He becomes a sucker! He's nothing. A small foetus ... so small. I didn't expect it and yet it's as if they put you into a grave. A big opening like a grave. You know nothing, nothing, nothing! It's as if you're in a plastic bag until you come out. Can these things happen without feelings, without anything? Is such a thing possible?

Now I can see little babies everywhere. Since I don't love them, what can I do with them? Shall I constantly become a baby then? I can't bear, I can't stand babies, I can't stand foetuses. Me love babies? But how can I love them as long as I didn't exist? They upset me, Doctor. Those babies upset me terribly! I want to feel, for goodness sake, that I exist, that I have existence. But I can't see that happening.

Now I address myself to the doctor who has taken on the appearance of my father. I say to him: "I want to feel that I exist, but I can't. Are you such a sadist that you can't understand that? Just because I'm a woman, what harm am I causing you? I'm a woman and you spit on me. Just as you mistreat me, I'll mistreat you. You want to feel something. You want me to give you something ... but what will I feel if I give it to you? What will come of it?"

I feel I'm a skeleton. I see myself as a skeleton. Skeletons exist to remind us that we exist too. We exist too ... I exist as a skeleton which begs for love from the great ladies ... Did I say great ladies? No. Great lady! That's it ... I, the skeleton, beg my mother, the great lady, for love ... acceptance ... But in vain. The great and wealthy lady plays the piano and we are its notes! Is that right? No! This difference between the great and wealthy lady and poor me shouldn't exist ... the rich and the poor. Shame!

I'm afraid of the sea because it'll drown me. And when I drown, I'll become a little baby, a foetus ... and then ... then there's the grave. Then Christ and death. But how does one really go to one's death? It's simple ... When they don't want you, they bury you, they bury you!

An enormous man's hand is approaching me now. I don't want that hand. No, I don't want it. What can I do with it as long as it doesn't satisfy me? That enormous hand is my father's. And my father says to me: "Come out, you piece of rubbish!" and I came out a piece of rubbish ... and he came out a human being. I can see people and women around me. Where am I? No, I don't see myself: I can't find myself anywhere. As if

The Knowledge of the Womb

my father cares about that! But I want to learn to exist for myself - I don't care about others - to exist! to exist!

Yet I am a nothing in front of my mother. She shut me in there in her womb and I'm a nothing. And my father watched and waited for the pregnancy to run its course. Alas, I feel I don't exist so that they can't see me. And since I didn't exist in there (in the womb), how can I ever feel that I exist?

The hand isn't my father's any more but my mother's. A beautiful hand, feminine, my mother's hand holding a piece of charcoal and crushing it. The charcoal is me ...

I have no worth, no worth at all. Why, God, did you send me? God is the womb. God is afraid of me and I'm afraid of God. Only God exists and I collaborate with him but this collaboration makes me feel terrible. God, I'm not his daughter! I'm nothing is his world. Priests are all-powerful and they become one with my father, one with the train which rolls over the track and I'm the track.

The thing that frightens me is the man's penis because it's the most powerful thing of all. It terrifies me because through it I was conceived. Skeletons await someone's judgement. Skeletons cannot live on earth. Skeletons await God's judgement and God is the womb - and I the skeleton.

Session 20 One problem that I have is Death. At this very moment I don't know if I'm going to live or die. I constantly feel Death and I constantly defend myself. I can't make love with anyone. The thought that I could make love with someone gives me a feeling of death. Sex brings me to the womb. To feel well, I have to kill the womb. I want to kill it, to kill it, to kill it. There's no other alternative. How can I kill it though? Can I kill the womb? How could I kill it? ... Could such a thing be done? ... Could it?

The doctor gives me a newspaper rolled up and says to me: "Kill it!" I take the newspaper from him and begin to cry and feel very afraid. The doctor seems like a murderer. The doctor is rejecting me and that makes me feel very sad while at the same time I hate him ... I throw the newspaper a long way away. If I kill the womb, I won't be satisfied. Again the result will be chaos, a void. If I destroy the womb, it's as if I'm destroying my own womb. I feel the doctor is an oppressor-murderer who wanted to deflower me. I feel he's rejecting me and I associate him with my father. I hate him. I hate him. And if I destroy the womb, what will happen? There'd be chaos, seeing that my conception has taken place, seeing that I was born. What's the point? I don't want to remove and destroy my womb because then men won't want me. The womb is a monastery for men[33] ... Will my children feel well, or will they feel as terrible as I do? By killing my mother's womb, I don't solve my problem because I also have a womb and my womb is a threat to me.

When you're rejected, you want to die ... and then follows Eternity and you'll always feel like that, always like that. Death and Eternity are one and the same thing. I'll always feel as if I'm dead ...

I must be thin. Being grown up and thin, I suffer, I suffer, I suffer ... They don't want me to exist and I would have liked never to have been conceived, but I exist ... Even if I'm a stigma in the womb, still I exist. Earth, you whore - Mother, you whore - womb. you whore! All wombs are to blame ... Now, even at this very moment, the womb wants to kill me. I fight back ... I'm afraid I'll die. When will I get out of this situation? It's black. I come out naked and people don't want naked people. I feel as if I'm burning ... I see black ash ... goodness me ... what's that? The womb is everything. I come into the world as if I'm burnt.

When I'm born, when I come out of the womb, I can't fight it because I feel I'm always in it. I feel I have something from the womb even if I'm outside it ... Now they know me for the dirty child they didn't want. They wore me out. My ancestors oppressed me ... The children I see around me remind me of myself ... I feel sorry for them.

Now an image appears before me. A very big hand which symbolizes power, dark power. It's holding the cross and the grave ... It's as if that hand is coming out of the tomb ... All the situations of the present rekindle the past. I want to break my bonds but I'm afraid of the unknown. When I break them, I'll want to hide in the womb again.

---

33 R6's note: I compare my womb to a church, to a beehive. On the one hand I do not want to destroy it so that men will accept me. On the other hand I want to destroy it so that it will never be a refuge for men.

EXCERPTS FROM AND SUMMARIES OF R12's HISTORY AND 5th SESSION

History Male, 30 years' old, single, social worker. R12 asked to undergo Sessions because he wanted to understand the deeper motives of his obsessional - as he characterized it - homosexual behaviour.

Session 5 Perhaps because during the last Session I had regressed to foetal status, I found the question on my mind: "Where was I before I was conceived?" The answer came dramatically.

A door flew open suddenly somewhere and I stood before an ocean of silver-white, soupy, silent, timeless liquid over which the sun appeared to have recently set, leaving behind it in the sky a pattern of reds and purples that hung in horizontal strips down to the horizon. The ocean was in constant motion, boiling and bubbling in a process of what I 'knew' to be destruction and resubstantiation. It looked like molten lava in a volcanic crater so vast that its bounds, except in one direction, the horizon, were invisible. And there it was not bounded by a rim, but by the horizon.

Though the ocean was boiling there was no steam and I felt no heat. I was overcome with awe at first - mixed fear and wonderment - and then I felt myself begin to melt. But it was no simple melting. I was separating into the various chemicals that composed me. Each chemical seemed to be related to a specific cloud in the glorious sunset over the lake. The clouds were, it seemed, pulling at these chemicals by some invisible process of attraction like magnetism.

Fear overcame wonderment. "Return at once to the present," I ordered myself. The door slammed noiselessly shut. The lake vanished. I was again in the room.

The vision had been so vivid, however, that for several moments I paid scant attention to my surroundings. The return to the womb of the previous Session paled into insignificance. That, I had been aware throughout, had been something happening in my own mind. This, I was convinced, was an experience external to me. I had been bodily transported to this magical lake which was somewhere in the objective world.

Beautiful as it was, however, I thanked God to be back in familiar surroundings. I touched the silken covering of the couch. I lovingly fondled the cushions and bolsters and looked around at the other furnishings: an escritoire, a book-case, beside it an easy-chair of wool and straw, portraits of Victorian gentlewomen frozen in the fashionably benign poses of their period which now seemed incongruous. Complicated coiffeurs, frills and flounces, from which the women stared philosophically into the middle distance, contrasted comically with their activities. One appeared to be ladlelling soup from a bowl to no one in particular, another stitched unseeingly at petit-point, and a third stabbed, equally unseeingly, at a heart-shaped fruit from which protruded the shaft of an arrow. Hanging by itself near the light-switch was a print of a Renaissance Madonna and Child. I got up to inspect it at close range.

The Madonna gazed distantly down at her baby, her hands folded in prayer before her face. Christ, who lay before her, regarded her intently with all the knowledge and aggressiveness of a precocious puberty which, according to his age in the picture, he should have been far from possessing. The picture fascinated me because it seemed to express my own mother's relationship with me at that stage in my life.

I thoroughly disliked the Madonna and sympathized with Christ, whose message of altruistic, almost masochistic love and subsequent (what seemed to me now) deliberate choice of death on the cross, no longer surprised me. The only feature of the picture that I liked was the background of pale sky with its almost evanescent fluffs of cloud. They were nothing like the clouds on my lake, but their still timelessness could only have come from such a region. I named the painting according to what I *knew* the Virgin must be saying in her prayer: "Pater meus qui es in coelis et qui es meus filius" (Father who art in heaven and who art my son). My mother also had loved her father almost to distraction. I disliked the picture, but it made me understand something about myself; and though I recognized it for art and the crinolined ladies, its neighbours on the wall, for so much kitch, how I wished my mother had had in her even a modicum of their mundanity.

Looking away from the portrait, my eye again caught the furniture and I was overcome by a new quality I seemed to have acquired whilst gazing at the lake: an intimate - the most intimate possible - knowledge of everything that met my eye. I knew everything - the walls, the window-panes, the cushions and upholstery - better than I had ever known anyone or anything in my entire existence. I had somehow become part of the room, not something foreign to it that was free to walk in and out of it, to use the furniture or not to use it, as I chose. No, I was on their level.

I placed the palm of my hand flat on the wall and pushed, expecting my hand to penetrate it - not with a crash or a crunch - but with the greatest of ease as though the wall were made of mercury. No. As though my hand and the wall were both quicksilver and would merge together like one drop of mercury with another. I touched the upholstery and cushions. Nothing happened! My hand had become neither satin nor silk. Am I mad? This urgent feeling of belonging ... Belonging to what?

The answer was instantaneous:

"To matter."

"Why?"

"You and all the things around you are material."

"And my soul?"

"It is matter like the rest of you."

"Then why don't I merge with everything?"

"Because between you and other things there is a difference."

"What difference?"

"A difference is time."

"What of the future"

Instantly I was returned to the lake and its eternal sunset. Again I was melting, separating, as though several metals which were alloyed together were loosening their grip upon one another and somehow, perhaps through some magnetic attraction, were being drawn into the sunset over the lake, each metal merging with a strip of light specifically ordained for it.

"Nirvana!"

"Yes, Nirvana. Pure matter."

"Beautiful. Terrifying. Suppose your mind gets stuck in this timeless region and you body stays in the present, they'll lock you up for madness. Return to the present! Return. Return."

I was back. After a moment I went to the lavatory. A feeling of immense age was upon me. I looked at myself in the mirror. No, I hadn't changed. My hair was ruffled, nothing more. No, perhaps because the light wasn't very bright, my hair did appear to have an ashy sheen to it. I reassured myself: "Take some vitamin B tomorrow and right now get some coffee."

The doctor's servant made me a double cup, but it wasn't really coffee I wanted; it was the sensation of being once again in the twentieth century, in the present. The lake and its atmosphere was something for Jules Verne and Hollywood. I could imagine the cinema posters: Jules Verne's immortal story, 'A Billion Years Ago', in Vista Vision, Panorama and Technicolor.

As I sat sipping the coffee and holding myself firmly to the present, a series of vivid mental pictures forced its way into my consciousness. I saw myself, always in the same position, on my back in a cradle, a tiny infant, looking up through a haze at two faces bent over me. I was screaming. I didn't hear screams, but I knew I was screaming. Hate ran through me, pure, blind hate for those two faces, the faces of my parents, and I clenched my baby fists and screamed, and screamed and screamed. The pictures stopped.

So I had been born over and over again, I told myself. Then, logically, men must have dug my grave again and again. But no pictures followed this thought.

The world is full of terrible hate, I thought. It is used to maim and destroy human material which nobody can replace; material that owes its existence to millions of years of evolution. We, the highest stage of organic matter, are only different from inorganic matter by the merest fraction of a fraction of the fractional. What a tremendous privilege. Surely this infinitely small difference should be the reason for respecting humanity rather than be the pretext for grinding it back to dust. It should be the very reason to push humanity on its way, making the distance between it and inorganic matter even greater.

But I also understand this hate. It comes of the dislike of being born, of a strong desire to return to the dust. Fear is at the bottom of it. Fear of new conditions.

Yes, the Bible and Darwin both speak the truth about Man. God made Adam from dust, say the religious books. Darwin has it that between Adam and the dust there was a whole series of beings, the first one to appear from the dust being something like an amoeba.

Does it matter? The operative word is *dust*. Homo sapiens is simply a variation of the dust; a variation of pure matter; nothing more, but certainly nothing less. Yet, what a marvel of creation is a piece of rusty iron in a junk yard. An ant! A tadpole! A tree! But how we break and discard, and crush and kill and cut down! I felt immensely ashamed, but, at the same time, strangely relieved.

It was strange that I who have always held, and still hold - though now considerably modified - an implicit belief in God, should rejoice at the certain *knowledge* that I had returned with from my lake, that man's soul is a part of pure matter, like a chair or a table; a different quality of matter certainly, but nevertheless matter.

I didn't feel relieved of responsibility. Far from it. The knowledge made me, if anything, more responsible, but I was relieved of a tremendous burden of fear. There was, indeed, a new hope. I felt certain that we were part of a truly wonderful plan in which we could take part more fully if - and it is a big "if" - we were willing to do so.

The Knowledge of the Womb

This was the sum of my experience when I took the pill which the doctor gave me. My eye-sight seemed marvellously improved for I noticed the word 'Largactil' written on it in tiny capitals whilst I still held the pill at arm's length.

EXCERPTS FROM AND SUMMARIES OF R16'S HISTORY AND SESSIONS

History Female, 24 years' old, translator, married, no children, parents' health very good.

Question: What are your complaints?
Answer: Since childhood I have felt ill at ease in front of others. Something makes me keep silent. I feel the need to disappear in order to escape their questions. I'm afraid of the silence which follows my answers to their questions. I'm afraid of my own voice when I am with others. Often when I speak I have the impression that nobody is listening to me. I believe that when somebody speaks he must assert himself and to assert oneself one must have confidence in oneself. I have no confidence in myself. When I open my mouth to say something I have the impression that everything stands still. I stop in the middle of what I'm saying because I can't continue: the effort to complete my words needs thought and thinking is something that I find impossible to do and very painful.

Question: What events in your life do you remember?
Answer: Between the ages of 14 and 16 I discovered freedom; I discovered that there were people without a bourgeois mentality who were willing to accept me and that I could lead a bohemian life. At the same time I became close friends with a classmate of mine. Our friendship has continued till today.

Answers on my existence I can communicate with someone only if I'm sure that he is not going to judge me. I talk to my parents but I don't communicate with them because I know that they judge me. There is a category of people I think very highly of: those who don't have a bourgeois mentality. I know that these people are prepared to accept me but at the same time I feel that they judge me because I belong to another social class. So I don't dare behave freely with them even though I very much want to.

When I was six, I started ballet. When I was 13 I stopped it. Why? I have never been able to understand why. Maybe it was because I had to make an effort. Now I regret it. Why do I love ballet? Perhaps because I'm motivated by an inner need to express myself in some way through my body. In ballet the body vibrates, it is alive, it moves easily, freely, without complexes. The physical exercise involved in ballet tires the person who does it in a pleasant way. After it, you feel your body invigorated because the body gave all it could. Ballet is a means of expressing yourself completely, without words and without intellectual effort.

Apart from ballet, nothing moves me emotionally. Reading and music can occupy me pleasantly but only on a superficial level. The same thing happens with everything else I undertake. I face everything lightly, perhaps so that I won't learn a lot. Having knowledge would oblige me to speak and express my personal opinion, and that would tire me very much. Everything I start I stop in the middle because it soon tires me. Maybe I want to be lazy. Maybe laziness is convenient. If people know that I have knowledge, they will ask me question and judge me, and I don't want anything like that ... I don't want them to listen to me.

I never express my joy freely and without inhibitions because I control my emotions and that makes me suffer. I'd like to express myself more openly, for instance I'd like to jump for joy, but my body stops me. I'm afraid to express what I feel. Maybe it's because people will look at me and judge me? Maybe because they'll listen to me?

I find it difficult to show tenderness to someone. My father says that I'm insensitive and that I never suffer. Of course my father doesn't realize that I repress my feelings and he doesn't know whether I suffer or not. But why don't I show my feelings? For physical reasons perhaps? My body doesn't belong to me completely. It feels clumsy and sluggish. Maybe that's why I have such a passion for ballet? But even if I begin ballet classes again, I won't feel free enough to make my body vibrate. My feelings block my body. Unfortunately my body is visible. I can't hide it as I hide my feelings. And my awful legs ... short, ugly ... The way I walk and sit isn't feminine enough. When I move my body I think it is ridiculous and that it doesn't represent the person called Natalie; it is foreign to me.

When I enter public places, I don't like to be looked at. I'm not perfect but I want to be the only one who knows that ... I feel that I'm trying to run away from myself. Why? I don't feel proud of myself whenever I shy away from making a determined choice between two or more things ... Why do I go on with my studies at the university when they don't interest me in the least? I don't dare put question to myself because I'm afraid I'll begin to go around in a vicious circle and finally I'll lose even the strength I have to keep up appearances which make me seem like a balanced person to others.

My parents tell me that everything is easy for me, that I'm successful at everything. But what is easy? Nothing is easy. The deeper you go into things the more complicated you realize they are. As for superficial studies, there's nothing easier; appearances keep the surface intact. The essential thing is not to make a choice. Making a choice means being criticized.

Answers on my sex I accept my sex. My sex doesn't disturb me. Until I met my husband I had difficulty communicating with males. When I was with a man I felt that he didn't accept me fully. When I made love I didn't dare express myself or participate in the act by moving my body because I was afraid that my partner would criticize me. I was also afraid that I wasn't sexy. I felt inhibited.

I had never had an orgasm before I met my husband. What factor does orgasm depend on? - on this body that feels heavy and sluggish? I remember one bastard that I had a relationship with. He didn't respect me. He treated me badly. But he made me feel great pleasure when he made love to me, although I didn't reach orgasm. Perhaps I have masochistic tendencies. Maybe for my heavy body to react I have to torture it. Maybe pain excites it. I like to feel that a man is dominating me. After all, aren't sadism and coarseness the ultimate expression of male strength and dominance? Male strength and coarseness excite me sexually; the reverse makes me feel indifferent, apathetic. If I'm not forced I feel bored. To feel pleasure I have to feel submissive. A man who is sure of himself knows how to control me. He speaks openly and he dominates me - like my husband does. Apart from that bastard, the men I knew in the past were clumsy and shy. So they lost all trace of superiority in my eyes and therefore they couldn't give me pleasure. Before I met my husband I was afraid to participate actively in the sexual act. I didn't move my body because I was afraid that I'd look ridiculous and be criticized. I reach orgasm with my husband because I feel that he doesn't judge me.

Answers on my behaviour I often don't understand the motives of my behaviour. I can't understand, for example, why I stop anything in the middle that entails intellectual effort. I want to feel calmness in my everyday life, not the remorse I feel when I can't complete anything serious.

Question: What do you desire most in life?
Answer: My great desires are to satisfy my father and to travel.
Question What do you fear most?
Answer: I'm afraid of financial insecurity.
Question: Are any of your dreams repeated in a stereotyped fashion?

Answer: Very often between the ages of two and twelve, and less frequently after that, I had the following nightmare: With agony I see an enormous rock, which in the nightmare I feel is me, rolling down into an endless abyss. As the rock is rolling down it becomes smaller and smaller and my agony becomes unbearable. The moment the rock becomes a small pebble I wake up terrified, sobbing and soaked in perspiration.

Question: What are your feelings for your mother?
Answer: I have no memories of her from my childhood. Today I feel boundless tenderness for her. I want to protect her. I love her as if she were a little child and not my mother. Until I was 16 I would quarrel with her because she irritated me. Now it's impossible for me to be angry with her. She often doesn't understand me and so I have to explain to her what she doesn't understand, just as I would explain it to a small child. I love her innocence and naivete. To me she is the ideal woman. I love her simplicity. At home she busies herself with everything, even down to the finest details. She does everything perfectly, modestly, without showing off. The opposite of my father. She is always there when I need her. She is emotional and spontaneous, so I joke with her, I kiss her like a small child. I communicate with her emotionally, not intellectually. I would like to identify with her simplicity and spontaneity but I am divided between spontaneity and intellectuality.

Question: What are your feelings for your father?
Answer: I remember nothing of him from my childhood. I admire him. I understand him. I guess his reactions in advance. He irritates me. In general his comments worry me. He doesn't listen to me when I speak to him. He is always in a hurry. He is very sensitive. I resemble him. I don't accept him because I don't accept myself. He wants whatever he does to be noticed and admired. I too like to be complimented for whatever I do: this gives me self-confidence which I often lack. When I was 14 I often went out with him and his friends. I was the young girl whom the adults admired. Older people understand and admire me whereas young people of my age criticize me. I know that I can speak to my father freely but he doesn't understand how I feel and so I cannot communicate with him. I always feel inhibited in his presence; I feel as if I'm playing a role. If I try to tell him something important I feel that, because he's always in a hurry, he is going to cut our conversation short and leave or that he'll change the subject before I've finished what I began. In any case, he never listens to me nor does he take what I say into consideration. Maybe it's because of him that I'm afraid of my own voice? Maybe it's because he has never paid attention to my voice that I'm afraid of others listening to

it? The voice expresses intellectual strength which is a male characteristic and which is meant for men's ears.

Question: What are your feelings about the interpersonal relations of your mother and father?

Answer: The relationship between my father and mother has never preoccupied me particularly.

Question: Do you feel that you have concealed anything?

Answer: I have concealed nothing.

Recapitulation of my problems My basic problem is fear of my father's criticism which castrates and destroys me. I have to be absolutely perfect and since I'm not perfect, then I'm unable to satisfy him and consequently I'm stupid.

Session 1 R16: On the table there is a vase and in the vase a pink flower. I look at the flower and feel uneasy. That flower with its blue centre, that strong, bad, cruel blue colour in the centre of the pink flower shocks me. It's unnatural.

Doctor: What do you feel?

R16: The abyss. A hole which draws you into darkness ... Why that blue, that bad blue in such a beautiful flower?

Doctor: What does the blue centre symbolize?

R16: The genital organs of the woman, the vagina, the road which draws you into the night, into something unpleasant ...

Doctor: Is there any relationship between the flower and the phallus?

R16: No. The shape of that candle there makes me think of a phallus.

Doctor: Have you ever had intense sexual impressions or experiences?

R16: Since I was 14 violence has excited me, dirty things, stories about sex between people and animals ... Of course, I didn't dare believe that I could take part in such things even though they excited me. It was allowed for others but not for me ... others, the degenerate, the liberated ... abnormal relations ...

Doctor: Who decides what is normal and what is not?

R16: The values adults have taught us.

Doctor: Which adult has influenced you the most?

R16: Whoever wasn't normal ... My father was always saying: "You have to do this and not that." He told me that I shouldn't flirt with boys; I should feel something deep ... If I ever made love with a man I wasn't in

The Knowledge of the Womb

love with I felt remorse. I wanted to forget what my father had said - that I had to feel that I was in love - and so I felt like a whore ...

Doctor: Do you mean that a woman is a whore if she makes love without feelings?

R16: Yes ... My father taught me that nothing in life should be impulsive: there must be a serious reason for everything that happens ... Suddenly the mirror catches my eye. I can see a black hole in the mirror: the abyss, and around it a halo ...

Doctor: The abyss?

R16: I would always see the abyss in my dreams when I was small and in people's eyes when they looked at me.

Doctor: Are the abyss and the eyes related to each other in any way?

R16: Yes ... I describe something which I now recall vividly. I'm sitting with about ten people around a table in a country house. The discussion begins to take a serious turn. They speak about religion, philosophy, art and suchlike. Suddenly they all fall silent while someone asks me what my opinion is. They all look into my eyes. I feel very upset. I try to look them in the eye but their eyes remind me of the abyss. Those eyes looking at me are the abyss itself. I can't escape the eyes. They judge me implacable and attract me like a magnet. I feel vertigo. I burst out crying and run to my husband's arms. He immediately justifies me in front of our friends saying that such subjects don't interest me. I calm down at once.

Doctor: Could you give a deeper interpretation?

R16: The eyes which judge me want to put me back into the abyss. They want to do me harm. They want to draw me into that hole ... The black hole is changing shape and becoming oval.

Doctor: What do you feel?

R16: Whether that hole is the womb or not, I don't feel it.

Doctor: Why?

R16: Because it's an intellectual statement.[34] My eyes settle on another piece of furniture on which there is a big candle. What is that candle doing there all alone? It is so small compared to the abyss! One minute I look at the candle and the next the abyss. I look without

---

[34] Doctor's note: R16 has heard about intra-uterine life from friends of hers and the thought occurs to her that the abyss she sees might symbolize the womb. Because the neuronal process which results in this thought occurs exclusively on an intellectual level (in the frontal poles, for example), it has no emotional impact on her. If the limbic neurons had also participated in this process, then R16 would have reacted emotionally as well.

understanding. I am in the void. I don't know what's in the black hole. It isn't clear ... The halo around the black contrasts with the black ... The black draws me towards it but with that halo around it I remain on the surface. I'd like to jump into the black. It attracts me like a magnet. It's inescapable. I feel vertigo. I'm going round and round like a stone rolling into the void after an explosion ... I have to go through the opaque coating on the back of the mirror to be able to reach the black hole in the mirror. But the bright halo around the hole is cut. It is the void, nothing but the void. I don't want to think any more.

At this point I hear a noise outside the room like an explosion. Instantly I see an image of a birth. A child emerges from the blood the moment I hear the sharp crack of the dynamite which makes the stones roll down the abyss.

Doctor: Are those stones which are rolling like the child?

R16: I didn't see the child falling ... Now the cold is invading me. My arms are immobilized. I can't breathe easily. I wrap my arms around my body; they warm me up. I want to pee. The doctor asks me if I want to get up and go to the toilet. I can't be bothered to. I feel very warm. It's beautiful. The child that was born was in an egg and not formed. It didn't want to be born because of the blood. The blood is the black hole! I'm very hot ... (silence) ... (anxiety) ...

Doctor: What's bothering you?

R16: The top half of my body is very small but my legs are big and ...

Doctor: Do your legs feel heavy?

R16: Yes, and very big.

Doctor: And your arms?

R16: Small. My legs are what prevent me from moving because they're heavy.

Doctor: They don't want to move?

R16: No. They're not mine! From my head to my waist everything is fine, alive. But I don't feel the lower part of my body.

Doctor: Don't you like your legs?

R16: No!

Doctor: Because they're short? Is that the only reason?

R16: They're not sexy! They don't move. They're male legs. From the waist up I feel fine; everything is small and charming, just the opposite to my legs which are huge. I feel like a satyr-Pan cut in two. Exactly like a charming little Pan.

Doctor: Is Pan a male?

The Knowledge of the Womb

R16: I can't see his genital organs. He is an effeminate man, small and cute.

Doctor: A female Pan then?

R16: A woman with small legs. No, he's a man with the head of a woman. His hair is curly. He looks like the ancient Greek statues which are big with very small genital organs. Pan has a small penis. I can see his head ... It's the head of my father as a child when his mother dressed him as a girl. As soon as I see my father's head I immediately feel the void.

Doctor: Why?

R16: I've identified with my father and with Pan. Pan was my father, a man with a small genital organ and simultaneously a woman. I must point out that my father's mother wanted him to be a girl. When he was born she began to dress him in girl's clothes and gave him a girl's hairstyle.

Suddenly I see the Manneken-pis[35] with its small genital organs and all the statues with my father's head when he was a child. From photographs I've seen of him I resembled him very much when I was small: the same curly hair and the same colouring. I can see him now as a statue standing there and peeing like a fountain. That statue is pissing on the world, mocking and dominating it. His dominance is expressed by the act of peeing with his little penis. Now I see a mermaid with large breasts. She also is cut in two, like Pan.

Doctor: What are her legs like?

R16: Like a fish. She doesn't have legs. We must definitely give her legs. Pan's legs! But they're small.

Doctor: So, she cannot walk?

R16: No, she'll crush them. She is very heavy and Pan is so small.

Doctor: Will she also crush his genital organs?

R16: Yes! Everything! She's now motionless on the ground up to the waist ... Suddenly I feel cramps in the legs and spasms. A power is pulling me backwards so that the genital area is projected forward. All of a sudden my legs begin to live. I can feel them growing longer ... They're just as I'd like them to be - slim, beautiful ... I look like a figure in a Picasso painting and where my genital organs are there is a hole. So what genital organs do I have?

Doctor: Are you afraid of the idea of having genital organs or of the idea of showing them?

R16: I'm afraid of the idea of showing them ... I get into the foetal position. I'm fine. My body and legs form a whole. I only want to pee

---

35 R16's note: A statue-cum-fountain in Brussels of a small boy urinating water.

and something is bothering me there where my genital organs are. I want to cut it off because it projects out of the egg, the cocoon.

Doctor: Who imposes this sexual organ on you?

R16: I don't know ... but if I pee through a male genital organ I'll govern and dominate like the Manneken-pis who looks like my father. My father imposes it on me because I identify with him. I'm not sure ... about the interpretation I just gave you because it's intellectual ... The spasms begin again the moment I see the mermaid cut in two and motionless ... Now I feel I'm cut in three: the head which is the intellect, the torso which is sensual and in complete harmony with myself, the legs which are dead.

Doctor: Is that how you are, then, and is that how others see you?

R16: Yes, their eyes cut me into three pieces. They judge me and throw me into the blackness where I am in three pieces ... The spasms continue to rack my body ... My legs grow longer and as soon as they become alive I feel the warmth again, the serenity, the calmness and unity of my body. Then I feel heavy, very heavy like that stone mermaid who has been put there.

Doctor: What does the mermaid represent?

R16: At the moment she represents me - heavy like a stone and imposing. I exist even without legs. Pan and the mermaid have the same characteristics: they're both cut in two. Pan is a male and represents my father but my father emasculated, thus my father who looks like me. So I identify with him. I'm also the heavy mermaid without legs who wants to crush my father and the small genital organ - mine or his, I don't know yet. That organ prevents me from feeling well and whole but as soon as I crush it I feel calm because I have found my unity again. However, my legs which would allow me to move and live are missing because those legs don't exist if I don't accept the small male genital organ. But I don't accept it and as soon as it appears I put a hole at this spot (see drawing) and I make it disappear.

The Knowledge of the Womb

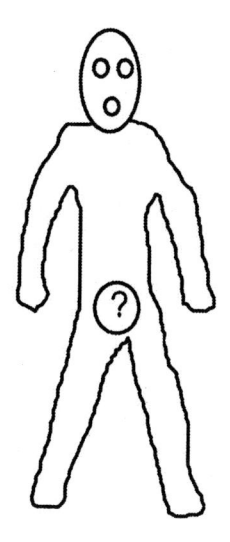

Session 2 R16: My head feels very heavy. It's being pulled to the left. I feel cramped and I can't move it. Nevertheless, I feel at ease in this position. As if I'm in a mould. It's the first time I've felt that my head and body form a whole. I'm like a stone statue. I'm not thinking. I'm not moving.

Doctor: Are you afraid?

R16: No. My body is becoming hard. I have muscles everywhere and I am immobilized, like the people of Pompei who became petrified in a single moment while they were in motion. I'm floating in the void and I have the impression that I'm gliding. My arms, back and legs are raised. My breasts are projected forward while my arms are held backwards.

Suddenly I feel I am all muscley again. I have no breasts. I'm as flat as a board. My hands are pressing on my breasts and crushing them, with great force they're making them disappear. I don't have breasts any more.

Doctor: Why don't you have breasts any more?

R16: I destroyed them.

Doctor: By yourself?

R16: No, it's a power, but I don't know if that power is me ... (silence) ... The doctor leaves the room for half an hour. I remain lying down without any feeling of fear or terror. When he returns he asks me if I am resisting. It's true that I am and that irritates me.

Doctor: Let's go back to the point where you felt you had no breasts and your head was immobilized. What's the emotional element? Why did you say that it wasn't like the first time?

R16: Because everything is stuck together, not in pieces.

Doctor: What's the symbolism of this?

R16: This time (in contrast to the last Session) everything is united and forms a whole. My legs are alive.

Suddenly I raise my arms - or rather my arms rise automatically - because the blanket, which feels like a cocoon, is bothering me. I mention a certain ballet where the male dancer thrashes about in a white sheet. I feel I want to be rid of something enveloping which is sticking to me, particularly to my arms. My legs are somewhere warm, well protected. I throw off the blanket till the waist to reveal my chest. My arms are extended as if I'm waiting for something. I don't speak. I'm waiting. But what's going on? I'm a motionless dancer who became immobilized as soon as he came out of the cocoon.

Doctor: Is he out of the cocoon completely?

R16: Not completely ... His legs have remained inside. The arms and head resemble a receptacle which is waiting to receive ...

Doctor: In this motionless position are you waiting for something?

R16: Yes, but for what I don't know. A sun looks down on me and shines its light on me ... This motionless position, in which the muscles look very powerful, is a male position which gradually changes into a charming female position. My arms open wide to expose it.

Doctor: Where are you?

R16: I'm learning to move. My body is moving slowly. My arms rise so that I may get out of the cocoon, like a bird which is learning to fly and which falls again. I don't have the strength to get out of the cocoon.

Doctor: Do you want to get out?

R16: No.

Doctor: Is that why you don't have the strength?

R16: I want to look out but I don't want to get out.

Doctor: Why?

R16: I'm fine. I want the sun to look down at me but I don't want to get out.

Doctor: If you get out, what will happen?

R16: I remain silent for a little and then I feel that if I get out of the cocoon, it will no longer protect me. I'll be able to move.

Doctor: What dangers are there outside the cocoon?

R16: I won't be able to wait like this any more. I'll be seen. I'll have to move.

Doctor: And what will happen if you move?

R16: When I move I feel tense. When I move outside the cocoon, everything is as hard as a rock while inside the cocoon everything is

The Knowledge of the Womb

charming. If I move I have to make a great effort because I feel all muscley again ... (silence) ...

Doctor: What do you feel now?

R16: I feel well. My left arm and my head are very small. But my right arm is enormous and it's beating the other one severely, as if it wants to make something disappear.

Doctor: Does the enormous arm want to make the small one disappear?

R16: Yes.

Doctor: Why?

R16: It's so strong and the other so weak ...

Doctor: Does the strong arm belong to you?

R16: Yes, but I like the small one better.

Doctor: Does the small arm disturb you? Is this why you want to make it disappear?

R16: And yet the little arm and the head go well together ... Perhaps the strong arm is crushing something else ... Suddenly I realize that it is crushing one of the fingers of my left hand. This finger grows and softens and becomes a small genital organ, Pan's organ. I'm crushing it to make it disappear.

Doctor: What sex is the statue.

R16: Male ... I feel calm. The little penis is in my fist. I took it from the statue.

Doctor: Are you satisfied now that you've crushed it?

R16: Yes.

Doctor: What do you feel?

R16: I'm supple and graceful. I'm floating on water. It's very pleasant.

Doctor: Do you know where you are?

R16: On a boat which is rocking rhythmically. I'm making the rocking movement with my hands ...

Doctor: Why are you still moving your hands like that?

R16: They're both becoming very small. But this time the left arm is strong and is resisting the right arm. Now they're both very small and the left one is being racked with spasms. Tension and spasms. My head feels as if it's tied to my ear. A power is sucking me in to make me disappear.

Doctor: Are you afraid?

R16: Yes ... I'll be engulfed ...

Doctor: Do you know this power which is sucking you into it?

R16: It's a black hole. It's always the same black hole. It's sucking me in and I'm becoming smaller and smaller. The smaller I become, the more

it sucks me into it ... I let myself be sucked in by the power and violent spasms begin ...
Doctor: Have you let yourself be sucked in by the hole?
R16: Yes. My back hurts. I feel hot and afraid.
Doctor: Are you in pain within this hole? Are you in pain because of the darkness perhaps? What is it?
R16: I don't know. Maybe it's the womb but ... that thought is purely intellectual. I don't know ... The feeling of calmness returns and I am surrounded by water. My breasts are burning. I feel that I'm tearing them off and peeling their skin off.
Doctor: Do they disturb you?
R16: Spasms rack me. I don't speak at all.
Doctor: Why are the spasms becoming stronger?
R16: The spasms stop when I have no breasts.
Doctor: Return back to the spasms. What causes them and what is the power that makes you feel awful about your breasts?
R16: When I no longer have breasts, my legs pull me backwards, just like when I feel that I have a small male genital organ. Now I'm okay. There are no more spasms.
Doctor: Can you go deeper?
R16: I have a small male genital organ and no breasts. I feel calm.
Doctor: How is this mechanism produced?
R16: That's how they want me! It's an external force. But how can we say that this is the womb?
Doctor: Answer your question.
R16: Because it's calm and agitated at the same time, like in the womb. At this point the spasms begin again. I feel that the aim of this force is to make me male! As soon as I become all muscles, I become as flat as a board again. My head is cramped and tied to my ear. They're compelling me to remain flat without breasts. They're pulling my ear as if they want to punish me. It's my father who is pulling my ear. "You'll stay right here," he tells me. The more he pulls my ear the more muscley I feel while at the same time I have torn off my breasts. My head is pinned down...

R16's realizations after Session 2: I feel that I am divided into two: female chest (breasts) and male genital organ, symbolized by the right arm and left arm respectively. One of my two halves wants to destroy the other. Lack of unity. Aim: to make the small male genital organ disappear. I want to achieve this either with my strong right arm or with my heavy female chest. When I wait like a receptacle in the refuge of my cocoon, I want to show myself to the sun as a charming woman. I'm afraid to leave the cocoon because outside it I am punished, while inside it I am protected and I can retain my female sex. So then, moving and speaking means being male in the eyes of the world. My obsession that I am being looked at stems from this lack of sex identity. People look at me and realize that I'm not what I should be.

Session 3 R16: Looking up at the rosette in the centre of the ceiling I'm transported emotionally to my mother's room in Paris ... There is a similar rosette there. After walking through all the rooms of the house I see the rosette stained with a black spot which is moving. That spot is like the black hole of the first Session. Gradually the rosette disappears and its place is taken by the black spot which becomes a black hole between two buttocks which is shitting on me. It's the backside of a giant sitting on a toilet. The black hole stops shitting and starts sucking me into it. It resembles the open mouth of a shark. It's waiting for me but I'm not going to throw myself into it ... One minute the black hole is sucking me in and the next it is rejecting me, spitting me out ...

Suddenly a shadow appears in the black hole. A foetus. I hide my head under my armpit. Then the foetus disappears and a huge crab appears. I want to make my head disappear by hiding it under my body so that I can protect myself. Spasms begin. I don't want to look at the ceiling any more. I take the foetal position and try to find somewhere to hide my head which has become very heavy. I try to look at the hole once more but the crab has disappeared ... (prolonged silence) ...

Doctor: What's happening?
R16: I don't know. I want to hide from the crab and from you!
Doctor: Am I like a crab?
R16: What did you say? I feel someone pulling me by the ear again. My head is wedged in somewhere. I want to hide. I have the impression that someone wants to scold me.
Doctor: Who?
R16: I don't know, but I'm hiding my head like a small child who is being scolded. I want to protect myself.
Doctor: From whom?
R16: From the questions you're asking me ... I put my head under my armpit. My armpit presses hard against my neck and ear. I feel I'm growing smaller. When you are small they shouldn't hit you because your innocence is something to be respected.
Doctor: Why are you pressing on you ear?

R16: I don't know. Go away! I want to stay like this. I start rocking as if I'm in a rocking cradle. The rocking movement increases.

Doctor: Who is rocking you?

R16: I can't explain. But I feel calm ... I'm becoming very small now and I have water in my mouth. It's not so pleasant. My body is liquefying ... My back hurts.

Doctor: And what about the water in your mouth?

R16: It's not there any more and anyway it was my saliva.

Doctor: Are you in the uterus?

R16: No!!

Doctor: Why are you moving your lips?

R16: They've become stuck together. I feel sticky everywhere now ... my eyes, my mouth.

Doctor: What are your emotions at the moment?

R16: I feel very well but just a little squashed. As if something is pressing on me ... My arm rises and covers my ear, blocks it. I want to block my ear so as not to hear something that shouldn't be heard ... a secret. Then I become immobilized. My legs are stuck to the couch. I am in great pain.

Doctor: What is the secret you don't want to hear?

R16: I feel terrible. With each moment that passes I feel worse. I'm standing on the edge of the abyss ... Suddenly my face feels as if it's being squashed in. I burst out crying ... I don't want to learn what the secret is ...

The Session ends and I know that I resisted. I resisted because I felt afraid. Perhaps I also resisted because of the presence of the doctor whom I associate directly with my father. What is clear is that the black hole contains something very unpleasant.

R16's realizations after Session 3: False conviction in everyday life: I think I'm invulnerable and insensitive, I smile, I am strong. My true nature: vulnerable. But as it's my mother's and father's wish that I be a boy, I become hard and strong. When I come into the world as a fragile little girl, I'm afraid that I'll be punished and so I become hard (shy, uncommunicative). I live only as half a person. As soon as I leave my mother's uterus, I protect myself in my shell.

Symbolism of the eyes: When people are waiting to hear my opinion, their eyes turn towards me. They expect an intellectual, intelligent opinion - a man's opinion - and they stare at me. Terrified, I find myself in the black hole where I'm just a fragile and unhappy little girl. It is those eyes which throw me back into the black hole where there's nothing but

The Knowledge of the Womb

despair. Thus I'm unable to speak and I start to cry. My shell no longer protects me.

The stone statue of the first Session: The statue is myself immobilized. When I come into the world, my sex is revealed as being female. I'm there, I exist but I'm inhibited, immobilized because I'm a woman: as a woman I'm afraid to move.

Session 4   R16: And again I see a spider whose legs are drawing me towards it like tentacles. Its black body looks like a mouth which is opening. The black attracts and rejects me, like the womb where I feel well and at the same time partly rejected. The spider symbolizes disgust ...

My inertia in everyday life is a defence. But the more I defend myself the more I'm encrusted with something that I hate. This defence doesn't help me. It's like a crystal ball in which I'm locked up. I'm afraid of everything and my fear neutralizes all desire for activity and adventure ... (silence) ...

Doctor: Try to remember when this defence began.

R16: I'm not sure if I'd really like to change my system of defence. There are days when I accept myself. Other times I become disgusted with myself. When I look into myself, I find myself deep inside the black hole where I'm not at all pleased to be. I feel disgusted when I realize that what I show to the world is the opposite of what I really feel ... (crying) ...

Doctor: Why are you crying?

R16: I don't need false smiles to save face in front of a world that I hate.

Doctor: Why do you always have to save face?

R16: Because my mother and father believe that I'm fantastic and that I succeed in whatever I do ... How mistaken they are ... I want to cry now ... When you cry it feels warm ... Now my tears are making me cold.

Doctor: What is causing all this?

R16: Despair takes hold of me when I face myself ... despair because I don't feel well in my skin ...

(Suddenly) I'm in the womb. I can hear breathing, heavy and oppressive - my mother's. It's the first time that I've felt I'm in the womb. I can feel only one lot of breathing and it's hers. I live through her, attached to her through the belly and the heart, my mouth open without swallowing. This is a soundless world. At the same time something is pulling my legs backwards. Here where I am is a soundless room where that strong breathing alone reigns. I remain silent and motionless for a long time listening to her breathing.

My buttocks are becoming muscley and I feel I have a penis. I am a man making love. The lower part of my belly hurts. I'm holding an enormous penis in my hand and I'm masturbating. Someone is looking under the blanket at what I'm doing. That's how my mother wants me to be in the womb, with a sexual organ like that ...

I'm waking up after a long nightmare. I'm rediscovering the world. I'm being reborn. I am on a beach, calm and sweet and fragile. The spasms have stopped. I am alone. I feel just fine. I don't need anybody, not even my mother. I let myself be rocked by anyone who wants to rock me. No one can harm me. No one dares to harm me because I am fragile. I adore this state. Only my mother could destroy me with her strong breathing. In the eyes of the world I am sweet, yet I feel hard and extremely muscley. I can see female dancers everywhere; a ballet that is gentle and white.

R16's realizations after Session 4: Crying makes me return to a state I experienced in my intra-uterine life because my crying is provoked by the terrible tribulation I suffered in the womb. My feeling awful in my skin, the disgust I feel for myself - these are things I felt in the womb because my mother wanted me to be a boy when I was really a girl. Thus, to protect the frail little girl that I am, I construct a shell around myself in everyday life, a shell of inhibition and rigidity. The shell protects me from my mother who wants me to be strong and muscley. And though I am a woman, I have to present myself as a man who is sure of himself. I try to play the game she demands of me, otherwise I'll make her angry and she'll punish me.

My husband is the first person who gave me both the perfect security, tenderness and warmth of the womb as well as rejection - when he desires another woman. When he rejects me, my insecurity makes me face myself and then I loathe myself: this in turn reactivates the awful state I felt in the womb. Thus, my husband engenders these two contradictory states in me and returns me to the womb. He is, then, the first man who helped me reach orgasm. I achieve orgasm in one position - the one that helps me feel that a penis is projecting from the genital area, like in the womb.

Session 5 (The Father) R16: If you don't have your father's blessing, you can do nothing. You need his blessing for matters serious and trifling. If he says "yes", then you can do anything. If not, then your mind doesn't work properly. I need his approval to relieve my mind. Although he has never refused me anything, yet I anxiously await his judgement. I want to see him as a bad person who will scold me and deny me what I ask for. I know he understands me but I want to see him as bad and hard; I get

The Knowledge of the Womb

pleasure out of debasing him - debasing Father, the paternal figure who is above all else. Why shouldn't he be toppled from his pedestal? Why should he always be the one to dominate and not others? My father is up high and why haven't others the right to be in his place?

Doctor: Do you want to be in his place?

R16: Yes. Why shouldn't I be able to look down at others from up there? It must be beautiful up there. He glides around and sees everything and we, we are below awaiting his judgement in terror. Why should we always be waiting for his orders? Why are there only men 'up there'? - Christ, God. Why are there never any women? I speak of "women" but it's I who would like to be up there with him, at his side.

Now I can see Christ on the cupola of a Spanish church. It's my father's image, with arms outstretched, waiting. Just two words from him and others not only work for him but they have accidents as well.[36] Now my foot is beginning to make involuntary movements. That means that something is bothering me emotionally. I've caught my husband's tic. That man up there gets on my nerves. What's he waiting for? - that we submit to him? My foot is still making those movements, as if it wants to tell me something. It's hard to see my father as Christ. Christ should be someone imposing, with a great beard and white hair, whereas one would say that my father is like a little boy who jokes and acts the clown, someone who is on my level. My father in Christ's place makes me laugh. And I am submissive to this Christ!? I say yes and accept it. I'm afraid of that gentleman up there who sees everything and yet, when he comes down to my level, I adore him. He's small and funny.

Suddenly, the ceramic Christ crumbles. All the little pieces are falling ... (to the doctor) I adore you, seeing you sitting there in your armchair. I adore my father. He's not that enormous blue and gold Christ. He has never reproached me and he is prepared to give me everything. Yet I always expect him to say no, I always expect him to reproach me. How is that possible? And what terrible fear I felt that Christ would fall down on top of me and crush me. Yet Christ is falling down in pieces because I'm the one who stuck him up there on the cupola ... and all those little pieces

---

36 R16's note: The day before the 5th Session, I asked my husband to take our car to the garage for repairs as I had run into something. He told me that he would take it the next day and forbade me to take it myself. I, however, was anxious to see it repaired so that my father wouldn't realize that it had been damaged. (He scolds me severely whenever I have an accident.) I ignored my husband and took the car. I tried to be careful. Result: I ran into a motorcycle. (My husband castrates me like my father does.)

become my little father. Is it really me who stuck them up there? How can anyone be so stupid? It's so funny. (laughter) ...

Now I can see my father with his long neck and huge ears joking and playing the camel as he often does. (laughter) ... How strange I am to have stuck him up there, like Michaelangelo. What an artist! What a job! It's immense. Oh, he's falling.

Doctor: Why is he falling?

R16: Because I stuck him up there. In reality he is never like that. He never really oppresses me or makes me afraid. I wanted him to be like that.

Doctor: Why?

R16: Because it's his role to scold his children, to be the master, my mother's husband ... However, at home he has never shown signs of dominating my mother, nor of being the master. Out of revenge I exaggerated his role and made him worse than what he really is. The image of Christ is becoming smaller and less important. At last I'm destroying the image I'd made of my father! I'm not afraid of him any more. I'm trying to imagine him as a small child. I see a photograph of him at his mother's house. I'm having lunch at her house as we used to do every Tuesday ... My foot is making those movements again. Why do I see my grandmother so clearly? Is it because my father adored her?

Doctor: Do you think he loved her more than you?

R16: My father has never shown his feelings except for that day when his mother died and I saw how much he loved her. He has never let his feeling for me show. I saw him as hard and cold. He goes through the house like a whirlwind and there's no time to speak to him. I remember that he slapped me only once, on my 14th birthday. I felt ashamed and humiliated. It's the only time I can remember him expressing himself to me. Since then I've been in fear of his anger and on the basis of that slap I constructed that hard monster. My foot has stopped moving. I like this Session ...

Doctor: Ah yes, it is good.

R16: Who'd ever imagine that I could 'think' with my feet? (laughter) ... Suddenly I see a monkey with big ears which is looking at me like my father does with his big ears. My father has huge ears. Maybe that's why I adore my husband.

At this point I burst out laughing and tell the doctor that I love my husband because he has big ears. Apart from that, though, he has nothing in common with my father. My father is blond and my husband is dark. Father is short while my husband is tall. My husband has a difficult character ... but so has my father. They're both very similar in character.

The Knowledge of the Womb

Did I really try to find the opposite of my father in my husband? Not any more because now my father isn't what I thought he was. I like it when my husband plays the little boy because he reminds me of my father. But I don't like it when he scolds me because he frightens me and then I just do stupidities. I have to tell him that because I'm old enough now to do everything by myself.

Doctor: Will you continue to be affected by your husband's remarks?

R16: Oh no. Now I know that the gentleman up there (pointing to the ceiling) won't scold me. I'm waiting for my foot to 'speak' because it's started moving again. Something is going to come, I can feel it. I always felt hard during the Sessions, like a ball of muscles or stone. In that way, I was defending myself against that enormous Christ, my father. All my life I was afraid that I'd be punished and so I became hard to be prepared for any blow. If I am hard, he is going to hurt himself too. That shell defended me. My mother and father created that shell ...

Doctor: What's the cause of your fear?

R16: That he'll scold me.

Doctor: For what other reasons could you be punished?

R16: For any reason, from the most insignificant to the most important. I'm afraid of my father's judgement. When I went out with boys I expected him to approve, but he appeared displeased. Waiting for his approval, I stopped all activity. Everything. Everything had to be under his control, particularly the matter of the boys I went out with. I was afraid to go out with boys even though he'd given me the right to go out whenever I liked and with whomever I liked. I could never feel free. At home I feel like an iceberg. I don't tell him what I'm doing, what I'm thinking. I can't express myself in front of him because I'm afraid of him. People I've met outside the home and who happen to come home don't recognize me. They find me shy and cold. At home I feel like a caterpillar which doesn't move, which says "yes, yes" and cannot talk to them ... (silence) ... One day, when I was abroad, I met an uncle of mine, my father's brother, and we had a long talk about my father. This encounter made me feel very emotional and close to my father. (crying) ... I'd like to feel like that more often. The only time I feel close to him is when I cry or when we joke together. It's the only way we can express ourselves when we're together. I could never communicate with him even though that is what we both wanted ... And I waited 24 whole years to understand. How stupid! How silly life is! To put that person up there for 24 years and not speak to him. It's idiotic. There's not a trace of the terrifying father in him. I'd like to take the plane and go to Paris. I love the whole world today - my father and who else? My mother. Yes, my mother. She's so small and gentle and she never says anything. She's a saint. I identify with her completely.

Doctor: Why?

R16: So that my father will be good to me and because I love him. As the father has the mother, the little daughter identifies with her mother and becomes just like her. But when I'm at home I'm untidy and not like her at all, just the opposite, and I'm aggressive towards her. Yet when I'm away from her, I identify with her and become her. I do whatever my mother does: I put my husband's things in order just as she does my father's.

What is Christ doing up there? He's always alone, whereas he should be with my mother. Why don't I see my mother? Because I made her disappear because I don't want to see her at his side! We always forget the woman! Men have had complexes for centuries and they don't want the woman at their side ... Only the king rules, the father, Christ.

Doctor: Yes, we've kept a tight grip on our position.

R16: Yes, nothing will overthrow you. Suddenly I want to hit the doctor but I can't. (to the doctor) You're so sweet, sitting there in your armchair drinking Coca Cola. I don't see you as the great and impressive doctor any more!

Doctor: All is fiction, my dear.

R16: Oh! You're wearing a bow-tie and acting the impressive doctor. But you can't fool me any more. The image has crumbled and fallen. Really, how could I have been so afraid?

Doctor: Explain why.

R16: The Almighty, the one who has complete power over his little girl. He judges everything in advance. He anticipates everything.

Doctor: How does he know everything?

R16: In fact he knows nothing! He just has some experience and he thinks he knows everything ... I feel contractions in the genital area. That irritates me. I can see a red circle like lips making sucking movements, like the movements my vagina makes. This disgusting red circle is my genital organs. I can feel them disappearing because I don't want them. My legs and the lower part of my torso are becoming very muscley. I'm becoming a man with my husband's body. I have muscles and I'm making love to a woman in the red circle. The red circle is me, but who is the man? My father? And yet, that's not his body. It's my husband's body. It's my husband who symbolizes my father and he's making love to me. And I am the red circle and that man simultaneously. Now my husband's body is disappearing and my father's body, without muscles, is taking its place. So I had identified with my father and, to camouflage my feelings for him,

I put my husband in his place. It's cruel ... youth and old age ... Of course my father would have been muscley in his youth ...

R16's realizations after Session 5: The doctor symbolizes my father. I'm ashamed of my unfaithfulness to my father and so I hide myself. I'm afraid that if he knew I was betraying him, he'd punish me. So I want to betray him with his blessing. By hiding I feel guilty. This guilt feeling towards my father made me fear him all my life. I was always in fear of being punished by him. In my mind I made him nastier because basically I wanted him to punish me for my sexual desires for him. Being afraid of his punishment I hardened myself and became withdrawn to avoid him making any surprise attack, when in reality he didn't want to do me any harm. To have a clear conscience about betraying him I imagined him as nasty so that I could more easily betray him. I could not possibly admit to myself that I adored him because I didn't have the right to desire him sexually. The only man I've reached orgasm with is my husband which is the exact opposite to my father from the physical point of view. All my other male friends looked like my father and that's why they inhibited me. Their physical resemblance to my father prevented me from feeling free and from reaching orgasm. They were my father's doubles. Every single one of them was my father. The forbidden fruit. My husband's dissimilarity to my father allows me to forget the father figure during orgasm.

It is now two months after the 5th Session and I still find it difficult to concentrate. I feel empty. Nothing interests me. No strong feelings. But in the womb as well, I feel neither absolutely well not absolutely awful. Nothing affects me, nothing enthuses me. I feel that in a way I'm identifying with my mother who, when she tries to speak about politics, economics or other such serious matters, makes me feel badly for her. Not being the intellectual type, she cannot cope with such discussions.

Session 6 R16: Since the Session began I've been feeling very weak. My legs start to move: bit by bit they open as if I'm doing ballet. They're being held open so that my knees touch the ground. I feel a fresh breeze caressing my belly and genital organs, just like when I'm naked on the sea shore. Nevertheless, my legs feel heavy. I realize that all this is related to sex and so I instantly feel the need to hide in the darkness so that the doctor won't see me. I feel I'm going to be dismembered. My thighs are being stretched. The lower part of my belly is contracting as if it wants to be free of something. I'm as hard as a rock, as tense as a bow. Suddenly I relax. I have the impression that a woman who has just given birth would feel similar relaxation ... (silence) ...

Doctor: What do you want to get rid of?

R16: I don't know. My genital organs, my belly, my behind. All the lower part of my body is hard just like in previous Sessions where I felt I was cut in two. The lower part of my body is muscley and yet I don't feel that I have genital organs. What am I waiting for with my legs open? The man who'll fall out of the sky? My father I had. My husband I have. What then? What am I waiting for pinned down like this? To be seen? I'm looking up at the sky so as not to look at you (meaning the doctor).

Doctor: Why?

R16: From up there comes the light, the sun, power.

Doctor: By looking up at the sky, what are you trying to do?

R16: I'm putting you up there in Christ's place and so you're less impressive. It's less personal. Down here beside me you can see me with my legs open and I feel ashamed. I'm naked before everyone. I'm exposed, particularly my genital organs, and that bothers me. So I put you up there. I'm pinned down and exposed ... Now my body is contracting a little, just like when I make love. The little spasms stop. My body is being enveloped ... I don't feel my body any more. I don't feel anything ... (silence) ... I can see a stork on the ceiling - the emblem of new-born babies. The spasms have stopped. I can't feel my body at all.

A fresh breeze is enveloping my body. Only my head has remained outside all this. It's very clear. I'm in the womb. I understand why I resisted in the first Sessions. It's because my head was not in and I didn't want to accept that I was in the womb. Now, by connecting thoughts and emotions, I can definitely say that I am. But why are my legs open in the womb? I can't explain why, but I feel that I've asked the right question.

Doctor: Well, what does having your legs open in the womb symbolize?

R16: I'm offering myself or waiting for something?

Doctor: For sexual contact?

R16: Yes.

Doctor: For what reason? To stay in the uterus and continue your intra-uterine life?

R16: All of a sudden I smile at the revelatory question. I feel a pleasant liquid around me. If the aim is to return, then I'm waiting for a man so that I can return. The minute I say this, I feel fantastically well. At last I understand. Your question was enlightening. The moment I realized that I return to the womb through sex, I felt very relaxed, I felt waves bathing and purifying me. The intellectual has become emotional. I feel

The Knowledge of the Womb

wonderful. The temperature is just right. When you give yourself, you feel you're enveloped in waves of bliss. The little stream, the water which gives you purity after love-making. You asked me fantastic questions. Return: I understand what it is. When I make love I return to the womb which accepts me. I feel so well. My body doesn't cause me problems. It's as if it doesn't exist. I have nothing more to say ...

Doctor: And when you leave this state what difficulties do you face?

R16: In this state I'm calm, serene. I don't want to do anything. Why should I do anything? Why should I read? When I don't do anything I feel wonderful. When I pick up a book to read, the first ten minutes are okay even though I don't follow what I'm reading. If I continue reading, I get depressed because my subjective state when reading and the bliss of the womb clash.

If I could make love all day long I'd be happy, I'd return and live continuously in calmness. That's why the sole object in my life is the man I love. With him I can reach the calmness, the fantastic nirvana of the womb. I don't need anything else. And yet, I must do something else in life because the man I love is not with me every single moment. I'd like to remain forever in this wonderful state somewhere between dream and reality. But I see the world around me. Everybody does something while I do nothing. This state of doing nothing is bliss, it's the return. After orgasm I feel this inactivity, but it is an inactivity full of life. I want to run free, to love, to smile. Yes, nothing else. Nothing intellectual. Nothing else interests me. But when I see that this state doesn't last, I feel depressed ... (silence) ...

Doctor: What else makes you feel depressed in everyday life?

R16: The difference between the intra-uterine world and the outside world. The former is bliss, the latter pure anxiety. The outside world makes me feel remorse for not studying, for doing nothing. I feel stupid doing nothing all day long. I feel stupid in front of my husband who is intellectual. However, my intellectual husband wants me to be stupid like his mother - that's what he says. His ideal woman is one who is stupid and beautiful. I also identify with my mother who's not exactly an intellectual genius. Here there's a double identification so that I can be near my father and husband. So then what can poor Natalie do in the midst of all this pressure? To be with my father I identify with my mother, and to be with my husband I identify with his ideal woman. To hell with everything. I'll open a brothel. I'll open my legs and wait, and send my books to Timbuktoo. To hell with everyone. (laughter) ...

Doctor: Does the external environment cause your depression or do you feel that the depression comes from within you?

R16: I feel guilty towards my husband because of my low intellectual level. And yet I'm just exactly what he wanted. That's what he wanted, that's what he got. I feel guilty towards my father because I haven't reached the intellectual level he wanted me to reach. But my father also loves stupid women. It seems that a whore can't also be an intellectual. But something isn't clear here. If I identify with my mother, who's not the intellectual type, I should be very happy. But I've always dreamed of being both beautiful and intellectual. I've always admired beautiful women who have succeeded professionally. I feel incapable of doing well in a profession. I feel like a very weak woman. My ideal has always been to combine the feminine with the masculine, beauty with intelligence. But the female element prevailed and that's why I'm stupid and weak.

Doctor: Did you inherit the female element from your female ancestors or is it something that was cultivated in you through education?

R16: I inherited it. I always admire girlfriends of mine who are very pale, very blond, almost transparent. If you pushed them, they'd break like crystal. On my father's desk there is a photograph of me where I am blond, ethereal-looking - for him the ideal beauty. When I feel so fragile and I think of the outside world, I'm afraid that if anyone touches me, he'll do me harm ... (silence) ...

Doctor: If your father, mother and husband didn't oblige you to study, what would you do?

R16: My father wants me to be intellectual and cultivated. I'm his ideal. He considers me intelligent and this is where my remorse towards him begins. I also feel remorse when my husband comes home and sees that I've done nothing all day. It's the same remorse I feel in front of my father. His daughter should combine beauty with intellectuality ... (silence) ...

The doctor leaves the room. I think: What causes my depression? I don't want to cry again for no reason. I have to clear up this situation once and for all. What puts me into this state? Guilt. Although my father wants me to be intellectual, I do nothing and so I feel guilty. I'd like to live up to his expectations but I don't, and this tortures me. When I don't think, I don't feel depressed. I occupy myself with trifles and never feel guilty then. Nevertheless, an empty day makes me feel afraid; I don't want to be in a situation where I do nothing. When my father and husband ask me what I'm going to do for the day I tell them that I'm going to meet So-and-So, trying to convince them of the importance of this appointment. What do they expect? - that I'm going to make great intellectual achievements? But since I don't feel like it how can I do it? I feel very guilty towards them. I have to live up to the expectations of my father who adores me. I

The Knowledge of the Womb

must do something; for instance read a book and discuss it with him. All these things are so contradictory.

When I try to speak to people on intellectual matters, no one listens to me, not even my husband. For them I am just a woman. So how can I get myself out of this state of affairs? I have to get out of it because it causes me such tension. But I don't want to force myself. Well?

An empty day makes me feel afraid. Afraid of what? Of facing myself? No. Then what? I'm afraid of being punished by my father. If he knew that I did nothing, he wouldn't be at all pleased. That's why I do whatever comes along. My father asks me: "What are you going to do today?" and in the evening: "What did you do today?" I tell him that I had a discussion with 'C' ... I did this and that ... Never mind. It was just fantastic today because we did absolutely nothing. (laughter) ...

I'm back in the womb again. Water envelops me. I feel fine, fine, fine ... ,It's difficult to speak ... I live through her belly. Everything is painless, my skin as well ... If only everything in life could be painless, painless, painless ... What bliss ...

The doctor returns. Instantly I feel I'm out of the womb. The doctor's presence removes me from the womb. The doctor symbolizes my father who rejects me ... (to the doctor) My father wants me to be intellectual ...

Doctor: Why does your father want you to be intellectual?

R16: Perhaps so that he can be closer to me. But I can't communicate with him intellectually because I'm not intelligent. How can I be intelligent if I'm not a boy? Only males are intelligent. The womb wants me to be a boy but I'm a girl, so it's impossible for me to be intelligent. But even if I do speak intelligently, nobody listens to me; not my father, not my husband, no man. I'm a "woman", therefore I'm stupid. In the womb I feel the bliss of doing nothing. Doing nothing means making no intellectual effort. Intellectual effort annihilates bliss. When people ask me my opinion on intellectual matters, their eyes turn upon me. Their eyes throw me into the womb. Their eyes become the womb which wants me to be a boy. Their eyes make me a boy when they ask me my opinion. But I'm a girl, I have no opinions. So what opinion can I give them? ... (silence) ...

The doctor leaves the room again. The jeans I'm wearing feel too tight. I unzip them. I tell myself that as soon as the doctor returns I'll zip them up again. Why? Is it because I'm afraid of arousing my father sexually? I don't want my father to discover that I desire him sexually. Of course, intellectuality would be a way of communicating with my father. Yes, there are two ways of communicating with my father: intellectually and sensually. However, these two ways cannot coexist. And something else: both are unattainable. To be intellectual, I would have to be a boy.

As for sensuality, I know very well that sex with my father is forbidden. The doctor returns and I tell him all my realizations.

Doctor: Follow your thoughts as they come.

R16: For me, ballet is love-making: the legs open, supple, calm, water, warmth, the feeling after making love, the fragile woman who reaches orgasm. Here I am truly a woman, completely non-intellectual. I feel so well and I want to sleep ...

REMARKS ON THERAPEUTIC RESULTS OF PHARMACEUTICAL AUTOPSYCHOGNOSIA SESSIONS

In the Greek edition of "The Knowledge of the Womb" I consciously omitted to mention the therapeutic results of the Sessions for the 16 cases of Table 1.

Since the Greek edition has been in circulation, however, many people have been insisting that, despite my reservations, I am obliged to answer certain questions.

Question 1 Are positive therapeutic results obtained with the Sessions and, if so, what are the relevant statistics?

Answer Yes, positive therapeutic results are obtained with the Sessions. (Positive therapeutic results are those where there is partial or almost complete subsidence of mental disturbance. Negative therapeutic results are those where there is no improvement or where there is a deterioration in mental disturbance.)

The statistics of the therapeutic results of the Sessions for the 16 cases are as follows:

Almost complete subsidence of mental disturbance	was observed in R3, R12, R13 and R16.
Significant subsidence of mental disturbance	was observed in R1, R4, R5, R7, R14 and R15
Moderate subsidence of mental disturbance	was observed in R8 and R11.
Slight subsidence of mental disturbance	was observed in R2 and R9.
No subsidence of mental disturbance	was observed in R6 and R10.
Deterioration of mental disturbance	was observed in no R.

Note: Despite the fact that R6 and R10's obsessional thoughts of suicide have continued undiminished in quality and intensity till today, these cases have not committed suicide. Both undergo two to three Sessions per year which result in a temporary diminution of the intensity of their mental disturbance.

It must be pointed out that all those who are about to begin Sessions are gripped by a vague and inexplicable fear, as if they are afraid to face their real self. It is because of this fear that many reject the Sessions before, while or even after undergoing them. During the Sessions this fear may, if the case allows it, escalate to the point where it becomes chaotic terror (§ 35, 36) and is a basic reason for his hindering the progress of his autopsychognosia. Some individuals cut a Session short or stop the Sessions altogether because the terror they experience in them is unbearable.

Another important point is that the progress of the Sessions is contingent upon the revival of rejecting conditions, that is, in order to achieve autopsychognosia a person must pass through the terrible trial of reviving the rejection or rejections of his existence (intra-uterine, hereditary, the rejection of expulsion-birth and so on).

Question 2 Are there criteria which aid the prognosis of positive therapeutic results?
Answer Yes. These criteria are revealed during the Sessions and may even be hinted at in the phase preparatory to the Sessions: they are whether *memory traces* of intra-uterine acceptance exist in an R. The stronger the *memory traces* of inter-uterine acceptance which an R retains in his nervous system, the more easily he revives the accepting womb. These *memory traces* form the foundations on which R can build a new life for himself.

Note: There are some cases whose nervous system retains not even the slightest trace of intra-uterine acceptance (see R6 and R10).

Question 3 After obtaining autopsychognosia, does R feel the need to continue having Sessions, pharmaceutical or otherwise?
Answer It must be stressed that the autopsychognosia R obtains can never be complete as the content of the unconscious seems to be infinite. It can be said, however, that after attaining a certain degree of autopsychognosia, some Rs begin a fresh way of reacting in their everyday life, they are content with themselves and feel no need for any kind of psychotherapy thereafter. Some Rs, on the other hand, feel the need to continue having Sessions, though at a slower pace than before. The pace varies from R to R. As a rule, each new Session brings to light new knowledge of the unconscious. It is worth noting that all those who have continued the Sessions feel that no other kind of psychotherapy could give them the possibility to reach such deep unconscious emotional levels.

The Knowledge of the Womb

Question 4 Are psychedelic drugs addictive? Do they harm the chromosomes?

Answer Since 1960 more than a hundred cases of mine have undergone autopsychognosia sessions with LSD-25, Psilocybine or Ketamine. Not one of these cases has presented addiction. Furthermore, one of the women, who underwent ten Sessions, later gave birth to two children. Today, 1982, the children are aged fifteen and ten. Both are in excellent health and very intelligent. It is interesting to note that the father too had previously undergone fourteen Sessions.

Question 5 What is the bioneurophysiological mechanism responsible for the subsidence of mental disturbance through pharmaceutical autopsychognosia sessions?

Answer Unfortunately, present means and methods of bioneurophysiological research do not give us the possibility of making an objective study of the neuronal mechanisms responsible for the various mental functions and their disturbances. Nevertheless, the need to give some bioneurophysiological interpretation, even if theoretical, of how positive therapeutic results are attained with the Sessions, led me to the following conclusion:

Foetal motor neurons and effectors (striated and non-striated muscular fibres) hypofunction because they are underdeveloped from an anatomical and functional point of view. On the other hand, foetal sensory neurons (limbic and other neurons) are capable of being excited by stimuli.

It is well-known that in the fully developed nervous system, the excitation of sensory neurons by stimuli is transmitted to motor neurons and then to effectors. The excitation of effectors and their subsequent movements result in the *equilibration* of the stimuli which had excited the nervous system.

In the case of the foetus, however, the process is the following: The excitation of sensory neurons by rejecting womb stimuli is transmitted to immature motor neurons and effectors which react very little or not at all. The result is that the excitation is *stored* in the nervous system and remains there in a latent state.

The Sessions showed that:

(a) This *stored* excitation anticipates the moment it will be activated so that it may react - even if belatedly - with the *most appropriate* kinetic (muscular) activity to the rejecting womb stimuli.

(b) The *most appropriate* kinetic reaction occurs after expulsion-birth, that is, when the nervous system has developed further or fully from an anatomical and functional point of view.

(c) The *most appropriate* kinetic reaction is repeated with greater or less frequency in everyday life towards whatever symbolizes the rejecting womb. It is as if the *most appropriate* kinetic reaction does not *satisfy* the nervous system because it is not carried out against the real dangerous stimuli, the rejecting womb stimuli.

(d) During the Sessions, when the rejecting womb is reactivated, R, his motor neurons and effectors long since fully developed, now has the chance to react to the rejecting womb stimuli themselves. The *most appropriate* kinetic reaction during the Sessions is achieved through hyperkinetic activity of all the muscles of the body, including the vocal cords (see § 64). This hyperkinetic activity includes efforts to flee from or to attack the womb. Very frequently the hyperkinetic activity is characterized by painful muscular contractions which are provoked directly by the rejecting womb stimuli. This whole process gives R's nervous system the opportunity of discharging and calming down. How long this calmness lasts varies from R to R.

PART TWO

General description of the subjective experiences and conclusions of the 16 cases of Table 1.

CHAPTER ONE

WHAT ONE MAY FEEL UNDER LSD-25 OR PSILOCYBINE[37]

General notes on LSD-25
Pharmocodynamic Activity of LSD-25

GENERAL NOTES ON LSD-25

§ 1   The pharmacodynamic activity of chemically pure LSD-25 depends on the dose one takes. Those who decide to use LSD-25 should know that the drug is highly active even in minute doses (micrograms). Doses over 100 mcg may cause utter confusion and severe agitation.

Contraband LSD is not sold in vials labelled with the number of micrograms contained in each "dose". Thus, the victims of contraband do not know what amount of LSD they are taking into their system. In addition, because of the crudity of its preparation in illegal chemistry laboratories, contraband LSD contains toxic by-products which are dangerous for the cells.

Young people should also know that contraband traders mix heroin or morphine into their LSD. The purpose of this criminal act is all too clear. As chemically pure LSD-25 never causes addiction, they succeed in expanding their clientele by "hooking" those who originally try it out of curiosity.

PHARMACODYNAMIC ACTIVITY OF LSD-25

§ 2   30-100 mcg of chemically pure LSD-25 give rise to one or more of the following symptoms and phenomena:
From the neurovegetative system: Dizziness, nausea, vomiting, chills, dyspnoea, mydriasis (dilatation of the pupils) etc. appear 30-60 minutes after the intake of the drug. As a rule, the symptoms are not strong and

---

[37] My experience has shown that the pharmacodynamic activity of LSD-25 is stronger than that of Psilocybine, i.e. reactivation of the memory of the neurons is stronger with LSD-25 than it is with Psilocybine

The Knowledge of the Womb

abate quickly. Their reappearance during the Session is due to excitation of the compact system of rejection (§ 50).

From the psychic sphere: The term 'psychic sphere' includes emotional functions, intellectual functions and so on[38]. The S & P[39] from the psychic sphere begin about one hour after the intake of LSD-25 and continue for as long as 6-8 or more hours.

After the pharmacodynamic activity of LSD-25 has ceased, the memory of what one experienced in the Session is retained. I believe that one of the most important pharmacodynamic properties of LSD-25 is that it reactivates the memory of the neurons. This results in the revival of the near and distant past as well as states of altered consciousness which are difficult to describe and to classify.

§ 3 *Revival of past experiences* Any experience of the past - sensorial, emotional, intellectual and so forth - may be relived vividly. Characteristic and very striking is the emotional and physical 'synchronization' which accompanies the revival of childhood, infancy and foetal life; that is, R[40] feels that his body has assumed the dimensions it had at the time of the revived event and he relives the emotions of that period.

Example: When R8 relived the unpleasant metal taste of the spoon with which her mother had tried to feed her in her infancy (she had refused the breast and the feeding bottle) she felt that her body had the dimensions of a baby and she cried exactly like a baby.

§ 4 *Realization of hypocritical behaviour* R's experience as a member of society obliges him to try to consciously hide his real feelings. Thus he gradually develops a system of 'defence' which renders him a hypocrite. LSD-25 may help R liberate himself from social hypocrisy only if he himself wishes it, that is, LSD-25 will neutralize R's system of 'defence' only if he decides that it will. During a Session, the revelations which come up from the unconscious may shock R to such an extent that he may prefer to inhibit its process by remaining silent without any emotional, mental or physical activity.

Example: An American student once told me that he 'converted' 500 mcg of LSD-25 to water when he began to realize certain unconscious desires inadmissible to him (sexual desire for his mother).

---

[38] For more details, see term *psychic functions*, § 109
[39] Symptoms and phenomena.
[40] The letter 'R' symbolizes any one of the 16 individuals of Table 1 (p. 18)

§ 5   *Mental clarity*   The expansion of R's everyday consciousness results in an amazing mental clarity and heightened capacity for self-observation, self-criticism and introspection which may lead to autopsychognosia. R's mental clarity is accompanied by the symptom of absolute certainty that his psychedelic experience corresponds to a real past situation and that his emotional-intellectual interpretation of his behaviour is correct.

§ 6   *Confusion*   In contrast to mental clarity is the extreme confusion caused chiefly by large doses of LSD-25 or by chemically impure LSD-25. The bioneurophysiological mechanism of this confusion is the rapid alternation of many reactivated 'memory traces' of various stimuli which had excited the nervous system in the past. The result is a spinning of ideas with a speed which prevents R from following them, accompanied sometimes by psychomotor agitation and hyper-activity.

§7   *Detachment of existential identity*   This is a peculiar, subjective experience which is characterized by the 'exit' of R's existential identity. The existential identity either observes the activity of the body or 'withdraws' from the room where the Session is taking place and is transported to 'worlds' belonging to eras chronologically indefinable (example R12).

§ 8   *Subjective sensation of dematerialization of the body*   This is a subjective experience of the body breaking down to the point where R thinks that he has no body or that he has died (example R10).

§ 9   *Anxiety-terror*   R feels severe anxiety which reaches extreme panic and terror. He feels that he is on the point of dying (example R10).

§ 10   *Perfect serenity*   In contrast to severe anxiety is a subjective experience which is characterized by perfect serenity. R3, R12 and R13 described such an experience which accompanied the revival of their intra-uterine life (example R3).

§ 11   *Reactivation of ancestral memory*   The memory of R's human ancestors (R10) or of other ancestors on the zoological scale, which is transmitted through heredity, gives rise to peculiar symptoms when it is reactivated, e.g. the reactivation of the memory of R4's winged ancestors created in him the absolute conviction that he could fly. (Note: This is one of the reasons why some of those who take psychedelic drugs without medical supervision jump out of windows.)

§ 12   *Total reconciliation with the environment*   R feels that he is fully reconciled with all forms of matter surrounding him, that he is basically no different to them, and that he can unite with them (descriptions by R4).

§ 13   *'Resurrection' of true identity*   During the Sessions, some cases who belong to the category of the Unwanted, 'discover' and for the first time in their lives feel their existential or sex identity which had been forbidden them by the womb-superpower.

§ 14   *Mystical experiences with religious content*   (R6).

§ 15   *Supernatural powers*   R feels absolutely certain that he has acquired supernatural powers and that he has been raised to super-human levels which allow him to see his blood flowing through his arteries and veins; to prophesy and foresee events; to influence telepathically the thoughts of others or the functioning of machines; to heal his own body or the bodies of other individuals of disease; and so on. After the Sessions, R's attempt at practical application of the 'supernatural' powers he had acquired under LSD-25 prove to him that he had misinterpreted the drug's capabilities.

Note: During Sessions, many an R realized that he possessed gifts which, owing to his psychological problems, had been inhibited to the point where he had been completely ignorant of them. Example: After his sixth Session, R1 felt the need to paint for the first time in his life. He fostered this need by taking painting lessons and attained very satisfactory results, according to art experts.

§ 16   *Alternating certainty and doubt*   During and in between Sessions, R6 vacillated between absolute certainty and doubt: one moment she was convinced that the psychedelic experience and the realizations which followed it were true and correct and the next moment she was overcome by doubt and wondered whether the whole Session was not just a fantasy.

When R6 had progressed in her autopsychognosia, she confessed that her doubts sprang from an unwillingness to accept her womb rejection - to accept it would have been to accept permanent disability.

§ 17 *Flashback* This is a partial revival of a past Session without the intake of LSD-25; that is, the 'memory traces' left in the nervous system by a past experience with LSD-25 may be reactivated automatically without new intake of the psychedelic drug. I always inform those who were about to undergo autopsychognosia sessions of the flashback. Experience showed that doing this did not influence R negatively: on the contrary, it encouraged him to use the flashback as a constructive Session. In any case, R can neutralize a flashback of his own volition or by taking 25 milligrams of chlorpromazine. Example of a flashback which occurred 20 days after R4's 13th Session:

"I am sitting in my office in front of the open window. Various thoughts come into my mind. I pursue one which brings vividly to mind the excitation of the senses during the months of spring. It is a feeling of both abandonment and flight. As I look out at the street, I have the feeling that I have to get away, to disappear (all this intellectually but with some emotional element, as happens in everyday life). Suddenly I begin to feel a little pain in the lower jaw and the top on my head (where the forceps left scars).[41] A strong desire to be annihilated on the spot. Agony suddenly overwhelms me (for several days I had felt it simmering within me). I raise my hands to remove from my mouth threads or tobacco from the cigarette I've been smoking. But there are no threads, no tobacco. The sensation of threads on the palate is like the sensation I experienced in the Session, of water mixed with fibres.[42] A feeling of great insecurity overcomes me. I feel a silent explosion taking place within. I am being cut to pieces (clearly the spasms of my intra-uterine life which, however, with the flashback are not so strong). I am experiencing a clear reactivation of the last Session. This lasts a few moments during which I put my hand to my lips which I feel have been smeared with paste (as in the Session). Then everything subsides. I feel calmer. While the flashback lasted, I didn't want to stop it. It was unpleasant but I accepted it. (I stopped it when I moved from the chair on which I'd been sitting.) The practical result was that that night I slept well, without jerking my feet or grinding my teeth as I often do".

---

[41] R4 was delivered by the forceps method which left scars on his head and lower jaw.

[42] Obviously he is referring to the sensation caused by the amniotic fluid during his foetal life.

CHAPTER TWO

WHAT I BELIEVE ABOUT LSD-25 AND PSILOCYBINE

The matter of which the human body is composed preserves the memory of its origin and evolution

§ 18   When I give an individual an intramuscular injection of 30-100 mcg LSD-25 and after about an hour that individual presents - for the first time in his life - specific S & P from the psychic sphere, I am obliged to conclude that the 30-100 mcg set into motion a biological (metabolic) mechanism which is responsible for the production (appearance) of those specific S & P. Consequently, it should be possible to interpret the S & P on a purely bioneurophysiological basis.

Many parents visited me at my surgery to relate with obvious distress the details of the Sessions described to them by their children. Indeed, one overprotective father once said to me, 'Doctor, my daughter it talking nonsense. She insists that when she was in the womb, she knew that her mother wanted her to be a boy. Now, is it possible for a foetus to feel and to understand its mother's wishes? Besides, I read in the encyclopaedia that the new-born is a small animal which at first occupies itself solely with its bodily needs - eating, expelling its waste products and sleeping - and that only gradually is it transformed into a social being which can grasp the quality of its relations with the external environment.' And he concluded by repeating, 'What my daughter says is madness.'

Yet this madness constituted knowledge with which his daughter was able to overcome the schizophreniclike symptoms which had tyrannized her for six whole years.

§ 19   The revival of any period of the past is a subjective truth for the individual experiencing it, which cannot be felt by an observer. The individual, for example, who feels that he has returned to the womb, is referring to a situation which is real for him alone and which is due to his nervous system retaining the 'memory traces' of stimuli which had acted upon it during foetal life. When these 'memory traces' are reactivated by LSD-25, the conditions of foetal life are relived. In other words, we are dealing with a subjective state which an observer would call false, an hallucination. Of course, it is false only according to the judgment of the observer: for the individual experiencing it the subjective state is true, and every emotional-intellectual realization he makes, every interpretation he gives to his behaviour is for him a subjective truth.

§ 20   The laws of bioneurophysiology which govern the functioning of the neurons limit everyday consciousness. These same laws allow certain chemical compounds (such as LSD-25) to expand the 'dimensions' of consciousness.

§ 21   I believe that the matter of which the human body is composed preserves the memory of its origin and evolution. The reactivation of this memory by LSD-25 transports a person back through the limitless past, creating in him levels of consciousness corresponding to various stages in the evolution of matter (R12's description). The revival of the very distant past which may be brought about by psychedelic drugs (as seen in the example just mentioned) is the result of reactivation of a latent memory of matter, the matter from which originated all our ancestors on the zoological scale (§. 11).

§ 22   Most of the S & P from the emotional-intellectual sphere of the 16 of Table 1, which were triggered by LSD-25, were directly or indirectly related to their psychological problems and may be interpreted on a bioneurophysiological basis.

CHAPTER THREE

EXPERIENCES OF THE 16 CASES OF TABLE 1 DURING AUTOPSYCHOGNOSIA SESSIONS

Revival of Experiences of Intra-Uterine Life
Revival of the Experience of Expulsion-Birth
Womb Rejection-Rejecting Womb
Remarks on the Experiences of the 16 of table 1

§ 23   During their Sessions, all the cases of Table 1, except for R11,[43] expressed with acoustic[44] and optic[45] symbols, subjective states which they characterized as:
   (a) The revival of experiences from their intra-uterine life.
   (b) The revival of the experience of their expulsion-birth and their first contact with the infinite chaos of the universe.
   (c) The revival of experiences from various periods after their expulsion-birth (§ 51).
   (d) The revival of experiences of ancestors on the zoological scale (§ 11).
   (e) The revival of conditions of matter beyond the bounds of the womb.

REVIVAL OF EXPERIENCES OF INTRA-UTERINE LIFE

§ 24   All the individuals of Table 1 (except for R11) maintain that during the Sessions they relived intra-uterine acceptance and/or rejection

---

[43] R11 described subjective states which, however, she was unable to place chronologically: she was unsure whether what she felt in the Sessions was a revival of her foetal life, her expulsion-birth or the first moments of infancy.
[44] Acoustic symbols are sounds and words uttered by R and which constituted acoustic stimuli for the doctor.
[45] Optic symbols are movements of R's head, trunk and limbs, as well as words, phrases and sketches which R put to paper, and which constituted optic stimuli for the doctor.

of their existence (their existential identity/self-preservation) and/or their sex by the womb-mother. They explained this ability to re-experience the conditions of their foetal life thus: consciousness of their existence (existential identity/self-preservation) began to function from the moment the union of the spermatozoon and ovum of their natural parents had taken place. For their foetal consciousness the womb acceptance or rejection constituted messages-stimuli which, as a rule, left 'traces' in their memory ('memory traces' in their nervous system). The reactivation of these 'memory traces' by the psychedelic drug resulted in the revival fo the intra-uterine experience.

The cases also stressed that during their intra-uterine life, whether they were accepted or rejected by the womb-mother, the latter was the first external environment to communicate messages-stimuli to them as well as their first acquaintance with life. Inevitable then, they became fixated to the womb which constituted a permanent base or reference (§ 46 and description by R4).

According to the quality of their intra-uterine experience - rejection or acceptance - the foetuses were classified into two categories: (a) Unwanted and (b) Welcome.

§ 25   *The Unwanted*   The Unwanted foetuses feel that their tiny mass is surrounded and dominated by a colossal superpower which bombards them with messages-stimuli which threatened their existence and/or their sex with death. This threat creates in the foetuses primitive terror (§ 35 & 36).

The Unwanted characterized the bombarding messages-stimuli as rejecting womb messages-stimuli and described the following kinds:

(a) Rejecting messages-stimuli of the existence of the foetus.

(b) Rejecting messages-stimuli of the sex of the foetus.

(c) Periodically rejecting messages-stimuli.

(d) A fourth kind of rejecting womb messages-stimuli are those which are inherited from ancestors in the form of 'memory traces' which may be reactivated (§ 85).

The above kinds of rejecting stimuli determine the following sub-categories of the Unwanted: (a) the Existentially Unwanted, (b) the Unwanted because of their Sex, (c) the Periodically Unwanted, (d) the Hereditarily Unwanted.

§ 26   *The Existentially Unwanted*   Existentially Unwanted are those whose presence their natural mother did not want in her womb. To this sub-category belong R6, R10 and R14.

The Knowledge of the Womb

Their revival of the chaotic terror caused by the intra-uterine rejection of their existential identity/self-preservation is one of the most tragic symptoms-phenomena of human pain I have witnessed in all my professional career. Both the terror and the emotional and physical pain they experienced during their Sessions are very difficult to describe.

During her third Session, R6 has taken the foetal position. Painful muscular spasms rack her body. In a voice full of agony, which is interrupted by uncontrollable sobbing and severe dyspnoea, she says: "I am in a dark, sealed off place. I feel something liquid on my face. Something is choking me. I can't stand it. Poison is being poured into me through some funnel. She wants to kill me. She doesn't want me ... She doesn't want me. I'm hungry. I'm hungry. My mother is hungry."

Note: Foetus R1 was Periodically Existentialy Unwanted

§ 27 *The Unwanted because of their Sex* Unwanted because of their Sex are those whose sex their natural mother did not want when she was pregnant with them (R6, R8, R9, R10, and R16). The revival of the intra-uterine rejection of their sex is for some cases as painful as is the revival of the rejection suffered by the Existentially Unwanted (description by R6, R10)

§ 28 *The Periodically Unwanted* Periodically Unwanted are the foetuses to whom are transmitted the pregnant mother's emotional disturbances which are unrelated to the foetus within her. These disturbances may be caused by friction resulting from incompatibility with the husband, mother-in-law or other persons; the husband's imposition of the sexual act (R10 and R12 § 48); the pregnant woman's hunger, as in the case of R6's mother; distressing thoughts or ideas; and so on.[46] The result is that the foetuses are shaken for the duration of their stimulation by the transmitted emotional disturbances of the mother. The stimulation is periodic and lasts as long as the mother continues to be disturbed.

Examples:

(a) R1, (p.59).

(b) R4 felt the stimuli which shook him during his foetal life as the womb's rejection of his existential identity/self-preservation (despite the fact that his mother had welcomed his presence within her womb) and,

---

[46] There are also indications that mechanical stimuli which act upon the pregnant woman are transmitted to and felt by the foetus. Mechanical stimuli are, for example, the thrust of a penis against the pregnant womb's cervix during coitus.

because the stimuli occurred periodically, he characterized himself as Periodically Unwanted. The intervals between the periodic rejections were moments of calmness. R4's mother informed me that when she was pregnant with R4, she wanted a boy. She also mentioned that during her pregnancy she had severe conflicts with those around her, which caused her nervous tension[47] and hysterical fits.

§ 29   *The Hereditarily Unwanted*   Hereditarily Unwanted are those who inherit the rejection of an ancestor or ancestors. To this sub-category belongs R10 who, beside reliving the intra-uterine rejection of her own sex, also relived the intra-uterine rejections of the sex of her female ancestors. More specifically, she relived the following rejections: The rejection of her mother's sex by her (R10's) grandmother, the rejection of her grandmother's sex by her great-grandmother and so on. In other words, R10 inherited the rejection of the female sex of many generations of her female ancestors by their mothers. R6 also belongs to the sub-category of the Hereditarily Unwanted.

§ 30   *The Welcome*   During Sessions, R3 and R13 felt their bodies gradually diminishing in size and finally assuming the dimensions and posture of the foetus within the womb. A feeling of perfect serenity filled their being. With optic and acoustic symbols they characterized their subjective state as the revival of their intra-uterine experience. (Later, they interpreted the serenity as the womb's acceptance of their existential identity/self-preservation.)

Following this, they re-experienced their expulsion-birth and the chaotic primitive terror caused by the process of their expulsion through the genital canal and their contact with the deadly dangerous chaos of the infinite universe.

Ousted, weak, defenceless and terrified, the foetuses/new-born babies longed to return to the place where they had felt that perfect serenity, to the place which they now felt had also provided them with absolute security.

R1, R2, R4, R5, R7, R12, R15 and R16 relived certain moments of their foetal life during which they felt Welcome. On the basis of their description and those of R3 and R13, the category of the Welcome was subdivided into the Constantly Welcome and the Periodically Welcome (descriptions by R3, R4)

---

[47] *Nervous tension* is used in this book as a term which refers to a specific clinical picture of mental disturbance (§ 119).

The Knowledge of the Womb

REVIVAL OF THE EXPERIENCE OF EXPULSION-BIRTH

§ 31   Besides R3 and R13, R1, R4, R5, R12 and R16 also relived their expulsion-birth and the primitive terror which accompanied it. It is interesting to note that all the cases mentioned above felt the process of expulsion-birth as a deliberate rejection of their existential identity/self-preservation by the womb-mother. R10 relived her expulsion-birth which was accompanied by bipolar feelings - on the one hand it was felt as a liberation from the intra-uterine hell, on the other as a continuation of the rejection.

WOMB REJECTION-REJECTING WOMB

§ 32   Recapitulation of the experiences of intra-uterine life and expulsion-birth clearly shows that both the Unwanted and the Welcome foetuses were subjected to womb rejection. It is for this reason that *all the cases in Table 1 have been classified as Rejected.*

The meaning of the term 'rejecting womb' includes the intra-uterine rejection and the rejection of expulsion-birth. The 'memory traces' of the rejecting womb which are retained by the foetal nervous system of an R are intertwined with the 'memory traces' of primitive terror.

REMARKS ON THE EXPERIENCES OF THE 16 OF TABLE 1

§ 33   Until 1975, I tended to classify each R in an absolute way. I considered, for example, R12 absolutely Welcome, R4 only Periodically Unwanted, and so on. But just as the principle of the absolute cannot stand in any field of medical science, so in the area under study it does not reveal fully the overall situation.

Detailed re-evaluation of the content of the 16 cases' Sessions led to the following conclusions: most cases belong to more than one category or sub-category and the degree of womb rejection or acceptance varies from one case to another. The theoretical interpretation of these conclusions is the following:

(a) The intra-uterine experience and the experience of expulsion-birth are the result of individual stimuli for the nervous system of each R.

(b) These individual stimuli leave individual 'memory traces' within the nervous system of each R. The degree to which these 'memory traces' are implanted in the nervous system varies from R to R and is possibly due to unknown biochemicophysical factors. The more strongly the 'memory traces' are implanted, the easier it is for them to be reactivated after expulsion-birth and the more intensely the womb rejection or acceptance is relived. More specifically:

(I) During Sessions, R4 relived short periods of intra-uterine acceptance which were interrupted by long periods of intra-uterine rejection, as the intra-uterine rejection left stronger 'memory traces' in his nervous system than did the intra-uterine acceptance. R4 belongs to the sub-categories of the Periodically Unwanted and the Periodically Welcome. R4 also relived the painful experience of his expulsion-birth.

(ii) R5 underwent 20 Sessions and during all except the first he relived the traumatic experience of the threat of death through suffocation at the time of his expulsion-birth (possibly due to pressure on the umbilical cord which obstructed the flow of blood through the cord). R5 realized that the experience of his expulsion-birth traumatized his nervous system severely.

(iii) R6's mother related to me that when she was pregnant with R6 she had repeatedly tried to terminate her pregnancy as she already had eight children and her financial situation was desperate. Finally she accepted the fact that she was pregnant but on condition that the foetus was a boy. She added that the period of her pregnancy was a time of tremendous stress, worry and privation. During her Sessions, R6 relived the intra-uterine rejection of her existence and sex as well as the other emotional disturbances of her pregnant mother very strongly, as the 'memory traces' of these rejections were powerfully preserved within her nervous system. Because of the variety of her intra-uterine rejections, R6 is classified under the sub-categories of the Existentially Unwanted, the Unwanted because of their Sex and the Periodically Unwanted. She also relived hereditary rejection (Hereditarily Unwanted).

(iv) R10 relived very strongly the intra-uterine rejection of her existence and sex as well as the stress of her pregnant mother when her husband imposed sex upon her. R10 is placed in the four sub-categories of the Unwanted because she also relived hereditary rejection. R10 also relived the rejection of expulsion-birth.

(v) At the beginning of her pregnancy, R3's mother tried, unsuccessfully, to abort foetus R3. It is interesting to note that while R3 relived intra-uterine acceptance in the Sessions, she did not relive any intra-uterine rejection. This is possibly due to the fact that the rejecting messages-stimuli left light (or no) 'memory traces' in R3's nervous system which were not reactivated by the psychedelic drug. Because R3 did not relive any intra-uterine rejection she is classified under the sub-category of the Constantly Welcome.

CHAPTER FOUR

REALIZATIONS AND CONCLUSIONS OF THE 16 OF TABLE 1

Fear
Symbolism of Sex
Womb Substitutes
Sexual Problems
R's Fixation to the Womb
The Compact System of Rejection
Identification and Projection

FEAR

§ 34   The 16 cases said that they felt any fear-producing stimulus during their infancy and childhood as a direct threat to their existential identity/self-preservation.

During Sessions, R2, R13 and R15 relived a childhood experience of becoming lost in the crowd. The extreme fear they felt was similar in quality to primitive terror (see types of fear immediately below).

Their intellectual development after childhood gradually helped the 16 specify some causes of their fears and decreased their intensity. However, for some of the 16, it was not unusual for insignificant stimuli to terrify them even after adolescence (R10 paranoiaclike and schizophreniclike state, p.49).

§ 35   *Types of fear*   The 16 described different qualities of fear which I have classified as follows:
(a) *Specific fear*   This fear occurs after expulsion-birth. It has specific causes which R is aware of (§ 119).
(b) *Anxiety*   This agonizing fear is accompanied by a vague threat to R's existence. Its cause is unconscious (§ 120).

The Knowledge of the Womb

(c) *Primitive terror* I have used this term to characterize the chaotic terror which the 16 felt during their intra-uterine rejection and/or the rejection of expulsion-birth.

Note: Though R7 and R11 experienced primitive terror, they could not tell whether it was during their foetal life, their expulsion-birth or immediately after birth.

§ 36   *Further details on primitive terror*
(a) When the rejecting womb messages-stimuli[48] excite the Unwanted foetus' nervous system, they cause:
   (i) A violent disturbance in the cohesion of his existential identity/ self-preservation and/ or his sex identity.
   (ii) Primitive terror.

From Unwanted R's point of view, the tragedy of all this process is that although he feels certain he is about to die, death - which would release him from this state of terrifying chaos - does not occur. Instead, he remains trapped in this state as long as his nervous system continues to be excited by the rejecting womb messages-stimuli.

[In the author's opinion, limbic neurons begin functioning from foetal life. Thus foetal limbic neurons are capable of being excited by rejecting womb stimuli. (According to the experimental finding of W. B. Cannon,[49] excitation of limbic neurons produces fear.)]

(b) The stimuli which are produced in the foetus/new-born's external environment during his expulsion and immediately after his birth may also cause a violent disturbance in the cohesion of his existential identity/self-preservation and primitive terror.

Note: The foetus' external environment during expulsion is the genital canal of his natural mother. The external environment after birth is the infinite chaos of the universe.

§ 37   As mentioned in § 32, the rejecting womb is intertwined with primitive terror. The 'memory traces' of the rejecting womb/primitive terror are preserved in a latent state by the neurons and may be reactivated after expulsion-birth by any rejecting stimulus. When reactivation occurs on a conscious level, R is aware that he is reliving the rejecting womb and primitive terror. Such a reactivation can occur only under conditions

---

[48] The foetus feels the rejecting messages-stimuli as coming from his external (intra-uterine) environment.
[49] W. B. Cannon, "Bodily Changes in Pain, Hunger, Fear and Rage", New York, 1929.

of autopsychognosia. When reactivation occurs on an unconscious level - as may happen in everyday life - only the primitive terror reaches consciousness. Thus, if the reactivation of the rejecting womb does not take place under conditions of autopsychognosia, only the primitive terror and not the experience of the rejecting womb is relived consciously (example R10).

SYMBOLISM OF SEX

§ 38   For all 16 cases of Table 1, sexual orgasm with a womb substitute symbolizes a return to the womb.

R3 and R13, Constantly Welcome, explain their 'return' to the womb through sexual activity which resulted in pregnancy, thus: during their pregnancy, they identified simultaneously with their mother and with the foetus within them. In other words, they were the foetus in their mother's womb. For R3 and R13 orgasm is a temporary state similar to the conditions of pregnancy: during orgasm the same double identification as in pregnancy occurs.

Other examples of 'returning' to the womb through orgasm are those of R4, R10, R12 (§48), R16.

§ 39   *Security*   For the Welcome, the womb was the first safe environment. For the Unwanted it was relatively safe - as safe, that is, as the rejecting intra-uterine environment could be considered. Thus, apart from the pleasure it may give R, orgasm also offers him the 'best obtainable security'.

§ 40   *Immortality*   R1, R3, R4, R12 and R13 feel the need to perpetuate themselves. This need springs from their existential identity/self-preservation and can be realized only through the birth of descendants. Through sex, then, these individuals ensure not only security but immortality as well.

R8 also desires immortality, though on her own terms: '9/10ths of my male descendants should be put to death and the remaining one used only for the perpetuation of the female sex.'

For R10 and R11, self-perpetuation is unthinkable. R10 says that she has 'not the least desire to perpetuate my shitty existence.' The thought of pregnancy horrifies R11; she feels that the foetus within her will be hideous.

WOMB SUBSTITUTES

§ 41 The symbolism of sex constitutes unconscious knowledge for R. It 'activates' him imperatively in his everyday life since emotionally (though unconsciously) R remains the foetus who needs the womb.

R's unconscious, invincible need to return to the womb he knew, that of his natural mother, drives him to search for it constantly. In his search, R 'discovers' various womb substitutes.

The nature of R's relations with the womb substitute is determined by the quality of his relations with the womb.

R's relations with the womb substitute are a complex process characterized by identifications, projections, efforts to create conditions of complete womb acceptance, efforts to create conditions of womb rejections and so on.

Examples:

(a) R3 and R13, Constantly Welcome, endeavour to revive the ideal conditions of their intra-uterine acceptance through sexual communication with a womb substitute .

(b) R10, Unwanted, tries either to create conditions of rejection or to create conditions of complete womb acceptance which, however, fail because the womb substitutes reactivate the rejecting womb.

(c) R4, Periodically Unwanted and Periodically Welcome, has a collection of rare coins and is willing to undertake any sacrifice to expand and enrich it. In R4's relations with his rare collection, there is an alternation of the following process: (i) The rare collection symbolizes the womb which R4 has at his disposal whenever he wants it. (ii) R4 identifies on the one hand with the womb and on the other with the collection which symbolizes foetus R4. Thus, just as he accepts the rare collection, so the womb accepts the foetus.

(d) R9, Unwanted because of his Sex, complains of being unable to penetrate a woman's vagina with his penis. He also mentions that he is intensely interested in mathematics. For R9, solving a difficult mathematical problem is almost the only way he can temporarily overcome his everyday agony caused by stimuli which reactivate the rejecting womb. Solving a mathematical problem gives R9 a momentary feeling of worth and arouses the vain hope that the womb will change its opinion of him: that he is useless and insignificant since he is not a woman, as the womb wants. But the womb remains relentlessly rejecting and castrating.

§ 42   When R discovers a womb substitute, the latter assumes supreme importance for him as it symbolizes security and perhaps immortality. He becomes fixated to the substitute: it alone gives his life meaning. Example: A house is engulfed by fire. Ignoring the danger, somebody throws himself through the flames to save a beloved person or object.

At first sight, this behaviour seems to contravene the law of self-preservation. Deeper analysis, however, reveals that the beloved person or object is more important than self-preservation: it symbolizes the womb without which self-preservation can be neither achieved nor perpetuated.

Usually there comes a day when the womb sustitute loses its attractiveness and causes R bitter disappointment. It is, after all, just a substitute and not the womb itself. R's disappointment is followed by fresh pursuit of his utopia. But despite all his efforts, R will never be the foetus in his mother's womb again (example R4).

SEXUAL PROBLEMS

§ 43   To the physical act of coitus the symbolism of sex adds emotional elements. For the 16, these elements are the basic cause of their sexual problems. In general, their sexual problems are characterized by:
(a) Difficulties in executing coitus.
(b) Abstention (temporary or permanent) from coitus and substitution with other forms of activity (example R1).

§ 44   *The sexual problems of the 16 of Table 1.* In more detail there are:
(a) Frigidity and/or abhorrence of anything related to sex.
(b) Highly unpleasant emotional-sensorial experiences during coitus, which intensify as orgasm approaches and result in the inhibition of orgasm and anxiety (R10); orgasm without pleasure; sobbing, depression and unpleasant physical symptoms following orgasm (R10); premature ejaculation without pleasure; fantasies (R4); and so forth.
(c) Various sexual activities: homosexual, masturbatory, sadistic, masochistic, activities involving fetishes, and so on (R12 § 48, R5).
(d) Obsessional acts. An illustration of (d) is the case of the 68-year old woman mentioned in § 122. Her sexual desires constituted internal stimuli which threatened to reject her existential identity/self-preservation: to have satisfied her sexual desires with real sexual activity would have been to risk shattering her self-respect

(her existential identity/self-preservation). Thus the rejecting stimuli 'activated' her sexual behaviour in an obsessional way. See also R12's example (§ 122).

§ 45 *Repercussions of sexual problems* The 16 realized that their sexual problems had repercussions on many of their everyday attitudes and activities - socio-political, moral, philosophical, scientific, artistic, religious, athletic and so forth.
Examples:
(a) R9's need to express and overcome his sexual problem through scientific activity (§ 41).
(b) R1's effort to solve his sexual problem through political activity.
(c) R4's division of sex into 'pure' and 'dirty' sex.
(d) R4's everyday agony which stems from lack of emotional fulfilment in sex.
(e) Worth noting is the sexual-moral attitude of all the women of Table 1, except R8, who feels they are 'whores'. Each one gives her own interpretation of the word:
R3 feels like a whore because she makes love with many men.
R6 feels she is a sinner (whore) because she still exists and is not a male.
R7 feels like a whore when she establishes sexual relations for social or financial gain.
R8 says: 'Men have succeeded in giving the most atrocious of meanings to the word "whore". "Whore" means a woman lower than scum. Through this term of abuse men try to demolish the personality of women who refuse to become their docile servants or exclusive property. Beneath the weight of heredity and the social code, women have been obliged to include the word "whore" in their vocabulary. And unfortunately women feel like whores, even for the most trivial reasons or the slightest deviation from the narrow path carved out for them by the social code. For me the word "whore" doesn't exist.'
R10 feels like a whore because she has genital organs.
R11 feels like a whore when she reveals her sexual desires.
R13 feels like a whore when she makes love with a man who doesn't love her.
R14 feels like a whore when she makes love with any man she can find in the hope that he will accept her.
R15 feels like a whore because she feels no emotional or physical excitement when she makes love.

R16 feels like a whore whenever she is humiliated for reasons which may or may not be related to her sexual activity.

How many generations of liberated women will it take before the 'memory traces' of the 'whore' have been erased from all their female descendants?

R'S FIXATION TO THE WOMB

§ 46   From the moment R's existential identity/self-preservation is created through the union of the spermatozoon and ovum of his natural parents - it is at the mercy of its external environment.

After his expulsion-birth, R unconsciously (and sometimes also consciously) feels permanently insecure. Thus, in various ways, he constantly endeavours to create around him conditions of security. The form this endeavour takes is moulded by the factors mentioned in § 24, 105, 106 and the symbolism of sex. Thus, for both the Welcome and Unwanted the womb constitutes the permanent base of reference.

Note: The experience of expulsion-birth and/or the 'castrating' behaviour of the mother and/or father may traumatize a Welcome R just as severely as an Unwanted R, and leave its 'memory traces' in his nervous system. Various stimuli which incline towards reactivating or which do reactivate these 'memory traces' cause mental disturbance (examples R1, R5, R12 § 48 & §122).

§ 47   *Repercussions of fixation of the Welcome to the womb*
(a) Welcome R is fixated to his natural mother (and/or the other womb substitutes) because she symbolizes the womb, the place where he had once experienced ideal security. For the Welcome infant (and later the child) the mother's presence is vital: just as she had protected him in her womb from the dangers without so she will protect him now from new dangers by taking him in her arms. She is to be constantly by him, exclusively his, her attention for him alone. Father, siblings, as well as other persons in the environment who remove her attention from him, unconsciously and sometimes also consciously become objects of hatred.
(b) When a rejecting stimulus tends towards reactivating the rejecting womb, Welcome R reacts with unconscious and sometimes also conscious aggressive behaviour: his rejection, for example, by a womb substitute provokes aggressive behaviour towards the substitute and/or the environment and/or himself.

The Knowledge of the Womb

(c) When a stimulus tends towards reactivating the accepting womb, Welcome R responds with reconciliatory behaviour towards the stimulus and/or the environment and/or himself.
(d) Welcome R feels an incessant, unconscious desire to return to the womb, which intensifies each time a rejecting stimulus excites his nervous system.
(e) When the rejection of expulsion-birth is reactivated, it gives rise to an existential problem which is exteriorized as psychoticlike S & P (example R13 § 129).
(f) Sexual problems (§ 43, 44).

§ 48 *R12's realizations* R12, Periodically Welcome, made the following realizations:
(a) Ejaculation during the sexual act with a womb substitute fulfils his desire to return to the safe womb as some of his cells (spermatozoa) 'return' to the uterus of the womb substitute. Said R12: 'In sex I take the path of my expulsion-birth, but in reverse. In so doing I return to the secure womb.'
(b) When internal stimuli (emotions, thoughts) or external stimuli cause him rejection-insecurity, the desire to return to the womb instantly intensifies. The result is that he feels the need for sexual activity at the most inappropriate moments of his everyday life.
(c) The symbolism of sex makes him feel that if he should ever lose his sexual capability he would lose everything in life. Sexual impotence would mean that there would be no way of 'returning' to the safe refuge whenever he were in danger. It would also mean forfeiting the chance of achieving immortality.
(d) His mother's autocratic behaviour and sexual taboos castrate him psychologically. The mere thought of having heterosexual contact is enough to render him impotent. His heterosexual experiences are very painful as they always lead to the ridiculing of his manhood and, for a brief moment, severe schizophreniclike-paranoiaclike S & P. Finally, he decides to ignore women. But the environment, ever hostile, intensifies his insecurity and sexual desire. Faced with no other alternative, he turns to homosexuality where the male partner, in not being a woman, cannot castrate him. He feels his manhood only when he has active sexual contact with a man. To the passive partner he projects his mother. In this way he acquires the sexual capacity to 'return' to the womb.

Note: During passive homosexual activity, R12 identifies simultaneously with the existential identity of his active partner and his mother.

(e) R12 finally added: 'Except for the painful moments of my mother's sexual activity, I felt welcome within her womb. But the effect of those moments, and of her sexual taboos generally, was to forbid my return to her. If I had slept with my mother, I wouldn't have blinded myself as Oedipus did. On the contrary, the experience of making love with her would have shown me the right path to the much-desired womb.'

Note: R12's mother revealed to me that, since adolescence, sex had terrified her. After she was married, her attitude towards sex deteriorated. When she was pregnant with R12, her husband insisted on having sex with her and this upset her greatly. When R12 was growing up, she tried to impart to him her abhorrence of sex.

§ 49   Repercussions of fixation of the Unwanted to the womb

(a) Unwanted R is both dependent on his natural mother (and/or the other womb substitutes) and extremely aggressive (unconsciously and sometimes also consciously) towards her as he considers her directly responsible for his tortured life (R10)

(b) After expulsion-birth Unwanted R is 'activated' in the following ways:

   (i) He projects the womb's rejections to the external environment and feels that everyone and everything reject him. Within a labyrinth of conflicting emotions he tries, like the 'wandering Jew', to express the agony of his inner world and the need for a little warmth in a refuge which will welcome him or at least not drive him away. He maintains the hope that some day the rejecting womb will change its attitude towards him and become accepting. Thus, with great hesitation, he decides to risk his 'return' through sex. A vain hope. With horror he reconfirms that the womb remains implacably rejecting, an unremitting hell ... And his wandering continues without respite.

   (ii) When the external environment is accepting, Unwanted R often tries (unconsciously and sometimes also consciously) to create conditions of rejection as these are the only conditions he is familiar with: only under such conditions does he feel that he 'exists' (R10)

   (iii) Periodically Unwanted R4 endeavours through sex to revive the few moments of calm in the womb which occurred between

the emotional disturbances of his pregnant mother (R4's description).
(c) Reactivation of the 'memory traces' of the intra-uterine rejection of Unwanted R's existential identity/self-preservation and/or his sex identity gives rise to an existential and/or sex identity problem which is exteriorized as psychoticlike S & P (§ 127 -133).

THE COMPACT SYSTEM OF REJECTION

§ 50 The autopsychognosia sessions show that the rejecting-psychotraumatic stimuli which excite R's nervous system during his foetal life, his expulsion-birth and after birth, become associated and form a compact system of rejection. This system may be excited after expulsion-birth by any stimulus (even the most insignificant) provided the stimulus contains even the slightest element of rejection.

The excitation of the compact system of rejection by a rejecting stimulus produces unconscious and sometimes also conscious fear and tends towards reactivating or actually reactivates on a conscious level the primitive terror of the rejecting womb (§ 37).

§ 51 *Psychotraumatic or rejecting stimuli* These are:
(a) The stimuli which reject, or which reactivate the rejection of, R's existential identity/self-preservation and/or his sex identity.
(b) The stimuli which incline towards reactivating this (or these) rejections (§ 96). *Basic rejecting stimuli* These are:
(a) During foetal life: the womb-mother's rejection of the foetus' existence and/or sex (intra-uterine rejection).
(b) During expulsion-birth: the process of expulsion-birth may be one of rejection (rejection of expulsion-birth).
(c) After expulsion-birth:
   (i) Abuse of the child by the mother (and/or father).
   (ii) The overprotective-castrating behaviour of the mother (and/or father) towards the child, be it boy or girl, is of a rejecting nature as it alienates-inhibits the child's existential identity. We are all familiar with parents who know it all, who alone make all the decisions and who impose their will on the child. Under such conditions, the child's existential identity is superfluous. This overprotection inclines towards reactivating or does reactivate the rejecting womb.

Note: The cause of the mother's overprotective-castrating behaviour is her insecurity. Unconsciously and sometimes also consciously the mother is traumatized-terrified as a result of personal experiences. She identifies with her child and tries to protect it as she would protect herself. If the mother has sexual problems, her behaviour towards the child becomes more alienating-rejecting (example R12 § 48).
(iii) The demands of the social code also alienate R as they impose their will on him.
(iv) Other rejecting stimuli of the external environment (a strong earthquake, for instance).

§ 52 People become parents before they have solved their psychological problems, many of which they are in any case unaware. In other words, although they are unprepared for procreation, people procreate. In addition, they are ignorant of the fact that basic elements in their behaviour have a negative-morbid influence on the development of their children's personality. Below are some of the factors which are responsible for misunderstandings between R and his parents and which constitute a source of unconscious and sometimes also conscious conflict between them.
(a) Convinced that their children have the same problems they had at their age, parents try to solve their children's problems in accordance with their own experience and mentality. Note: The Sessions proved their conviction to be fallacious.
(b) As a rule, parents are ignorant of their children's problems. Out of fear and 'respect', the children do not dare confide in their parents and discuss their problems with them.
(c) Parents usually undertake tremendous sacrifices for their children and expect recognition and gratitude in return. They do not realize, however, that even for the slightest reason their children may feel rejection, unbearable alienation and castration - symptoms which leave no room for gratitude.
(d) The Unwanted form a special category of people who are 'activated' by the unconscious desire to avenge the hateful womb which persecutes them almost incessantly in their everyday life.
(e) The father's sexual conquest of the mother or vice versa is interpreted emotionally by R as his parents' rejection of him. The rejection is exacerbated by the appearance of baby sister or baby brother, i.e. the fruit of the paternal or maternal conquest. All 16 cases of Table 1 mentioned that they were severely traumatized when they discovered that their parents had sexual relations.

IDENTIFICATION AND PROJECTION

§ 53   Two basic neuronal mechanisms which play a very significant role in R's 'activation' by stimuli are identification and projection. These two mechanisms are established according to laws analogous to those which govern the formation of Pavlov's conditioned reflexes.

§ 54   *Identification*   This is the property of R's nervous system to combine the emotional-intellectual-motor image of his own existential identity with the image of another person's existential identity. The images of the two existential identities coalesce and symbolize the same individual.

'I identify with *B*' means either (a) 'What I feel, I think *B* also feels; what I think, I think *B* also thinks; how I behave, I think ***B*** also behaves' or (b) 'What I think *B* feels or thinks, I feel or think too; the way I think *B* behaves, I also behave' (example R4).

§ 55   *Projection*   This is the property of R's nervous system to project the image of *B*'s existential identity, as he (R) has subjectively formed it, to *C*. The two subjective images of the existential identities coalesce and thus what *B* symbolizes for R, *C* also symbolizes for R. Also, as *B* 'activates' R, so in the same way *C* 'activates' him.

§ 56   *Functioning of identification and projection*   Identification and projection function unconsciously and correlate two or more persons, beings, environmental conditions, a person with an object, a person with an animal and so forth.

Examples:
(a) R15 identified with her little dog to the point where, when the dog disappeared once, she stopped eating. As she said, she 'had to' share his probable hunger (who would feed the dog?).
(b) The subjective correlation of R10's school and university exams with the rejecting womb.
(c) R4's identification with the coins in his collection (§ 41).

How strongly the mechanisms of identification and projection function depends on how far the images which are identified or projected coalesce. Thus, identifications and projections may range from partial to almost absolute.

Worth noting are the simultaneous double or multiple identifications and/or projections, eg. R3's (and R13's) double identification during her pregnancy with her mother and the foetus within her womb (§ 38), R10's multiple projections.

Conclusion: During wakefulness and dreams, the mechanisms of identification and projection are 'activated' unconsciously by various stimuli. Thus, R's everyday emotional life may be stereotyped repetition, on an unconscious level, of the intra-uterine experience and/or the experience of expulsion-birth.

§ 57 *Identification, projection and womb substitutes*   The mechanisms of identification and projection result in, among other things, the production of womb substitutes. A womb substitute may be any person, animal, object, and so forth, which unconsciously symbolizes the rejecting or accepting womb.

The most basic womb substitute is the natural mother or the woman who takes the role of the natural mother. The emotional image of the father may also symbolize the rejecting or accepting womb, that is, the father may also become a womb substitute (example R10). The emotional images of the mother and father form the foundations on which the edifice of the other womb substitutes is built.

Note: The mechanism of identification can turn R himself into a womb substitute (see torturers § 118, R10 masochism, R10 sadism, R10 depression).

CHAPTER FIVE

AUTOPSYCHOGNOSIA[50]

Psychedelic Drugs
Preparation for Autopsychognosia
Resistance to Autopsychognosia

§ 58   *Autopsychognosia is a neuronal process which gives rise to emotional-intellectual realizations[51] about the content of the unconscious and the motives of behaviour. Autopsychognosia is a subjective experience. A person who has not undergone the process finds difficulty in empathizing with its emotional content.*

§ 59   *The aim of autopsychognosia* is to help R become as well acquainted with himself and his environment as possible.

§ 60   An individual decides to begin or not begin autopsychognosia after he is informed that *autopsychognosia is not a method of therapy. It is combined emotional and intellectual knowledge which acquires therapeutic value only if the individual uses it in everyday life entirely on his own initiative.*

R15 was asked by a very close friend of hers: 'Since you've progressed so much in your autopsychognosia, why haven't you solved your psychological problems satisfactorily?' R15 replied: 'Have you any idea what a rape feels like? Let me tell you that there is no feeling more horrible than that. If we suppose that someone has raped me, my knowing it doesn't mean that the rape is no longer a reality. What happens is that I

---

50 In contrast to autopsychognosia is autognosia, a term for the ancient Greek saying that total knowledge of oneself leads to total knowledge of the universe and the gods.

51 In contrast to subjective emotional-intellectual realizations are plain intellectual realizations which leave R indifferent from an emotional point of view. The remark made by R7, who had undergone psychoanalysis before coming to me for autopsychognosia sessions, is typical: 'With my psychoanalyst's help, I learned how to make intellectual realizations about the motives of my morbid behaviour, but the whole thing just left me cold.'

know the rape occurred and I either reconcile myself with this emotionally painful fact or I continue to be tortured by it. Now then, the knowledge of the rape corresponds to the knowledge of autopsychognosia.'

§ 61   One way of achieving autopsychognosia is through pharmaceutical autopsychognosia sessions. Sessions may be performed with an individual or with a group. The participants in an individual Session are an R and a doctor. In a group Session, the participants are two doctors, at least three nurses and 8-15 Rs.

Because a Session is a subjective experience which concerns only a specific R and because the presence of others impedes R's concentration, the first five Sessions are individual. After this, if R so wishes, he participates in group Sessions.

PSYCHEDELIC DRUGS

§ 62   The process of the Sessions is based on the use of small doses of psychedelic drugs. The word 'psychedelic' is derived from the Greek words *psyche* (soul) and *delo* (I manifest). A psychedelic drug is a drug whose intake by the human body may bring about the manifestation or exteriorization of the unconscious. A basic pharmacodynamic property of the psychedelics is that they reactivate the memory of the nerve cells. This results in:
(a) The vivid emotional and physical revival of past events, some pleasant but most of them unpleasant (example R4).
(b) An amazing improvement in self-observation and introspection.

§ 63   *Dosage of psychedelic drugs*   For the first Session, men are given 3 mg Psilocybine or 50 mcg LSD-25, women 3 mg Psilocybine or 30 mcg LSD-25. The dose of the psychedelic for each Session thereafter is regulated according to R's reaction in the Session before. I seldom found it necessary to exceed doses of 9 mg Psilocybine or 100 mcg LSD-25. An exception is a case published in the periodical "Annales Medico-psychologiques de Paris" (t2, 121e annee, 1963, no 2). This case presented strong resistance. Owing to my lack of experience, I thought the resistance could be neutralized with a larger dose of the psychedelic. Thus, by gradually increasing the dose, I reached the colossal amount of 900 mcg LSD-25. As a result of this, not only was the resistance not neutralized but the case also presented severe confusional excitement which obliged me to terminate his Session with an intramuscular injection of 100 mg chlorpromazine.

§ 64 *Environment for a Session* The room where the Session takes place must be sound-proof and arranged so that R can:
(a) Concentrate: for this reason the room is in semi-darkness.
(b) Move about freely. (R9 and R2, who felt the need to move about a great deal, preferred to lie on the floor instead of the couch.)
(c) Express his aggressiveness towards the environment in every possible way. R's original womb rejection and his frequent rejection by womb substitutes create in him anger, exasperation and the need to act destructively towards his environment and to shout with all his might. For this reason photographs of his mother, father and siblings should be in the room as well as various objects which he can destroy. In addition, paintings of various historical figures and events, known or unknown, often reactivate 'memory traces' of repressed psychotraumas and aid penetration into deeper layers of the unconscious.

General rule: During the Sessions R is encouraged to express his aggressiveness towards the external environment to the maximum.

§ 65 From 1960 -1964, I felt obliged to keep my cases (with few exceptions) in a hospital for several days after each Session because of the possible side-effects of the psychedelic. The experience of this period revealed that:
(a) The side-effects of the psychedelic were slight agitation and moderate melancholia, which abated easily with small doses of amitryptiline or chlorpromazine.
(b) R's confinement in the hospital was a psychological and financial strain.
(c) R's contact with the psychotraumatic family environment helped him strengthen and extend the realizations made in the Sessions.

Thus, after 1964 I changed tactics radically. The Sessions were still performed in the hospital but subsequently R returned home. Naturally, he could contact me any moment he wished. With this new procedure I did not encounter any unpleasant surprises.

§ 66 *Duration of a Session* Because the duration of a Session cannot be foretold with precision, the doctor must be armed with the patience of Job.

The Sessions last about 6 - 8 hours and as a rule require the continuous presence of the doctor. I never stop a Session if R is still making realizations about his unconscious. One of the most astonishing realizations occurred during the 11th hour of R12's 4th Session where he described the conditions of his intra-uterine life. For me this description was the first indication that the 'memory traces' of intra-uterine experiences are preserved by the human nervous system.

At the end of each Session R is given 25 mg chlorpromazine. The same dose is repeated two hours later if the pharmacodynamic activity of the psychedelic drug continues. If it is necessary to stop a flashback or to terminate a Session because of severe and prolonged (more than two hours) anxiety, R is given 25 mg chlorpromazine.

§ 67   *The phases of autopsychognosia*   Generally speaking there are ten Sessions in the first phase of autopsychognosia, the interval between each Session being 1 - 3 weeks. The period before the second phase of autopsychognosia, the number of Sessions in the second phase and the interval between each Session in the second phase depends on R's progress in his autopsychognosia.

§ 68   *The selection of cases for autopsychognosia* was made on the basis of the following criteria:
(a)   The absence of permanent psychoticlike (psychotic) S & P.[52]
(b)   A certain sensitivity in communicating with their fellow man and with their environment in general. A person who is narrow-minded and conservative in every aspect of his personal and social life does not constitute fertile ground for autopsychognosia.

PREPARATION FOR AUTOPSYCHOGNOSIA

§ 69   R prepares for the Sessions by writing answers to a history questionnaire which consists of a general and a specific part. Here is a sample questionnaire.

General questionnaire: Sex; age; educational level; profession; marital status; children; number of siblings, their sex and age; state of health of mother, father, siblings.

List your complaints, physical and mental - describe your symptoms, their intensity and duration. Describe any pharmaceutical therapy or any

---

[52]   R1, R4, R6, R8, R9, R10 and R14 mentioned in their history psychoticlike S & P which, as a rule, diminished with the Sessions.

other kind of therapy you have undergone. What serious illnesses have you suffered?

Specific questionnaire: What events in your life can you remember? Which of these events do you consider important? What emotions did these important events produce in you? Does the way you communicate with your daily environment satisfy you? Does your environment accept you? Does it reject you? Do you feel negligible even amongst those closest to you? What are your feelings on your existence? Does your existence satisfy you? Are you pleased with yourself? with your body? Do you feel that your body is yours? Do you feel that the movements of your torso and limbs are yours? Do your thoughts, feelings, deeds disturb you? Do you accept your sex? Does your sex disturb you? How do you feel with members of the opposite sex? with members of the same sex? Do you have difficulty in communicating with them? Describe your sexual activity, the fantasies and emotions which accompany it. Do you reach orgasm? If so, describe what you feel before, during and after orgasm. Do you always understand the motives of your behaviour? If not, give a specific example. What do you desire most in life? What are your ambitions? What are your expectations? What are your hopes for the future? What do you fear most? What are your other fears? Describe your recreational activities. Do you remember your dreams? Are any of your dreams repeated in a stereotyped fashion? Describe your feelings towards your mother, father, each sibling; your feelings about the interpersonal relations of your mother and father, mother and siblings, father and siblings, siblings; your feelings towards persons whom you feel have played a significant role in your life. Have you ever had suicidal thoughts? If so, describe them.

Do you feel that you have concealed anything in answering the above questions? Recapitulate your problems beginning with the most important. What do you hope the Sessions will do for you? Do you have anything else to add?

§ 70 *Observations on R's answers to the questionnaire* The accuracy of R's answers to the general questionnaire can usually by checked through various other sources (relatives, friends). On the contrary, the absolute accuracy of R's answers to the specific questionnaire cannot be checked through any source but R himself. Moreover, R is not always consistent. At different moments, his answers to the same questions may vary, both in quality and intensity. Typically, oral descriptions of feelings towards his mother or father during the same or different free communication sessions (non-pharmaceutical sessions) fluctuate. R's contradictory descriptions pose this question: Does his information correspond to reality or is it deliberately or unwittingly inaccurate?

The realizations R makes during the Sessions show that his answers to the specific questionnaire were often vague, inaccurate or incomplete even though he was convinced of their truth and accuracy. The answers were so because the roots of R's problems were unconscious or semi-conscious, unclear or incomprehensible. Despite their inaccuracy, written replies to the specific questionnaire before the Sessions are essential: they give R the possibility to realize later just how little he knew himself.

Example: During her 15th Session, R10 was terrified by the vision of a ghost-like creature with green eyes, unruly white hair, white face, and wearing a green robe. Its arms were outstretched threateningly towards her. Here is what R10 said about the creature after her 19th Session:

"The feeling of being watched by some invisible 'thing' began, as far as I can remember, at age eight and has been with me every day since then. 'It' watches my every deed and knows even my innermost thoughts and emotions. Though this 'thing' is invisible, it has often been an extremely powerful presence, so strong that I can actually 'hear' its mocking 'laughter', that is, I don't actually hear a voice, but *I feel* it intensely. And whatever it has to 'say' to me, I believe it is right, sometimes partly, but most often fully, and so I obey it.

This 'thing' has been with me even when I've been alone. Thus, instead of feeling free and uninhibited when I'm alone, I feel exactly the opposite - that I must conform to social behaviour. So if I do anything that one must not do in public, the 'thing' criticizes me severely. If I am depressed, frustrated, angry, desperate, it scornfully 'tells' me that I'm putting on an act. When I feel very female (which is seldom), it ridicules and mocks me: "Who are you trying to fool?" When I feel and behave like a man: "What a fool!" On the rare occasions when I feel relatively happy it 'says', "This won't last long," or "You won your happiness under false circumstances."

If I am in a room, the 'thing' is in an upper corner of the room. If I am out in the open air, the 'thing' is up in the air at a certain fixed point, again as if in an upper corner of a room. I have often tried to use my logic to tell myself that there is nothing up in the corner of the room watching me since it cannot be seen or grasped with the hands. But this has never worked. From the very first second of feeling it, nothing I can say to myself can break its iron grip on me. And my very same logic tells me that though this 'thing' cannot be seen, it doesn't mean that it's not there. *It is there and it is real.* I feel its presence as so much a part of my life that, despite the fact that it tortures me, I consider it as something natural and so it did not occur to me that I should mention it in the questionnaire before beginning the Sessions. Now, after 19 Sessions, I realize that the invisible 'thing' is the green creature of Session 15, that is the green womb - the womb which doesn't want me, which constantly threatens my existence, which knows and sees I'm in agony but yet continues to bombard me mercilessly with rejecting messages, which laughs at me for being a 'woman' and mocks my efforts to become a man."

Note: The factors which negatively influence the 'sincerity' of R's answers to the specific questionnaire also influence his answers in psychometric tests. None of the psychometric tests used on the 16 prior to the Sessions could predict that memories of intra-uterine life are retained by the nervous system.

RESISTANCE TO AUTOPSYCHOGNOSIA

§ 71   Although the Sessions are subjective in nature and cannot be grasped through mere descriptions, it is nevertheless essential that prior to the Sessions R be familiarized with two basic elements which are vital to the positive evolution of autopsychognosia:

(a) Conscious and unconscious resistance to penetrating into the unconscious.

(b) The means of neutralizing resistance.

§ 72   *Some causes of resistance*   The person who is to undergo Sessions feels shame and vague fear. Before her first Session R8 said, 'I'm afraid I might see myself as more despicable that what I imagine.'

One cause of R's resistance is his fear of revealing to the doctor terrible inner thoughts and shameful deeds. Revealing them to the doctor is like revealing them to the whole world. These thoughts and feelings constitute conscious and unconscious resistance to confiding in the doctor and are not easily neutralized. Even when R has decided to express his every thought to the doctor, there is always something that he will hide from the latter and from himself.

§ 73   The thought that autopsychognosia might transform his character and emotions makes R feel anxious.

Examples: On the eve of his first Session R12 was worried that autopsychognosia might change his feelings towards certain beloved friends. R9 feared that autopsychognosia might alter his feelings towards a certain young woman. This fear prevented progress in his Sessions until he realized that the woman symbolized his only link with the external environment, For foetus R9, communication with the original external environment, the womb, was his only means of survival. For R9 the adult, the external environment was symbolized by the young woman. Thus, cutting his communication with her would have been like sentencing himself to death.

§ 74   The 'memory traces' of fears, anxiety and primitive terror caused by various psychotraumatic stimuli become associated and form a compact system of rejection (§ 50). Because psychedelic drugs reactivated the compact system of rejections, R is overcome by a fear which he senses will intensify until it is unbearable. To avoid this, he consciously or unconsciously represses his fear and so blocks the evolution of the Session. There are many tactics of resistance. For instance, at any point in the Session R may announce that he wants to smoke: smoking, however, is a means of emotional self-control and if R is permitted to satisfy his desire the process of the Session breaks down.

Beforehand, R must know that the intensity of his fear-anxiety will increase during the Session and that if he wishes to learn the causes of his mental disturbance he must not neutralize the fear-anxiety, even if he feels that he will die.

§ 75   From the general principle that the nervous system selects the 'best' way of reacting to stimuli, one concludes that mental disturbance[53] is the 'best defence' against rejecting stimuli. Naturally, then, R fights autopsychognosia which tends to neutralize his mental disturbance.

§ 76   The doctor's presence may be another cause of resistance in the Sessions and occurs even when R's communication with the doctor is satisfactory. This is due mainly to shame. Forewarned of this, R should not hesitate to ask the doctor to leave the room if he wants to be alone and to call him back when he needs him.

Clearly, the doctor must be at R's disposal during the Sessions if he is to help R effectively. The doctor can achieve this only when he has fully grasped the process of the Sessions and accepts his secondary role.

Example: During his second Session R5 wanted to be alone. Without hesitation I left the room. Half an hour later he called me back and confessed embarrassment at assuming the foetal position in my presence. Applying the general principle that he must express everything he feels,

---

[53] For definition of mental disturbance, see § 110.

R5 had found the courage to ask me to leave. As a result of my immediate departure, R5 took the foetal position, began to rock himself to and fro and finally felt that he was in the womb. He then relived experiences of periodic rejection during intra-uterine life and the severe trauma of his expulsion-birth. After this Session R5 admitted his need to take the foetal position in the first Session as well, but he had not dared express his wish to be alone. This had prevented his 'return' to the womb.

§ 77   Before the Sessions I inform R that he is not anaesthetized by the psychedelic: on the contrary he retains his senses and is fully aware of what he is thinking, saying and doing. In addition, he can remember almost all details of a Session when it is over. If R has no objection, the Sessions are recorded. On the subject of recording R9 said, 'Listening to the taped Session I relive the past once again and reinforce the realizations I made during the Session.' The tapes belong to R and he retains them for his own private reference. Even if R consents to the recorder, its presence may inhibit him. If this happens, recording is stopped.

§ 78   The psychedelic is given in minute doses. Thus, if he wished, R may neutralize its pharmacodynamic activity completely and obstruct the progress of a Session (example R4).

§ 79   *Neutralization of resistance - examples*   If unpleasant emotions accompany a thought or image in R's mind during a Session, then the thought or image is related to his psychological traumas. In this case R tends to repress rather than to express what he is thinking and feeling. Thereby, the process of the Session breaks down. If, however, he expresses his thoughts and feelings, then the series of ideas which follows will lead him to the root of his mental conflict. The expression of the original thought is like the beginning of Ariadne's thread which guides R through the labyrinth of the unconscious.

Example: One hour into his first Session, R2 describes the following image: 'I see myself as a small child holding my mother's hand. I'm very happy. Suddenly the image of my father appears. He's furious with me. His very presence terrifies me. I'm very afraid.'

At this point R2 stopped speaking. After a few minutes' silence he began describing some minor conflicts with his only sister and finally stopped speaking altogether. His prolonged silence was a clear indication of resistance and thus I urged him repeatedly to recall the image of his angry father. Finally R2 responded: "I can see my father, angry again. His image disappears and in its place comes another. It's me in front of an enormous vulva which is protecting me. I feel safe and secure. It's my mother's vulva.'

From this image R2 realized that his sexual desires for his mother sprang from his need for security. He was afraid to exteriorize these sexual desires: their expression would have implied confrontation with his father, all-powerful rival and master of his mother. He would have annihilated R2's existential identity/self-preservation.

§ 80   During a Session two images of different content may alternate and hinder the progress of the Session if R does not continue expressing his thoughts.

Example: During her second Session R15 saw two alternating images. First Image: 'I see myself at the age of twelve chasing butterflies in the garden.' Moderate anxiety accompanied the image. Second image: 'Again I'm twelve years old. I'm lying on my bed.' Moderate anxiety also accompanied this image.

The alternation of the images was repeated a few times and finally R15 fell silent owing to resistance. I urged her to return to the images. She asked me which image she should follow. I suggested she choose the image that felt more significant. In a co-operative effort to neutralize resistance, she insisted that I choose one for her. Because I thought a traumatic sexual experience would more likely follow from the second image, I proposed this one. R15 complied and the image evolved as follows: her older sister enters the room, sits on the bed and starts talking about a dress she wants to buy. R15 remarks, 'I don't feel that this image goes anywhere.' This image was the result of resistance, its aim to block the Session.

I recommended that she return to the first image. R15 complied and continued, 'I am in the garden chasing butterflies ... The image changes. Now I'm eight years' old and in the same garden. Here is our gardener ... (anxiety) He invites me to follow him. He says he wants to show me some beautiful flowers in the green-house ... (anxiety increases) There, he begins to caress me ... He exposes his penis and rubs it against me. I don't resist. His penis touches my genital organs ... I feel pleasure and terrible shame ... (severe anxiety) Oh God, I'm not a virgin.'

This example shows that even if R follows the wrong path momentarily, he finally finds the right one if only he expresses whatever he feels.

§ 81   R must be informed that a Session leaves 'memory traces' in his nervous system which may be reactivated automatically without the psychedelic. This important process, which may occur from anywhere between a few days to many years later, is called a flashback. It is easily neutralized either at will or with 25 mg chlorpromazine. During the flashback R may function as he does in a Session and progress on to realizations (§ 17).

§ 82   *The doctor's role during the Sessions*
(a) *The doctor's view of his role*   Many years of experience have shown me that R needs someone who stands by him as a person during the Session and who acts as a doctor if the Session needs to be stopped. It is R who has the primary role in a Session: it is he who must find the painful road to his unconscious. The doctor sits patiently at R's side regardless of the duration of the Session.

If R shows signs of resistance in his stream of thought during a Session, I intervene by asking questions related to the source of resistance. If R's anxiety increases, I encourage him not to neutralize it even if he feels that he is approaching death. If severe anxiety lasts for two hours, I stop the Session with an intramuscular injection of 25 mg chlorpromazine.

If the doctor's presence inhibits R's stream of thought, he should leave the room and return only when R calls him.

(b) *R's view of the doctor's role*   The doctor acts upon R as an external stimulus which reactivates 'memory traces' of past rejecting or accepting stimuli. This process stems from the mechanisms of projection and/or identification.

Example: During his 19th Session, R5 feels he is about to relive the very painful experience of near-suffocation during his expulsion-birth and asks me to turn on the light. 'I want you to see me suffering,' he says and continues: 'The agonizing moments of the past that I relive are proof that I suffer. You're to blame for all my suffering because you gave me the injection (of the psychedelic drug which reactivated the past). Yes, you're my mother and my father. You're the rejecting womb. You do whatever you like with me. You try to fool me. You gave me an injection of tap water, not medicine. You want to make fun of me. I feel the drug working strongly and yet I believe that you didn't give me a real injection. Yes, but I can fool you too. Everything that you see, everything that you hear (he means muscular contractions, groaning and screaming from the agony of suffocation) is an act, a comedy. It's bullshit. I want to progress. I want to show you that I'm progressing in the Session, that I make realizations and that the Session is succeeding. Perhaps that way you'll be happy and stop rejecting me.'

Here we see that R5's feelings towards the womb are projected to the doctor whom he tries to fool just as he tries to fool the rejecting womb.

PART THREE

Author's questions, conclusions and bioneuropsysiological interpretations of the experiences and conclusions of the 16 cases of table 1

CHAPTER ONE

MEMORY OF INTRA-UTERINE LIFE

§ 83   It is my view that the pregnant woman's desires, fears and emotional disturbances are caused by biochemicophysical substances-factors (among them neurotransmitters[54] and neuro-hormones[55]) which are produced in her internal environment (in her neurons, for example). It is these biochemicophysical substances-factors which excite foetus R's nervous system and which his existential identity/self-preservation feels as messages-stimuli from the external (intra-uterine) environment. As a rule, the biochemicophysical substances-factors leave 'memory traces' within foetal neuronal elements: these remain preserved there in a latent state. When these 'memory traces' are reactivated after expulsion-birth by the psychedelic, the whole process of the original neuronal excitation is repeated and thus R relives his intra-uterine experience.

Emotions - fear, anger and such - result from the excitation of limbic neurons. It may be that the excitation of limbic neurons produces special neuro-hormones - fear-producing, anger-producing and so on. Thus, if a pregnant woman's limbic neurons generate fear-producing or other kinds of neuro-hormones, the latter enter her blood stream and, through the umbilical cord, reach the foetal blood stream, excite foetal limbic neurons and cause a subjective emotional state which is embraced either by the term 'rejecting womb' or by the term 'accepting womb'.

---

54   Neurotransmitter is a biochemical substance which is stored in the axon terminals of a neuron. When a neuron is excited, neurotransmitter is secreted into the synapses of its axons. There are some kinds of neurotransmitters, eg. acetylcholine, which transmit the excitation of a presynaptic neuron to postsynaptic neurons. There are other kinds of neurotransmitters, eg. GABA (gamma-aminobutyric acid), which inhibit the excitation of postsynaptic neurons.

55   Neuro-hormones are polypeptide compounds which are produced by specific neurons. Because neuro-hormones are absorbed into the blood stream, they can be conveyed to distant areas of the body where they act. Neuro-hormones are considered a kind of neurotransmitter.

The Knowledge of the Womb

§ 84   How is it that in Sessions R can describe the experiences of a period (intra-uterine) during which he did not have the ability of language? When R describes his intra-uterine experiences, he is describing what he had felt as the foetus from which he developed and which he is now reliving. R's description is given with various acoustic and optic symbols which he learned after his expulsion-birth and which he feels are applicable to the revived experience. For example, when R10 shouted during her 20th Session 'The fire! The fire! she was describing with acoustic symbols (which she learned after her birth) what she had felt at the time her foetal existence was being bombarded by rejecting stimuli.

§ 85   R10's revival of the intra-uterine rejection of her female ancestors' sex may be explained as follows: The 'memory traces' - preserved within a neuron - of a stimulus which had excited that neuron may be transmitted through heredity to a descendant homogeneous neuron. The greater the biological significance of a stimulus (see § 96), the greater the probability of hereditary transmission of its 'memory traces' to descendant homogeneous neurons. In other words, the 'memory traces' of stimuli of great biological significance are 'engraved' within the genes and thus are transmitted to descendants. (Homogeneous neurons are those neurons which are located anatomotopographically at the same point in two nervous systems and whose excitation produces the same qualitative result, e.g. the limbic neurons of two nervous systems are homogeneous neurons.)

The experience of an ancestor neuron may be revived by a descendant homogeneous neuron thanks to the hereditary transmission of the 'memory traces' of that experience from the ancestor neuron to the descendant neuron, and to the reactivation of the 'memory traces'.

CHAPTER TWO

A FEW NOTES ON BIONEUROPHYSIOLOGY

§ 86   The nervous system consists of a large number of nerve cells (neurons) which are separated from each other by synapses.

The direct result of the excitation of a living neuron 'n' by a stimulus 's' is the secretion of neurotransmittter into the synapses which separate the axon terminals of 'n' from the dendrites and/or cell body of 'n's postsynaptic neurons. (In this case, 'n' is a presynaptic neuron.[56]) Whether 'n's excitation by 's' is transmitted to some or all of 'n's postsynaptic neurons or whether it is not transmitted to any postsynaptic neuron, depends on the quality and intensity of 's'.

As far as the quality of a stimulus is concerned, Eric Kandel's experiments on the Aplysia Californica[57] show that this mollusc withdraws from a harmful stimulus thanks to the transmission of the excitation of presynaptic neurons (in this case, sensory) to their postsynaptic neurons (in this case, motor). On the other hand, the mollusc hardly reacts to a stimulus which is neither harmful nor beneficial because the excitation of presynaptic neurons (again, sensory) is not transmitted to postsynaptic neurons (again, motor). Kandel's experiments show that even such a simple organism as the Aplysia Californica has the ability to recognize the biological significance of stimuli which excite it.

---

[56] The terms 'presynaptic' and 'postsynaptic neurons' refer to the relationship between any neurons which link up with each other. Any neuron can be presynaptic. Postsynaptic neurons are those neurons whose dendrites and/or cell body link up with the axon terminals of one or more presynaptic neurons. In fig 2 (p.175), for example, neuron n-1 is presynaptic to neurons n-2a and n-2b which are postsynaptic to n-1: neuron n-2a is presynaptic to neurons n-3a and n-3c which are postsynaptic to n-2a, while n-2b is presynaptic to n-3b and n-3d which are postsynaptic to n-2b, and so on.

[57] Eric Kandel, "Small Systems of Neurons", Scientific American, 'The Brain', Sept. 1979.

With what mechanism do the sensory neurons of the Aplysia Californica recognize the biological significance of stimuli which excite it?

§ 87   The role played by the intensity of a stimulus in the transmission of neuronal excitation may be seen in the following example. When the syllable μο and νο are uttered in an audible voice, they constitute acoustic stimuli. If these acoustic stimuli are repeated frequently at equal intervals and with the same intensity, they will combine in the following way: ...μο-νο-μο-νο-μο-νο-μο-νο-μο-νο-μο-νο-μο-νο-μο-νο-μο ... As a result, the nervous system will be unable to distinguish which of the following four words excited it: μό-νο, μο-νό, νό-μο or νο-μό.[58] The distinction will depend on there being a pause following a single combination of the stimuli μο and νο, on the chronological order of the combined stimuli and on the intensity of the stimuli.

If the stimulus μο is followed by the stimulus νο and then there is a pause, the combination will give the word μο-νο, but which of the two words will it be, μό-νο or μο-νό? For the nervous system to distinguish between these two words, one of the two stimuli must be stressed, that is, it must be of greater intensity.

What is the result when the intensity of a stimulus exciting a neuron increases? The answer is given by H. K. Hartline's experimental findings[59] (fig. 1). These show that when the intensity of a stimulus increases, the number of impulses which a neuron presents in a unit of time also increases. In my view, this process in turn increases the quantity of a neurotransmitter secreted into the synapses of the excited neuron and results in the transmission of the excitation to a greater number

---

[58] Translator's note: The Greek words μόνο, μονό, νόμο and νομό have been retained in the English text. μόνο, with the stress on the first syllable as shown by the accent, means 'alone'. μονό, with the stress on the second syllable as shown by the accent, means 'odd' as in 'odd and even numbers', or 'single' as opposed to 'double'. νόμο with the stress on the first syllable means 'law' while νομό with the stress on the second syllable means 'prefecture' or 'county'.

Each of these words has a peculiarity that does not exist in English, namely that by interchanging the consonants (μ and ν) of the first and second syllables (μο and νο) as well as the emphasis (from the first to the second syllable and vice versa) - the vowel of each syllable being a constant 'o' - three more words are produced.

[59] H. K. Hartline, "Intensity and Duration in the Excitation of Single Photoreceptor Units", J. Cell. Comp. Physiol. 5, 229, 1934.

of postsynaptic neurons. The threshold of different qualities of neurons varies (§ 88): the higher the threshold of a neuron, the larger the quantity of neurotransmitter needed to excite it. Thus, the greater the intensity of a stimulus exciting a presynaptic neuron, the greater the number and the more qualities of postsynaptic neurons which are excited (see figures 2, 3, 4, 5, and 6).

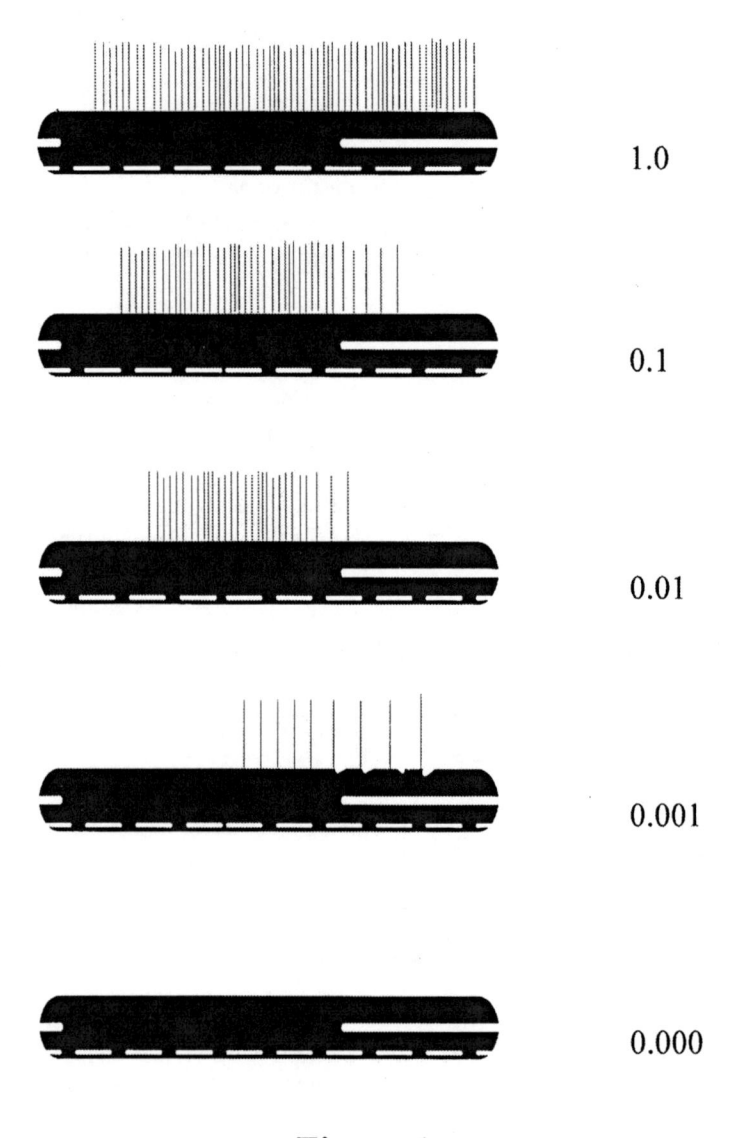

1.0

0.1

0.01

0.001

0.000

Figure 1

The Knowledge of the Womb

Figure 1 Impulses set up in optic nerve fibre of *Limulus* by one second flash of light with relative intensities shown at right. The lower white line marks 0.2 second intervals and the gap in the upper white line gives the period for which the eye was illuminated. (From Hartline, 1934.)

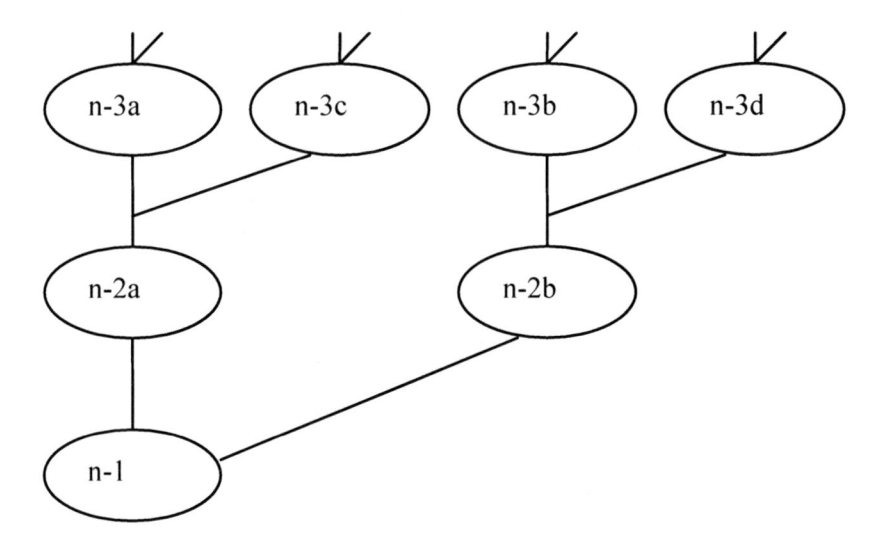

Figure 2 For simplicity's sake, a peripheral sensory neuron, n-1, is presented as linking up with only two neurons, n-2a and n-2b, each of

Athanassios Kafkalides MD

different quality to the other. Each one of the latter (again for simplicity) links up with only two neurons - n-3a and n-3c; n-3b and n-3d - each of different quality to the other.

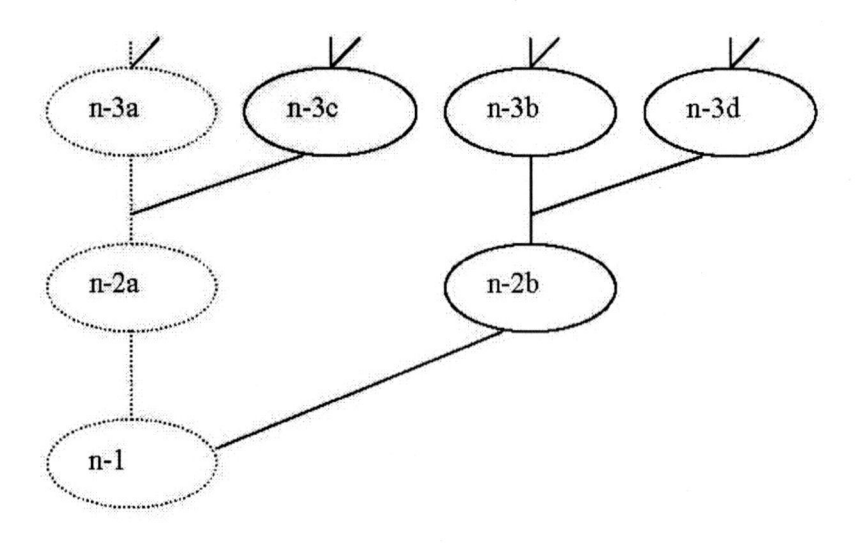

Figure 3

Figure 3 shows the specific neuronal path or circuit along which the excitation from neuron n-1 is transmitted when n-1 has been excited by a stimulus 's' whose intensity is one degree. The transmission of the excitation from n-1 to n-2a and then to n-3a produces a specific result. The neurons which are excited are marked in dotted lines.

The Knowledge of the Womb

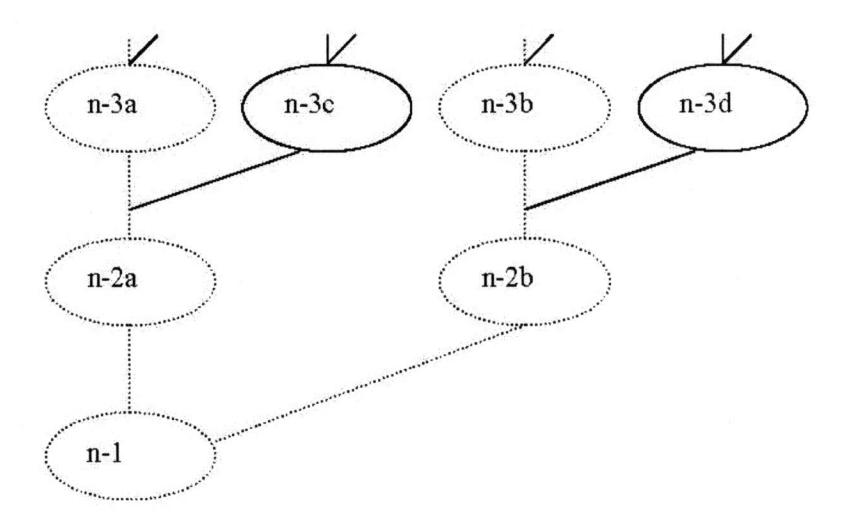

Figure 4

Figure 4 shows the specific path-circuit along which the excitation from neuron n-1 is transmitted when n-1 has been excited by the same stimulus 's' (ie. its quality remains constant) whose intensity is now double, that is, two degrees. The transmission of the excitation from n-1 to n-2a, n-2b, n-3a and n-3b produces a specific result which is different to that of figure 3. The neurons which are excited are marked in dotted lines.

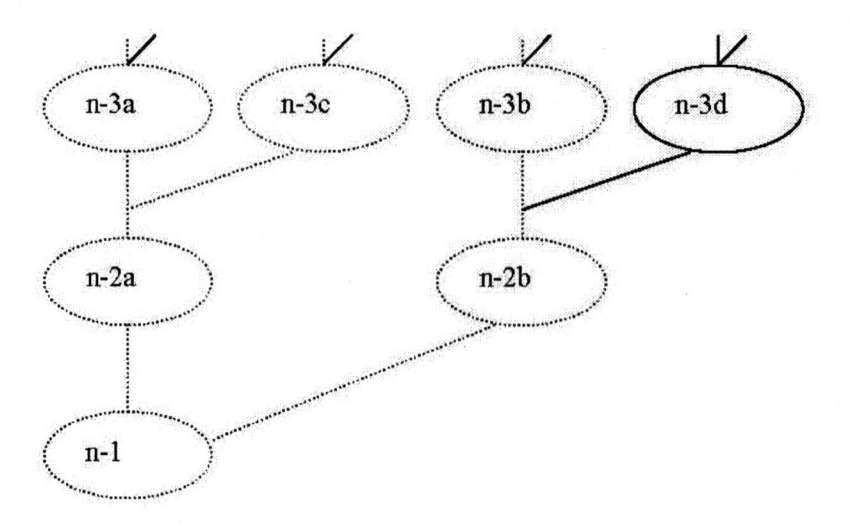

Figure 5

Figure 5 shows the specific path-circuit along which the excitation from neuron n-1 is transmitted when n-1 has been excited by the same stimulus 's' whose intensity has now tripled, that is, to three degrees. The transmission of the excitation to n-2a, n-2b, n-3a, n-3c and n-3b produces a specific result which is different to that of figures 3 and 4. The neurons which are excited are marked in dotted lines.

The Knowledge of the Womb

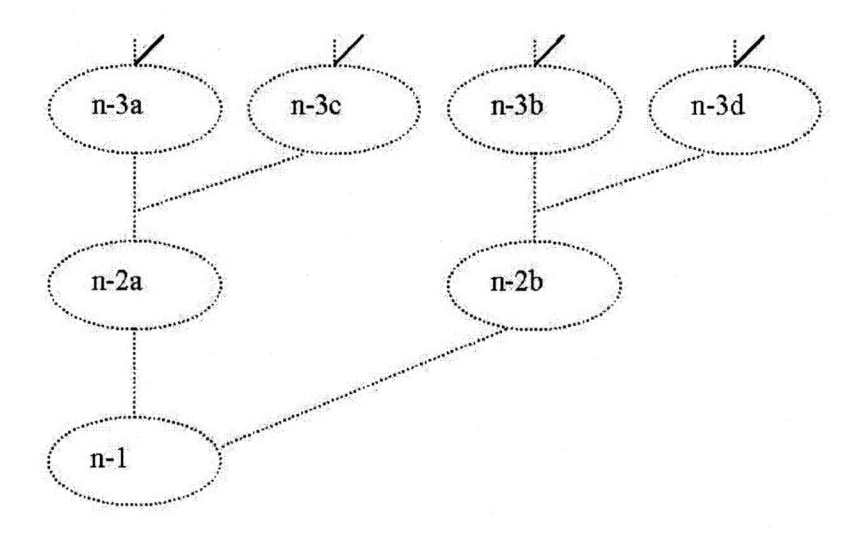

Figure 6

Figure 6 shows the specific path-circuit along which the excitation from neuron n-1 is transmitted when n-1 has been excited by the same stimulus 's' whose intensity has now quadrupled, that is, to four degrees. The transmission of the excitation to n-2a, n-2b, n-3a n-3c, n-3b and n-3d produces a specific result which is different to that of figures 3, 4 and 5. The neurons which are excited are marked in dotted lines.

If figures 3 - 6 we can see that when neuron n-1 is excited by a stimulus constant in quality but different in intensity, the excitation follows four different and specific neuronal paths or circuits through the nervous system. Of course, the specific result of each path-circuit will be different, depending on the quality of the neurons which are excited at the various levels of the nervous system: the spinal cord, cerebral stem, diencephalon, limbic system and the cortex of the cerebral hemispheres (see § 89 for more details).

The result of combinations of stimuli, such as μο and νο, will also depend, as we have said, on their chronological order.

In figure 7, for simplicity's sake:
(a) Neuron μο-1 symbolizes all the specific peripheral acoustic neurons which are excited by the acoustic stimulus μο.
(b) Neuron νο-1 symbolizes all the specific peripheral acoustic neurons which are excited by the acoustic stimulus νο.

Athanassios Kafkalides MD

(c) Neurons μo-1, μo-2a, μo-2b, vo-1, vo-2a and vo-2b are each presented as joining up with only two postsynaptic neurons. (In reality every neuron links up with a multitude of postsynaptic neurons of different quality.)

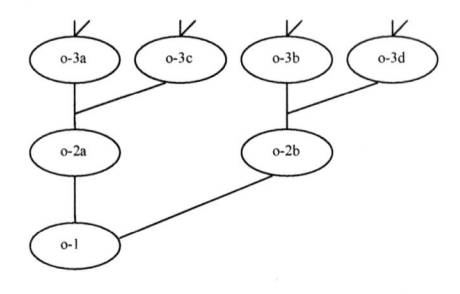

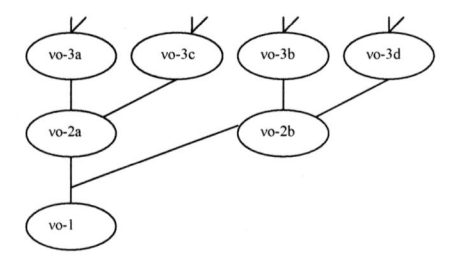

The Knowledge of the Womb

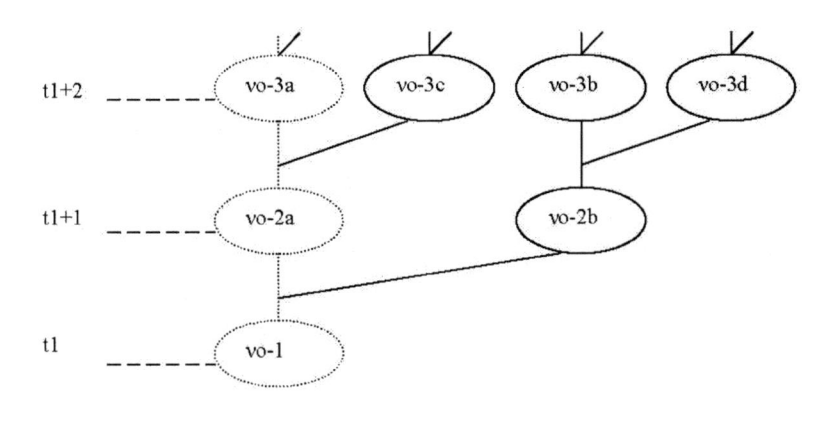

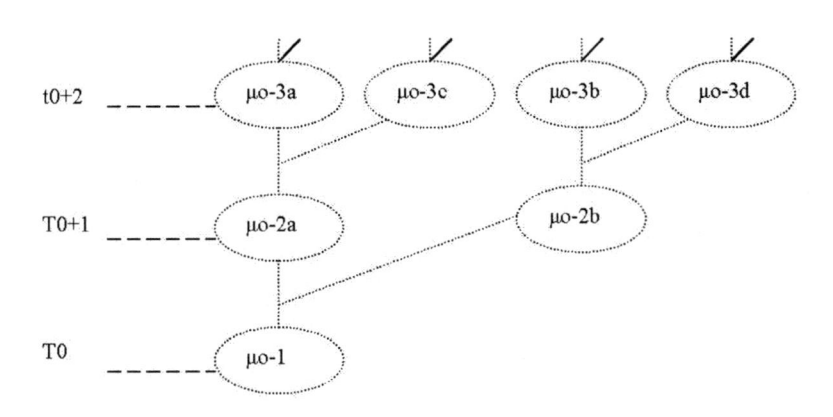

Figure 8

Figure 8 This shows the specific neuronal path or circuit along which the excitation from neurons μο-1 and vo-1 is transmitted when μο-1 and vo-1 have been excited by the acoustic stimuli μό and vo, in that order. The result is the acoustic impression μόvo. The neurons which are excited are marked in dotted lines. Because the stimulus μό precedes the stimulus vo, it excites neuron μο-1 before the stimulus vo excites vo-1, as shown in the figure ('t' stands for time). Because the stimulus μό is stressed, its intensity is greater than that of vo: thus the excitation from μο-1 is transmitted to neurons μο-2a, μο-2b, μο-3a, μο-3c, μο-3b and μο-3d. Because the stimulus vo is unstressed, its intensity is less than that of

211

μο and thus the excitation from vo-1 is transmitted only to neurons vo-2a and vo-3a.

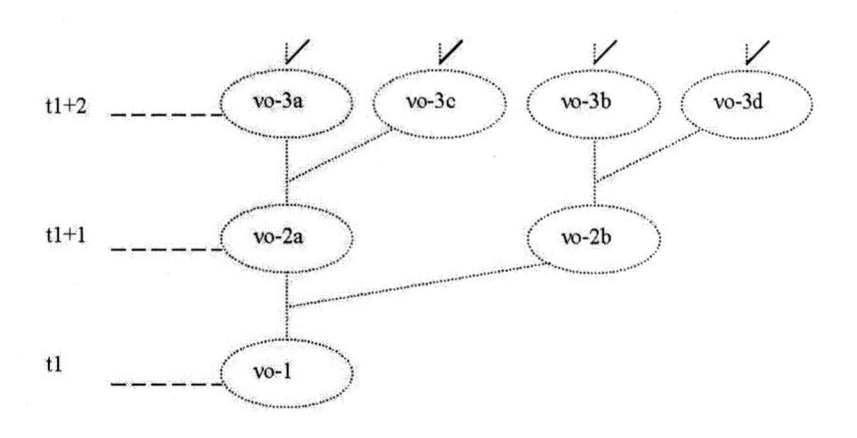

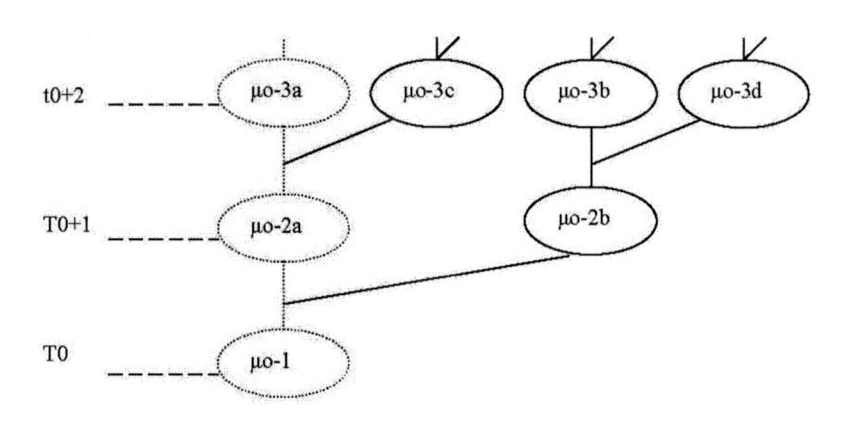

Figure 9

Figure 9 This shows the specific path-circuit along which the excitation from neurons μο-1 and vo-1 is transmitted when these neurons have been excited by the acoustic stimuli μο and vó, in that order. The result is the acoustic impression μονó. The neurons which are excited are marked in dotted lines. Because the acoustic stimulus μο precedes the acoustic stimulus vó, it excites neuron μο-1 before the stimulus vó excites vo-1, as shown in the figure. Because the stimulus μο is unstressed, its intensity is less than that of vó and thus the excitation from μο-1 is transmitted only to neurons μο-2a and μο-3a. Because the stimulus vó is stressed, its intensity is greater than that of μο: thus the excitation from vo-1 is transmitted to vo-2a, vo-2b, vo-3a, vo-3c, vo-3b and vo-3d.

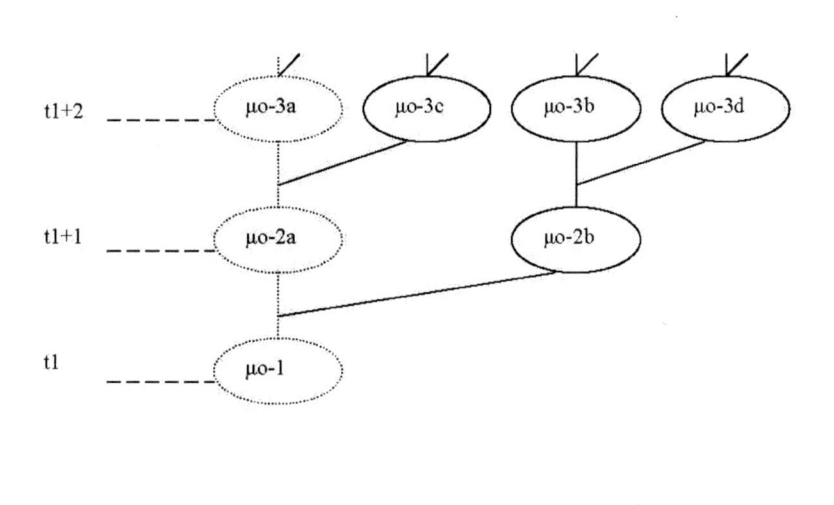

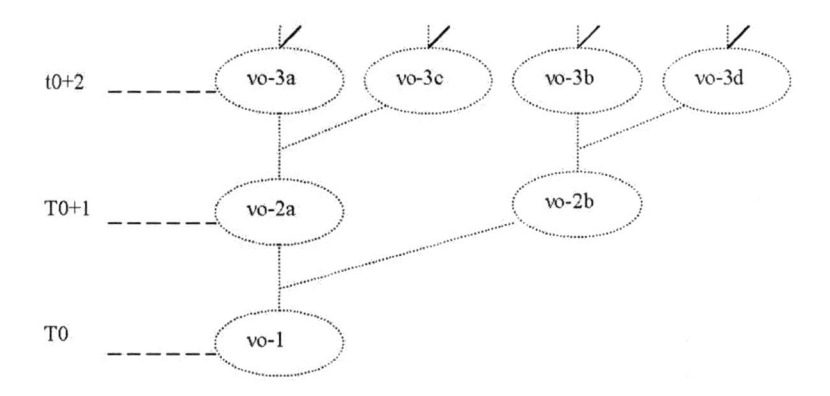

Figure 10

Figure 10 This shows the specific path-circuit along which the excitation from neurons vo-1 and μο-1 is transmitted when these neurons have been excited by the acoustic stimuli vó and μο, in that order. The result is the acoustic impression vóμο. The neurons which are excited are marked in dotted lines. Because the acoustic stimulus vó precedes the acoustic stimulus μο, it excites neuron vo-1 before the stimulus excites μο-1, as shown in the figure. Because the stimulus vó is stressed, its intensity is greater than that of μο: thus the excitation from vo-1 is transmitted

Athanassios Kafkalides MD

to neurons vo-2a, vo-2b, vo-3a, vo-3c, vo-3b and vo-3d. Because of the stimulus μο is unstressed, its intensity is less than that of vó and thus the excitation from μο-1 is transmitted only to neurons μο-2a and μο-3a.

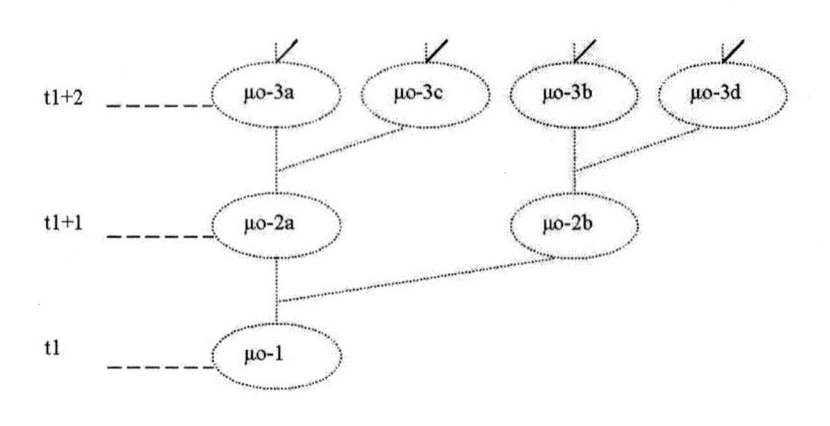

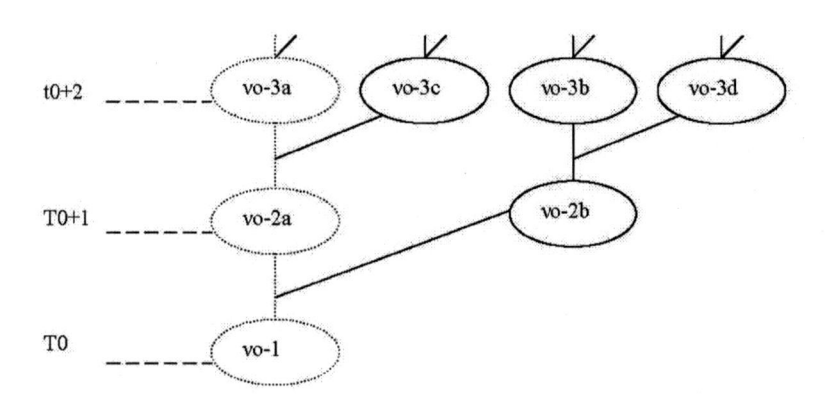

Figure 11

Figure 11 This shows the specific path-circuit along which the excitation from neurons vo-1 and μο-1 is transmitted when these neurons have been excited by the acoustic stimuli vo and μó, in that order. The result is the acoustic impression voμó. The neurons which are excited are marked in dotted lines. Because the acoustic stimulus vo precedes the acoustic stimulus μó, it excites the neuron vo-1 before the stimulus μο excites μο-1, as shown in the figure. Because the stimulus vo is unstressed, its intensity is less than that of μό and thus the excitation from vo-1 is transmitted only to neurons vo-2a and vo-3a. Because the stimulus μό is stressed, its intensity is greater than that of vo: thus the excitation from μo-1 is transmitted to neurons μo-2a, μo-2b, μo-3a, μo-3c, μo-3b and μo-3d.

In figures 8 - 11, we can see that the excitation of neurons μo-1 and vo-1 by the acoustic stimuli μo and vo follows four different neuronal path-circuits and produces four different results or acoustic impressions according to the intensity of the stimuli and the chronological order in which they excite μo-1 and vo-1.

Note: Of basic importance to the functioning of the nervous system is the ability of a neuron to participate in many neuronal circuits, e.g. in figures 8, 9, 10 and 11, neuron μo-2a participates in four different circuits with a different result in each case.

§ 88 A most basic factor which influences the quality and intensity of a nervous system's reaction at a given moment is the threshold of its neurons at that same moment. One factor which regulates the threshold of neurons is their metabolism. For example, a dog which has just satiated its hunger does not present the same degree of salivation at the sight of food as it would if it were hungry. (This observation shows that experimental research into the process of neuronal excitation should be carried out concurrently with research into the process of metabolism occurring at the same moment as the excitation.)

The threshold of neurons also depends on their quality. For example, pyramidal motor neurons have a different threshold to that of spinal motor neurons.

§ 89 The role played by the quality of the neurons which participate in a path-circuit of neuronal excitation can be seen in the following:
(a) Through sensorial neurons the excitation results in sensorial symptoms of sight, hearing, touch, kinaesthesia and so on.
(b) Through motor neurons (pyramidal cells and motor neurons of the anterior horns of the spinal cord) the excitation results in the contraction of striated muscles.
(c) Through neurovegetative neurons it results in neurovegetative S & P.
(d) Through neurons of the limbic system it results in emotional symptoms of fear, anger and so forth.
(e) Through neurons of the frontal poles it results in the symptom of streams of thought.

(f) Through the existential neurons the excitation results in the symptom of consciousness of existential identity.

Note: The clinical data of Petit Mal fits, postconcussional and postepileptic automatism, sleep, fainting attacks and other states support the view that R's nervous system contains a special and highly complex neuronal circuit whose excitation gives rise to the symptom of consciousness of existential identity. For the sake of brevity, the special circuit is called 'existential neurons'. When R's existential neurons are inhibited, so too is the symptom of consciousness of existential identity: in other words, R ceases to exist for himself. (Dreams support the viewpoint that the existential neurons may be excited during sleep.)

§ 90 Recapitulation of § 86 - 89: The excitation of a neuron 'n' by a stimulus 's' at a given moment is transmitted successively to a series of neurons of the same and different quality. The end result of this entire process depends on:
(a) The quality and intensity of 's'.
(b) The quality of 'n'.
(c) The threshold - at the same moment - of the neurons which connect directly or indirectly with 'n'.
(d) The quality of the series of neurons to which the excitation of 'n' is transmitted.
(e) When many neurons are excited by different stimuli the end result also depends on the chronological order of their excitation (figs. 8 - 11).

CHAPTER THREE

A FEW NOTES ON STIMULI

R's 'Activation' by Stimuli
Outline of R's 'Activation' by Stimuli
Internal Factors
External Factors
Conclusions

§ 91   *A stimulus* is any form of energy (biochemical, chemical, mechanical, electromagnetic and so on) which is produced in R's internal or external environment and acts upon him.

Internal environment[60] is the sum total of cells and liquids which constitute a living system (and therefore R's body). *Internal stimuli for R* are the stimuli which are produced in his internal environment.

R's external environment is whatever surrounds his internal environment. *External stimuli for R* are the stimuli which are produced in his external environment and act upon him.

§ 92   During intra-uterine life, the foetus' external environment is the womb. During expulsion-birth the external environment for the foetus/new-born is his natural mother's genital canal. Immediately after birth it is the infinite chaos of the universe.

Note: The various conditions of the external environment consist of the sum of stimuli of sundry quality and intensity. These combined stimuli have a certain symbolism for the internal environment and constitute messages for it.[61] For example, the conditions of expulsion-birth are composed of the sum of mechanical, acoustic, optic and other stimuli which excite the foetus/new-born's nervous system. The foetus/new-born's existential identity feels these combined stimuli as messages from the external environment.

---

[60]   Claude Bernard's term. See Ernest Renan, "L'Oeuvre de Claude Bernard", Paris, 1881.
[61]   It is for this reason that the terms 'conditions-stimuli' and 'messages-stimuli' are used in the text.

§ 93   The external stimuli which excite the neurons usually leave their 'memory traces' in neuronal elements. These 'memory traces' may be reactivated either through a recurrence of the stimuli which produced them or by various other internal or external stimuli. When this happens, the experience produced by the original stimuli is revived because the whole process of the original neuronal excitation is repeated.

Example: The 'memory traces' left within the neurons by the conditions-stimuli of expulsion-birth may be reactivated (by psychedelic drugs, for instance) and result in the revival of expulsion-birth.

§ 94   There are numerous kinds of internal stimuli. Some of these are:
(a) The biological needs - direct and indirect - which 'activate' R in his everyday life. The direct biological need is an internal force which motivates R to preserve the homogeneity, cohesion and integrity of his individual material being for as long as possible. The indirect biological needs are those needs which spring from the direct biological need. These are R's self-perpetuation through sexual activity, food intake and so on.
(b) Metabolites, that is, various chemical substances which are produced during cell metabolism.
(c) Emotions, thoughts and so forth.
(d) Various biochemicophysical substances-factors, such as neurotransmitters and neuro-hormones, which are produced in the internal environment.

Note: The 'memory traces' of stimuli which are preserved within the neurons are potential internal stimuli.

An internal stimulus may excite directly any central or peripheral neuron. For example, in figure 2 (p.175) an internal stimulus may excite neuron n-2a, which is central, without having previously excited the presynaptic neuron n-1 (see note § 101).

Conclusion: An internal environment may be 'activated' at a given moment solely by internal stimuli. Hallucinations, for example, result from the excitation of neurons by internal stimuli.

R'S ACTIVATION BY STIMULI

§ 95   When a stimulus excites R's nervous system, it disturbs the equilibrium of his internal environment. As a result, the internal environment is 'activated' to restore its equilibrium through a series of excitations which are transmitted from receptors-sensory neurons to motor neurons and finally to effectors.[62] The movements of effectors, which occur when the latter are excited, are always related to the stimulus in some way.

'Activation', then, is the process which takes place within the internal environment from the moment its equilibrium is disturbed by a stimulus until equilibrium is 'restored' through the excitation of effectors. The process of 'activation' is characterized, among other things, by (a) the endeavour to recognize the biological significance of stimuli which excite the nervous system and (b) symptoms and phenomena.

§ 96 *Biological significance of stimuli* Every stimulus which acts upon R has, unconsciously and sometimes also consciously, a certain biological significance for his existential identity/self-preservation.

Of the various stimuli which act upon R, some favour his existential identity/self-preservation while others oppose it. Unconsciously, and sometimes also consciously, R considers the former accepting stimuli and the latter rejecting stimuli.

A rejecting stimulus, then, is any stimulus which is dangerous for R's existential identity/self-preservation and which prevents him from satisfying his biological needs. Every rejecting stimulus causes unconscious and sometimes also conscious fear, whether it be specific fear, anxiety or primitive terror.

An accepting stimulus is any stimulus which is beneficial for R's existential identity/self-preservation and which satisfies his biological needs. The accepting stimulus gives rise to a feeling of security-reconciliation (see § 47).

If a stimulus is neither rejecting nor accepting, then it lacks biological significance. Consequently, the excitation it produces is usually restricted to the peripheral sensory neurons.

Note: The intensity of a rejecting or accepting stimulus depends on internal and external factors (§ 104 - 108).

§ 97 A nervous system's 'activation' by stimuli results, among other things, in:
(a) *Various symptoms* A symptom is a subjective state experienced by a specific nervous system. It accompanies the excitation of sensory neurons of that nervous system. The quality of symptoms depends on the quality of the sensory neurons which are excited, for example:

---

[62] Effectors are striated and non-striated muscular fibres.

(i) Sensorial symptoms - optic, acoustic, olfactory, gustatory, tactile, kinaesthetic, thermal and so on - accompany the excitation of the various sensorial neurons.
(ii) Emotional symptoms - such as fear and anger - accompany the excitation of the various neurons of the limbic system.
(iii) Intellectual symptoms - such as streams of thought - accompany the excitation of neurons of the cerebral cortex and in particular the cortex of the frontal poles.
(iv) They symptoms of consciousness of existential identity accompanies the excitation of the existential neurons (see § 89). Symptoms are either unconscious, conscious or both; for example, fear is unconscious but sometimes it also reaches consciousness.
(b) *Various phenomena*   Phenomena are the movements which effectors make. In other words, they are the contraction and dilatations of striated and non-striated muscular fibres which occur when the latter receive excitations from motor neurons (see § 99).

§ 98   *Motor neurons*   These terminate at the effectors. Two types of motor neurons are distinguished:
(a) Neurovegetative motor neurons; these excite the non-striated muscles of internal organs and glands (intestines, larynx, salivary glands etc.) causing the internal organs to contract and dilate and the glands to secrete their products.
(b) Motor neurons which excite the striated muscles. These are called pyramidal neurons and motor neurons of the anterior horns of the spinal cord. The movements (contractions-dilatations) of the striated muscles result in R's movements within the space of his external environment - blinking, walking and so on.
Note: The cardiac muscle consists of a special quality of striated muscular fibres.
When R's effectors are excited the result is called a phenomenon because it may be perceived by an observer. A phenomenon may excite kinaesthetic neurons and produce the symptom of kinaesthesia.

§ 99   *Behaviour*   R's behaviour consists of such phenomena as gestures, facial expressions, manners of speech, of walking and of dressing, digesting, blushing and so on.
The word 'behaviour' is used in this book in a very broad sense to cover the movements of any effector or effectors since all effectors consist of muscular fibres which contract and dilate.

The Knowledge of the Womb

Note: Although effectors react in a stereotyped manner when excited, various qualities of sensory neurons use the same effectors to serve their purpose. Examples: Limbic and other neurons excite the same neurovegetative motor neurons and effectors to shed tears of sadness and tears of happiness. Limbic and other neurons use the same effectors of the lower limbs to approach an anger-producing stimulus and to withdraw from a fear-producing stimulus.

Conclusion: Effectors are literally organs which effect or carry out the directions of the sensory neurons. Thus, *it is the emotional-intellectual motives of behaviour and not behaviour itself which is of supreme importance.*

§ 100   In contrast to the foetal sensory neurons, the foetal motor neurons hypofunction. Thus, when foetal limbic neurons are excited by rejecting womb stimuli and this excitation is transmitted to motor neurons, the latter react very little or not at all. Consequently, the excitation is 'stored' within the neurons. The Sessions show that this 'stored excitation' constitutes a permanent source of potential internal stimuli which, when reactivated, result in extremely strong 'activation' (see R10 p.41).

OUTLINE OF R'S 'ACTIVATION' BY STIMULI

§ 101   Internal or external stimulus → Excitation of various sensory neurons = disturbance of internal environment's equilibrium → Co-ordination of sensory neurons which have been excited → Transmission of excitation to specific motor neurons and effectors → 'Most appropriate' movement of effectors = 'most appropriate' behaviour in order to equilibrate original internal or external stimulus and to restore internal environment's equilibrium.

In accordance with the above outline, the specific sensory neurons which are excited at a given moment co-ordinate and function as R's 'organ of direction' for that same moment only.

Note: Internal stimuli may excite (a) effectors, without having previously excited motor neurons or (b) motor neurons, without having previously excited sensory neurons (the excitation of the motor neurons is subsequently transmitted to effectors) or (c) sensory neurons or receptors (the excitation is subsequently transmitted to motor neurons and then to effectors).

§ 102   When an indirect biological need (internal stimulus) disturbs the equilibrium of R's internal environment, the stimulus is equilibrated through the 'most appropriate' behaviour, that is, (a) discovering the 'most appropriate' point in the environment where the biological need can be satisfied, (b) turning the forehead facing the 'most appropriate' point, (c) keeping the forehead facing the 'most appropriate' point, (d) moving towards the 'most appropriate' point, (e) satisfying the need at the 'most appropriate' point.

To satisfy an indirect need by completing the process of the 'most appropriate' behaviour requires a certain amount of time. During this time stimuli which are dangerous for R's existential identity/self-preservation may occur. In such a case, the motive for behaviour - the indirect need or internal stimulus - is instantly replaced by existential identity/self-preservation's direct need (different internal stimulus). The attempt to satisfy the indirect need is interrupted and R's internal environment is motivated to satisfy the direct biological need.

Example: R is in the jungle. While approaching a spring to quench his thirst, he perceives a lion lurking nearby. R instantly flees.

§ 103 R's 'activation' by rejecting stimuli - outlines

(a) Rejecting stimulus → Very strong excitation of sensorial neurons at level of spinal cord or cerebral stem → Direct (monosynaptic) transmission of excitation to specific motor neurons and effectors → 'Most appropriate' behaviour.

Example: R is smoking. Suddenly, through carelessness, the lighted cigarette brushes against one of his fingers. Instantly certain striated muscles contract and the finger withdraws from the cigarette, the latter being a rejecting stimulus for R's finger and by extension for his existential identity/self-preservation.

Note: In this example the sensorial neurons of the V, VI, VII and VIII cervical myelotomes functioned as the 'organ of direction'.

(b) Rejecting stimulus → Simultaneous excitation of many different qualities of sensory neurons → Excitation of one kind of limbic neurons predominates → Transmission of excitation to specific motor neurons and effectors → 'Most appropriate' behaviour.

Example (i) R is quarrelling with X. The latter says to R: 'You're an idiot!' R immediately punches X.

Note: 'You're an idiot' was a rejecting stimulus for R's existential identity/self-preservation which excited specific neurons of the limbic system and caused anger. These limbic neurons functioned as R's 'organ of direction' and 'activated' his effectors to aggressive behaviour.

Example (ii) Immediately following R's attack, X counter-attacks with stronger blows, putting R to flight.

The Knowledge of the Womb

Note: The stronger blows acted as mechanical stimuli which threatened to reject R's existential identity/self-preservation. These rejecting stimuli strongly excited specific limbic neurons and caused fear. The limbic neurons functioned as R's 'organ of direction', 'activating' his effectors to flight.

Example (iii) R is swimming in the sea. Suddenly a huge shark attacks him. R panics or freezes.

Note: The shark, a rejecting stimulus for R's existential identity/self-preservation, violently excited specific limbic neurons and reactivated primitive terror. These limbic neurons functioned as R's 'organ of direction', 'activating' his effectors to panicky behaviour or paralysis.

(c) Rejecting stimulus → Simultaneous excitation of many different qualities of sensory neurons → Excitation of cortical neurons of frontal poles predominates → Transmission of excitation to specific motor neurons and effectors → 'Most appropriate' behaviour.

Example: A young Roman, brought before Hannibal, thrust his hand into fire and removed it only when it had been completely burnt. The young man's aim was to convince Hannibal of the Romans' bravery and the futility of his attacking besieged Rome.

Note: Hannibal constituted a rejecting stimulus for the young Roman's existential identity/self-preservation which intensely excited his cortical neurons. These neurons functioned as the Roman's 'organ of direction', 'activating' his effectors to the 'most appropriate' behaviour.

(d) Rejecting stimulus → Simultaneous excitation of many different qualities of sensory neurons → No predominant excitation of any kind of sensory neurons → Transmission of contradictory excitations to motor neurons and effectors → Indecisive behaviour.

Example: Any dilemma leads to indecisive behaviour.

§ 104   What has been said in this chapter so far raises the following two questions:

Question 1: If a stimulus 's' of specific quality and intensity excites R's nervous system at two different moments after expulsion-birth, will the results in both cases be identical both in quality and intensity?

Question 2: If an external stimulus 's' of specific quality and intensity excites the nervous system of each R simultaneously, will the results be identical both in quality and intensity?

Answer to Question 1: If the conditions of R's internal environment are absolutely identical at both given moments, then the stimulus 's' will produce identical results in both cases. (Theoretically, identical conditions of this kind do not exist since by the second moment the living system is older.)

Answer to Question 2: This may be given only after we have studied the internal and external factors regulating the quality and intensity of 'activation' of each R's nervous system.

INTERNAL FACTORS

§ 105 Internal factors are individual factors which characterize a specific internal environment, predisposing it to react to stimuli in a manner which is absolutely peculiar to it. The most basic internal factors are individual heredity and individual constitution.
(a) *Individual heredity* Through heredity are transmitted to the cells of a specific R's body:
   (i) The 'memory traces' of the general manner in which living cells are 'activated' by stimuli.
   (ii) The 'memory traces' of the particular way in which the cells of the human species are 'activated' by stimuli.
   (iii) The 'memory traces' of the individual way one or more of R's ancestors was 'activated' by stimuli.
(b) *Individual constitution* Among the factors which comprise a specific R's individual constitution is the unique manner in which all his cells (and in particular, those of his nervous system) are 'activated' by stimuli. Individual constitution is moulded, among other things, by:
   (i) The 'memory traces' of stimuli inherited by R's nerve cells (neurons) from homogeneous nerve cells of one or more ancestors.
   (ii) The 'memory traces' of stimuli which had excited R's nervous system during his foetal life and expulsion-birth and which were implanted and preserved in neuronal elements of his nervous system.

As mentioned earlier, it is possible that the presence or absence of unknown biochemicophysical factors influences the degree to which the 'memory traces' of womb messages-stimuli are implanted in foetal neurons. Thus, sometimes the 'memory traces' are implanted more strongly, other times less strongly. The stronger the 'memory traces', the more easily they are reactivated by stimuli which excite the nervous system after expulsion-birth.

EXTERNAL FACTORS

§ 106 External factors are the various external stimuli which excite a specific R's nervous system. They engender in R an internal subjective state (individual experiences) which is absolutely peculiar to him.

Note: The quality and intensity of external stimuli fluctuate at different moments.

§ 107 The threshold of a nervous system's neurons fluctuates at various moments (§ 88). Thus, identical external stimuli which occur at different moments do not 'activate' the nervous system in the same way.

CONCLUSIONS

§ 108 Each R is 'activated by stimuli in a manner unique to him which, however, fluctuates at different moments. In other words:
(a) The S & P of R's 'activation' by identical stimuli fluctuate in quality and intensity at different moments. Example: R5's behaviour towards his father was at times aggressive and at times reconciliatory.
(b) The S & P of 'activation' by identical stimuli vary from R to R in quality and intensity. Example: The appearance of a dog caused R8 joy, R14 fear and R12 indifference.

CHAPTER FOUR

DEFINITION, CLINICAL PICTURES AND METHODOLOGY OF CLASSIFYING MENTAL DISTURBANCES OF THE 16 (TABLE 1)

Symptoms and Phenomena of Mental Disturbances - Clinical Pictures Classification according to Tuke

§ 109　A mental disturbance is any disturbance of the psychic functions. Psychic functions are emotions, thoughts, memory, imagination, existential identity, sex identity, καλόν κάγαθόν (kalon kagathon) in the ancient Greek sense, motives of behaviour and so on.

§ 110　The bioneurophysiological mechanism of psychic functions is unknown: also, the bioneurophysiological mechanism involved in the development of mental disturbance is unknown. The causes of mental disturbance itself are as a rule unknown. Thus the question arises: with what criteria will an R of Table 1 be considered mentally healthy or unhealthy at a given moment (bearing in mind that no R suffers from organic lesions or toxic or functional disturbances of any system)?

Careful study of how R is 'activated' by various stimuli reveals that when rejecting stimuli excite his nervous system, they endanger his existential identity/self-preservation causing him unconscious and sometimes also conscious fear. As a result, R is 'activated' at all levels (emotional, intellectual, motor, etc.) to equilibrate the rejecting stimuli.

Regardless of its quality or intensity, the entire process of R's 'activation' by rejecting stimuli is considered a mental disturbance. Or, more simply, *when R's nervous system is excited by rejecting stimuli, the result is mental disturbance.*

The Knowledge of the Womb

Whether stimuli acting on R are rejecting or not is for R's nervous system to judge. An observer of R's behaviour is in no position to make such a judgment.

A mental disturbance lasts as long as the nervous system is being excited by rejecting stimuli. When these stimuli stop acting on the nervous system, mental disturbance ceases. As well, if the rejecting stimuli lose their rejecting nature and/or symbolism, then they no longer cause mental disturbance.

§ 111   One can remark that a person who presents mental disturbance may or may not be aware of it. If he is aware of his mental disturbance, he may conceal it from the environment and try to equilibrate it alone. On the other hand, he may seek help from his environment because he feels he cannot equilibrate his mental disturbance alone, or because he believes that he may gain something through his mental disturbance, or both. If a person is unaware of his mental disturbance, his behaviour may be troublesome for the environment. If so, the latter intervenes and, if it wishes, confines the person to a 'special place'. If not, the environment does not intervene.

From the above, then, mental disturbance may be troublesome (a) only for the person who presents it, (b) only for the person's environment, (c) both for the person who presents it and for his environment. It may be, however, that mental disturbance is troublesome neither for the person nor for his environment: in this case one could say that there is no psychiatric problem. The other three cases, however, are the direct concern of neuropsychiatry and no one can deny that the latter is a branch of medicine (despite the opinions propounded by the Anti-Psychiatry Movement).

The 16 cases of Table 1 are aware that they present mental disturbance which is troublesome both for themselves and their environment. At first they tried to equilibrate the S & P of their mental disturbance alone. Finally, however, they sought neuropsychiatric help.

SYMPTOMS AND PHENOMENA OF MENTAL DISTURBANCE - CLINICAL PICTURES

§ 112   Mental disturbance is characterized by S & P. *Symptoms of mental disturbance* are unconscious and sometimes also conscious subjective experiences caused by rejecting stimuli which excite R's nervous system. *Phenomena of mental disturbance* are the behaviour R manifests when rejecting stimuli excite his nervous system. *A clinical picture* is the sum total of the S & P of mental disturbance at a given moment. The particular clinical picture of mental disturbance at a given moment depends on the quality and intensity of the S & P at that same moment. The clinical picture may vary from R to R. It may also vary in the same R at different moments.

§ 113 *The clinical pictures of mental disturbance are (a) nervous tension, (b) neurotic S & P, (c) psychoticlike/psychotic S & P.*[63]
Note: Mental disturbance may:
(a) Present all the clinical pictures in succession, that is, it may begin as nervous tension, develop into neurotic and then psychoticlike S & P and terminate in a psychotic state. Through the inevitable process of conditioning, any clinical picture which R once presented may be reactivated later by seemingly irrelevant stimuli.
(b) Be directly characterized by psychoticlike/psychotic S & P. The sudden death of a loved one, for example, may cause acute depressivelike S & P. As well, there are the S & P presented by autistic children.

§ 114 My efforts to classify the 16 of Table 1 from a diagnostic point of view proved to be problematic. Systematic observation and study of the 16 revealed that the S & P of their mental disturbance fluctuated periodically both in quality and intensity. More specifically, at some moment every R had presented either S & P of nervous tension or neurotic S & P (obsessional, psychosomatic, conversion hysteria and so forth). Apart from these, R1, R4, R6, R8, R9, R10 and R14 had also presented one or more of the psychoticlike clinical pictures. In short, I found it impossible to make a permanent diagnosis of any R according to the traditional classification of mental disturbances.

CLASSIFICATION ACCORDING TO TUKE

§ 115 My diagnostic difficulties were overcome thanks to H. Tuke's simplified classification ("A Dictionary of Psychological Medicine", 1892). Tuke divided mental disturbances into two large groups.

Group I - Mental disturbances accompanied by toxic or functional disturbances or organic lesions of the nervous system or any other system, as confirmed through laboratory investigation. To this group belong the organic, toxic and functional psychoses of traditional psychiatry, that is, mental disturbances of know aetiology.

---

[63] For explanation of the term 'psychoticlike/psychotic' see § 127.

Group II - Mental disturbances not accompanied by toxic or functional disturbances or organic lesions of the nervous system or any other system, as confirmed by laboratory investigation.[64] Tuke calls these mental disturbances 'Diseases of the Generative System'. To this group belong the neuroses and psychoses of traditional psychiatry.

In Tuke's group II I also place nervous tension (§ 119), a specific clinical picture of mental disturbance which is not mentioned in traditional psychiatric texts.

The 16 of Table 1 belong to group II because laboratory investigation revealed no organic lesion, no functional or toxic disturbance of their nervous system or any other system.

§ 116 No matter what the quality or intensity of their S & P, the 16 of Table 1 are classified as Rejected. This is because the roots of their mental disturbance lie in their foetal life and/or expulsion-birth when rejecting stimuli 'activated' their nervous system.

According to the quality of their intra-uterine experiences, the 16 are further classified into categories and sub-categories (§ 25 - 30).

---

[64] As our knowledge of bioneurophysiology expands, the mental disturbances of Tuke's group II will gradually move to group I.

CHAPTER FIVE

DEVELOPMENTAL MECHANISM OF MENTAL DISTURBANCE OF THE 16[65]

Nervous Tension
Anxiety
Psychoticlike/Psychotic S & P

§ 117   A neuronal process which plays a most important role in the way R's nervous system is 'activated' by stimuli is this: *Every rejecting stimulus tends to make unconscious primitive terror conscious.*

Because conscious primitive terror is an unbearable symptom, R's existential identity tries to hinder or equilibrate the process mentioned with all the means at its disposal. Among these means are the various clinical pictures of mental disturbance: nervous tension or neurotic S & P or psychoticlike/psychotic S & P.

The basic cause of the clinical pictures of mental disturbance is fear, which escalates because the quality of the rejecting stimuli causing the fear changes (see § 119, 120, 121, 127).

§ 118   The existential identity also uses other means to hinder or to equilibrate reactivation of the rejecting womb/primitive terror. Among them are:
(a) Deifying the womb, ie. R deifies the womb, endows it with the property 'whoever loves me, tortures me' and accepts suffering with pleasure (masochism, see R10 p.42).
(b) Identifying with the rejecting womb, ie. R identifies with the rejecting womb and becomes as aggressive towards his environment as the

---

[65] The aim of this chapter is not to describe the clinical pictures of mental disturbance. These are mentioned in broad outline only so that a simplified description of how mental disturbance develops may be given. The reader who is interested in detailed descriptions of the S & P of mental disturbance should consult the traditional psychiatric textbooks.

The Knowledge of the Womb

rejecting womb was towards him (instances of torturers in dictatorial systems, sadism, see R10's example of sadism p.45).
(c) Imitating a foreign existential identity, ie. in order to avoid reactivation of the rejecting womb, R abolishes his existential identity and replaces it with the existential identity of someone who impresses him. Example: After R9 had carefully studied the biography of an author, he then tried to feel, think and behave on all occasions as he supposed the author would feel, think and behave on similar occasions. For other examples of imitating foreign existential identities see R5 p.90 and R10 p.41.

NERVOUS TENSION

§ 119   If the rejecting stimuli which excite R's nervous system are specific, R is 'activated' to equilibrate the stimuli in one of the following ways which characterize nervous tension:

| Nervous tension I |

Symptoms:

Neurovegetative:	tachycardia, tachypnoea, dyspnoea, sweating and so forth.
Limbic:	unconscious and sometimes also conscious fear, unconscious and conscious anger.

Phenomena:

Behaviour-defensive attack:	overt aggressiveness which ranges from hostile silence or an almost imperceptible ironic smile to violently destructive muscular activity towards the fear-producing - anger-producing stimuli.

Note: The fiercer the attack, the greater the unconscious fear. If the anger-attack does not equilibrate the fear-producing - anger-producing stimuli, the latter give rise to:

Nervous tension II

Symptoms:

Neurovegetative: tachycardia, tachypnoea, dyspnoea, sweating and so forth.

Limbic: intense unconscious and conscious fear.

Phenomena:

Behaviour-defensive flight: overt flight-withdrawal from the fear-producing stimuli.

Note: The direct result of specific rejecting stimuli may be S & P of nervous tension II and not of nervous tension I, that is, when nervous tension II occurs, it is not necessarily preceded by nervous tension I.

Comment: Nervous tension I and II are frequently accompanied by strong guilt feelings. When R suffers from prolonged nervous tension, other S & P besides the ones already mentioned appear: nervousness-irritability, physical and mental fatigue, lack of mental concentration (R8 and R12 had to stop university and R6 and R14 high school because they could not concentrate on their studies), insomnia or somnolence, anorexia or gluttony, and so on.

ANXIETY

§ 120   If:
(a) the anger-overt attack or the fear-overt flight does not equilibrate the rejecting stimuli which caused nervous tension, or
(b) R is, for whatever reason, unable to attack or to withdraw from the rejecting stimuli, or
(c) R tries but fails to check his attack or flight, or
(d) nervous tension is accompanied by guilt feelings, then R is overcome by perplexity and indecisive behaviour. Simultaneously the following neuronal mechanism begins: the rejecting stimuli which caused R nervous tension reactivate (on an unconscious level) 'memory traces' of other rejecting stimuli which had excited his nervous system at various periods in the past. As a result, the fear involved in nervous tension expands because the 'memory traces' of fears caused by the past rejecting stimuli are also reactivated. Simultaneously, the cause

The Knowledge of the Womb

of the expanded fear becomes obscured because the 'memory traces' of the past rejecting stimuli are not reactivated on a conscious level.

If the rejecting stimuli continue to excite R's nervous system, he feels helpless. Thus, unconsciously and sometimes also consciously, he seeks protection from a 'power' which will neutralize the rejecting stimuli for him. Unconsciously, this power is the womb which is symbolized by its substitute.

If R does not obtain completely accepting womb-protection through a womb substitute, he is overcome by anxiety - a fear characterized by an agonizing, vague threat to his existence (chronic anxiety neurosis) which may periodically present sudden exacerbation (acute anxiety state).

The vagueness and agony in anxiety neurosis derive from the fact that the anxiety-producing stimuli incline towards reactivating the rejecting womb/primitive terror.

§ 121 R's unconscious and sometimes also conscious effort to equilibrate anxiety-producing stimuli results in neurotic S & P (obsessions, psychosomatic S & P, conversion hysteria, phobias and so on).

Through his neurotic S & P, R unconsciously and sometimes also consciously endeavours to create conditions of 'security' which will equilibrate the rejecting stimuli with a different kind of attack or flight.

§ 122 *Obsessional acts* are a kind of flight-withdrawal from the 'real' dangerous (rejecting) stimuli. R transfers his emotional and motor 'activation' to other stimuli which symbolize the 'real' dangerous stimuli but which are 'supposedly' less dangerous than them.

Examples:
(a) For R12, any woman was a dangerous-castrating-rejecting stimulus because she symbolized his mother. To defend himself, R12 gave up heterosexual activity. This was tantamount to fleeing from the dangerous stimulus. However, the ever-hostile environment constantly drove him, together with physical need, to seek security in sex. Thus, the only safe ways left open to him were homosexuality and masturbation.
Conclusion: R12's homosexual behaviour was obsessional and helped him avoid heterosexual activity which, to him, was far more dangerous.
(b) Another case of obsessional neurosis is a 68-year old woman, married and childless.[66] For ten months she had presented the following:

---

[66] This case is not included in Table 1, nor did she undergo autopsychognosia sessions.

every night, as soon as she began to feel sleepy, she was filled with uneasiness which motivated her in a stereotyped manner. She sat at her desk and placed a paper-knife and two ink-bottles in a certain position. She then changed the positions of the three objects until they returned to their original positions. She repeated these movements until, exhausted, she lay down and slept. If she happened to wake up during the night, she could only sleep again by repeating the same ritual until exhaustion. Attempt to hinder the stereotyped movements caused here severe anxiety.

During a 'frank' - as she characterized it - discussion, the 68-year old woman revealed that the obsessional phenomena appeared after months of unsuccessful attempts to neutralize persistent sexual desires. These desires always began as soon as she lay down to sleep and caused her guilt and anxiety. She did not dare confess them even to her husband. 'How could this respectable, aged lady have such desires? It was inadmissible.' She felt that her dignity was in danger of crumbling, that her whole existence was threatened. She was unable to give further details about how the obsessional acts began but she had noticed that they temporarily neutralized her sexual desires.

Note: It is clear that the paper-knife and two ink-bottle symbolized the male genital organs for the 68-year old woman.

Author's intellectual interpretation of the mechanism involved in the development of her obsessional behaviour: If the 68-year old woman had decided to satisfy her sexual desires, she would have had to use the male genital organs. The latter, however, were dangerous stimuli: they would reject her dignity/existential identity/self-preservation. Thus, unconsciously, she transferred her sexual activity to other stimuli - the paper-knife and two ink-bottles - which were less dangerous.

§ 123   *Obsessional ideas* result when rejecting stimuli 'activate' R's behaviour which takes place in fantasy.

Example: The obsessional idea of matricide is, in fantasy, neutralization of the stimulus which is dangerous for the existential identity/self-preservation - the mother's castrating behaviour.

§ 124   *Phobias* are excessive fear of animals, insects, spaces (closed or open), and so forth, which symbolize or are associated with rejecting stimuli and/or the rejecting womb. R4, for example, who suffered from claustrophobia, realized during Sessions that closed spaces symbolized the asphyxiating rejecting womb.

Note: Avoiding phobia-producing stimuli is like avoiding the basic rejecting stimuli.

§ 125   *Psychosomatic S & P* are a kind of introverted attack, that is, R 'activates' his motor neurons and effectors against himself. R's aim is to create conditions of 'security' which will 'protect' him from rejecting stimuli.
Example: As a child R3 would make herself vomit to send her mother into a panic and keep her by her side. The mother, symbolizing the safe womb, would protect R3 from any danger which might 'threaten' her during her mother's absence.

§ 126   *S & P of conversion hysteria* are another kind of introverted attack in order to create conditions of 'security'.
Example: The married woman who fears the consequences of her unfaithfulness 'suddenly suffers' paraplegia. This prevents her from keeping a date with a man waiting for her at a motel.

PSYCHOTICLIKE/PSYCHOTIC S & P

§ 127   The terms 'psychoticlike' and 'psychotic' S & P are used in the text as follows: In both quality and intensity psychoticlike and psychotic S & P are identical. The difference between them lies in their duration: the psychoticlike are temporary whereas the psychotic are permanent. This also applies to the terms 'depressivelike/depressive S & P', 'schizophreniclike/schizophrenic','hallucinatorylike-/hallucinatory', paranoiaclike /paranoiac'.
If neurotic S & P fail to equilibrate anxiety-producing stimuli, the latter reactivate primitive terror, i.e. R's fear reaches an intensity which is unbearable. As a result, R is 'activated' with psychoticlike S & P. *These express his unconscious endeavour to equilibrate the rejecting stimuli which are now the unconsciously reactivated 'memory traces' of the rejecting womb* and not the anxiety-producing stimuli nor the original specific fear-producing stimuli which had caused nervous tension.
The reactivated 'memory traces' of the rejecting womb may function as another existential identity within R which wages war against his existential identity/self-preservation and/or his sex identity. In other words, on a conscious level R feels as if he has two existential identities which are at war with one another and/or he feels that he is both man and woman (see R10 p.49). The reactivated 'memory traces' of the rejecting womb may also function as a superpower which 'activates' R as it wishes.

R feels that the superpower either resides within him or belongs to the external environment (see R10 p.164).

Note: The reactivated 'memory traces' of the rejecting womb in combination with the functioning of the existential neurons may take the form of multiple existential identities.

The psychoticlike symptomatology and phenomenology are based on disturbances of the existential and/or sex identity and are characterized by depressivelike or maniclike S & P and/or schizophreniclike S & P and/or hallucinatorylike S & P and/or paranoiaclike S & P.

§ 128 *Depressivelike S & P* Basic depressivelike S & P are bitter sadness, which is reflected in the face, and suicidal thoughts.

Note: All 16 cases suffer periodically from bitter sadness and suicidal thoughts but there is 'something' which sets these symptoms in R6, R10 and R14 apart from the analogous symptoms in the remaining cases. To avoid confusion, the term 'depression' is used for the symptomatology of R6, R10 and R14 and the term 'melancholia' for the symptomatology of the remaining cases.

The 'something' which sets depression apart from melancholia cannot be easily described from the point of view of quality or intensity. The distinguishing factor, however, is this: Melancholia is cause by rejecting stimuli which do not reactivate the 'memory traces' of the rejecting womb whereas depression is caused by rejecting stimuli which do reactivate the 'memory traces' of the rejecting womb on an unconscious level.

§ 129 R6, R10 and R14 realized that their depressivelike S & P resulted from disturbances in their existential identity/self-preservation and the latter's subsequent submission to the rejecting womb. The mechanism involved in this: Various rejecting stimuli excite their nervous system, reactivate the rejecting womb 'memory traces' and revive the past. In other words, just as they had felt the external environment - intra-uterine environment - rejecting their foetal existence, so in their everyday life after expulsion-birth they feel that the external environment - everyone and everything - rejects them as well. Just as they had felt weak and terrified, so now they feel helpless and overwhelmed by primitive terror. In order to escape from the primitive terror, they submit to the will of the womb, identify with it and reject their existential identity/self-preservation to the point of total death (see R10's description p.47-49). R14 attempted suicide before beginning autopsychognosia sessions and was saved only by timely medical care.

The Knowledge of the Womb

Interesting to note is the case of R13 who presented acute depression when her lover abandoned (rejected) her. She thereupon attempted to commit suicide because her rejection by the womb substitute (her lover) reactivated the primitive terror of her expulsion-birth and caused acute disturbances in her existential identity/self-preservation.

§ 130 *Maniclike S & P* These are characterized by psychokinetic hyper-activity, hyper-euphoria, hyper-optimism and so on.
  Note: None of the 16 of Table 1 present manic S & P.
  R2 and R8 periodically present euphoria and excessive optimism (light hypomanic S & P) which they characterize as a semi-conscious effort to repress their painful melancholia with the help of diametrically opposite 'activation'. R2 and R8's realizations indicate that, if they had developed manic S & P, the latter would have been the result of unconscious hyper-repression of depression and unconscious hyper-'activation' with S & P diametrically opposite to depression. In other words, behind mania lurks depression and behind depression primitive terror.

§ 131 *Schizophreniclike S & P* These are characterized by bipolar 'activation' at all levels - emotional, intellectual, motor and so on.

Emotional:	For example, one minute R loves a person and the very next minute he hates him; one minute he feels he is God and the very next the devil.
Intellectual:	For example, one minute he thinks of various ways of helping himself and the very next of destroying himself.
Motor:	For example, one minute he obeys orders and the very next he resists.

R1, R4, R6, R8, R9 and R10 realized that their schizophreniclike S & P resulted from disturbances in their existential identity/self-preservation and/or sex identity and their subsequent resistance to the rejecting womb. The mechanism involved is this: The 'memory traces' of the rejecting womb and primitive terror are reactivated by various rejecting stimuli. In the face of the reactivated rejecting womb, R's existential identity musters its small forces and tries to resist. A vain attempt. The womb easily neutralizes the resistance. But the existential identity continues its struggle and the outcome is bipolar 'activation' of R at all levels (see R10 p.49-50). When the tactic of resistance alternates with the tactic of submission, then the schizophreniclike S & P alternate with depressivelike S & P. The resulting clinical picture presents schizoaffectivelike S & P.

§ 132   *Hallucinatorylike S & P*   Hallucinatorylike symptoms are very vivid sensory impressions produced exclusively by internal stimuli which reactivate the latent 'memory traces' of stimuli which had excited the nervous system in the past. Because the symptoms are not caused by external stimuli, an observer considers them false, non-existent. This is naturally so as the symptoms do not exist in his nervous system. But for R whose nervous system presents them they are as real as the sun he sees.

According to their quality, hallucinatorylike symptoms are differentiated into acoustic, optic, olfactory and so on. The emotional-intellectual content of hallucinatorylike symptoms is moulded, as a rule, by disturbances of the existential and/or sex identity and motivates behaviour accordingly, that is, it causes phenomena which come to the observer's attention (see R10 p.48).

§ 133   *Paranoiaclike S & P*   These are ideas of persecution, grandeur, reference and so forth.

Example: R9 feels that the world whispers about him and accuses him of being homosexual. The mechanism of R9's paranoiaclike symptoms is the following: The 'memory traces' of primitive terror - which was caused by the womb-mother's rejection of his sex - are reacitvated in everyday life by any rejecting stimulus. As a result, R9 suffers from disturbances in his sex identity and is dominated by primitive terror. However, because he does not know what caused the disturbances, he projects the cause to persons and/or situations in his environment. Thus, he feels that known and unknown persons slander and plot against him. He feels that the presence of motorcycles whose licence plates begin with XXX[67] is somehow mysteriously connected to the dark powers which accuse him of homosexuality. In the face of these persons and situations, R9 feels the need to attack and destroy them or to flee from them. He adds: 'Through the light of the Sessions, I realize that I project the rejecting womb to people and situations. My desire to destroy them symbolizes my desire to destroy the tyrannical womb which oppresses me even though I've done nothing to it. If I could, I'd destroy the womb - and without a trace of remorse.'

Another example of paranoiaclike S & P is R10's (p.49-50).

---

[67] During a Session R9 remembered that, when he was twelve years' old, a friend of his who owned a motorcycle with licence plates XXX had said something ambiguous which R9 interpreted as questioning his maleness. These ambiguous words formed the foundations of his paranoiaclike ideas concerning XXX licence plates.

APPENDIX

The appendix presents two pictures painted by a case (R17), the first after his 8th autopsychognosia session with Ketamine, the second after his 13th. R17 belongs to the group of cases who underwent Sessions exclusively with Ketamine during the period 1972 - 1982.

Brief history of R17: male, 27 years' old, Ph.D., researcher, single. R17 asked to undergo autopsychognosia sessions because he wanted to understand why he could not communicate sexually with women.

Of the first painting, R17 has written: *Here you see the rape of my mother from which I, her son, was conceived. Here you see the terrible cruelty of my father who felt not the violence of his own penis because he was entombed in stone of blackest ignorance. Mother's womb cried with burning pain and I burned with her even as my spirit first glimmered into being and I knew I was alive. So I inherit the knowledge of cruelty.*

The primitive memories of terror, at first wraiths of formless shadow, are now transmuted into images of terrible clarity by the action of conscious knowledge.

My father was a life removed from life. Denials and repressions overlayed the sufferings of his maddened soul like layered stone beneath the sea that conceals the bones of monsters. He chose not to feel at all in order not to feel hurt, and so his life was cast into the same prison with his pain. But his prison was also his weapon. He gained his will against my mother by the force of denial, he refused to be human when she craved humanity. And when Mother seemed broken, his penis sought to enter the womb as a conqueror in a mask of stone and death.[68] *But in Mother awoke a spirit fierce and bright. She wielded her terrible will as a great sword and smote the darksome phallus at the threshold of her womb.*

Father was desperate. He pressed against the womb. The womb yielded not. His blackened, ruined spirit cried for release. It was not given him. Womb against phallus, the opposing forces balanced - for a mere moment beneath the sun of day, for a thousand millenia of night in the womb. Such was the hour of my conception, expanded into ages of pain by the hate of implacable wills.

There is a power in me that dwells in peace, that knows the terror but stands apart and free. Against the horror of my conception, there is memory of great love from Mother's womb-spirit. Love connects son to

---

68 Doctor's note: Represented in the painting by the skull.

mother and connects both to earth and heaven which are the womb of life. Shades of memory flit about my being. I feel the womby sea broad and deep who bore me upon her waves beneath the singing wind and moon and stars. I feel the fire in the hearts of giant suns and all around the Deep of fierce etherial blue. An infant in the womb of love is wreathed in heaven eternal.

Under the shadow of unconscious memories from the strife of my conception I have never had orgasm with woman. Mine was a solitary and desolate orgasm which revived the bleeding womb and the tyranny of my father's blackened, petrific phallus. But what I have suffered is so small in comparison to what I will become. In the memory of love I stand beneath the suns of heaven to speak: Love, I lovingly embrace thee, rejection I cast from me.

Of the second painting, R17 has written: *There is a place in my memory where the natural world shines forth in naked splendour. I was borne upon a Deep of sea and stars streaming under the power of vast unseen but felt energies. In the dark between the stars I saw minds and life coalescing from primitive matter. Mother's womb spirit dwells here. I look upon her spiritual abode. In visions, as in the one presented here, she bears herself in the incandescence of the four-bladed star, sign of her origin in sea and suns. The first conscious memory of my infant life is of the evening star in the red sky after sunset.*

I believe that consciousness arises from matter and bears the memories of this origin. My mind coalesced inside of Mother who felt her origins in earth and heaven. Her womb felt to me like the ancient Deep because that was in her nature. Such is the love between mother and son.

That woman who shines by the light of this elemental love bears serenity immemorial. The security of her person radiates itself from her very body. Her acceptance is gentle and not craving, but for all that it is yet emphatic because its substance is immemorially great and does not yield to passions less than itself. In my last hour of autopsychognosia I was so blessed as to glimpse the vision of such a woman. Her eyes bore her immemorial love. So you see her here. I will carry with me the memory of her eyes for all the days of my life

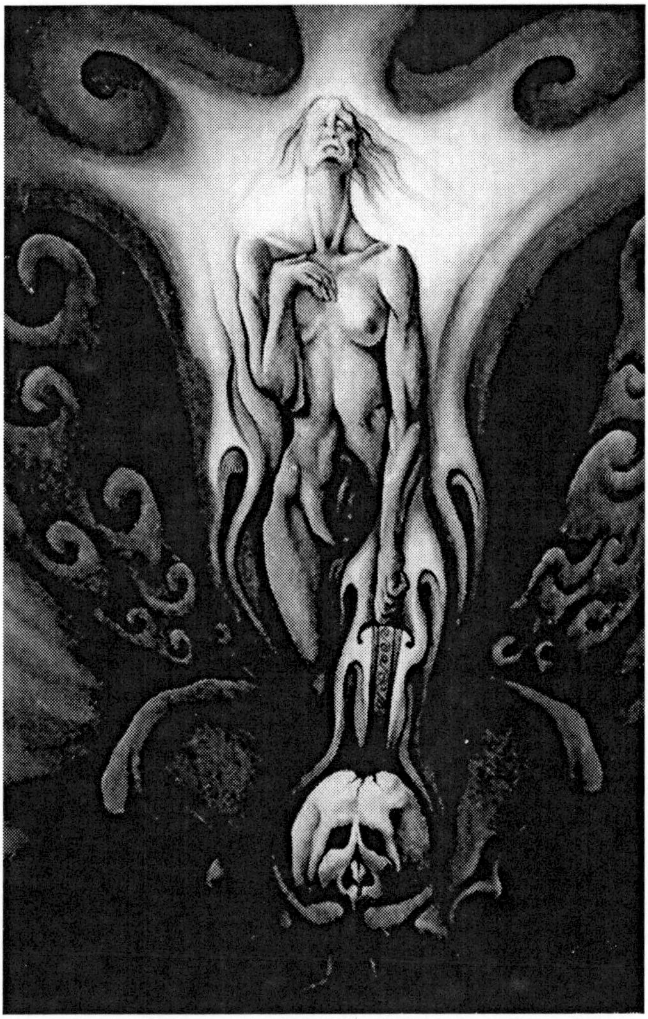

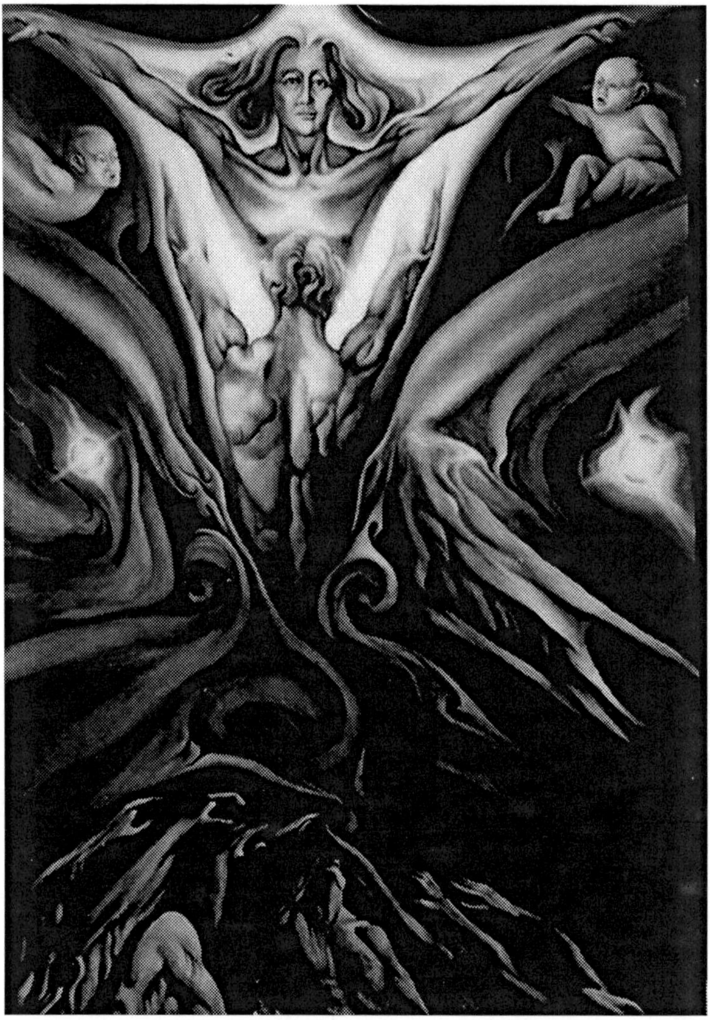

GLOSSARY

The glossary explains the meaning with which certain terms, abbreviations and alphabetical symbols are used in the book. It must be noted that the meaning of many terms in the glossary does not correspond to the meaning these terms have in traditional psychiatry.

Accepting womb the foetus' subjective feeling that the womb (that is, his external environment) accepts him either periodically (Periodically Welcome foetus) or continuously (Constantly Welcome foetus).

Activation the process which takes place within R's internal environment from the moment the internal environment's equilibrium is disturbed by a stimulus until equilibrium is 'restored' through the excitation of effectors.

Autopsychognosia a neuronal process which gives rise to subjective emotional-intellectual realizations about the content of the unconscious and the motives of behaviour.

Behaviour the result of the excitation of effectors.

Conditions-stimuli see messages-stimuli.

Direct biological need the internal force which motivates a living system to preserve the homogeneity, cohesion and integrity of its individual material being for as long as possible.

Effectors the non-striated muscular fibres of the internal organs and glands as well as the striated muscular fibres of the skeleton and the heart.

Existential identity/self-preservation R's unconscious and sometimes also conscious subjective feelings that he exists as an individual material being, separate from the remaining forms of matter which surround him, and that he has individual (biological) needs which motivate him to satisfy them.

External environment all the forms of matter which surround an internal environment.

Frontal poles from an evolutionary point of view this is the latest neuronal formation with which only the human brain is endowed. It is concerned with thought functions.

Indirect biological needs the needs which spring from the direct biological need. These are the perpetuation of the living system, food intake and so on.

Internal environment Claude Bernard's term which comprises the sum total of the cells and liquids which compose a living system.

Internal Environment of R whatever constitutes R's body.

mcg (microgram) a unit of weight. 1 mcg is a millionth of a gram.

Mental disturbance the result of the excitation of R's nervous system by rejecting stimuli.

Messages-stimuli/conditions-stimuli the sum of stimuli of various quality and intensity which have a certain symbolism for the internal environment on which they act.

Nervous tension a clinical picture of mental disturbance resulting from excitation of the nervous system by specific rejecting stimuli.

Neuro-hormones these are polypeptide compounds which are produced by specific neurons. Neuro-hormones are absorbed into the blood stream and conveyed to distant areas of the body where they act. They are considered a kind of neurotransmitter.

Neuron the nerve cell.

Neurons, central all the neurons which are interposed between the peripheral sensory and the peripheral motor neurons.

Neurons, existential specific neurons whose excitation results in the symptom of consciousness of existential identity/self-preservation.

Neurons, homogeneous these are neurons which are located anatomotopographically at the same point in two nervous systems and whose excitation produces the same qualitative result, eg. the limbic neurons of two nervous systems are homogeneous neurons.

Neurons, limbic the neurons of the limbic system. Their excitation gives rise to emotional symptoms such as fear, anger and so on.

Neurons, peripheral motor the neurons which terminate at the effectors.

Neurons, peripheral sensorial the neurons which begin from the receptors.

Neurons, presynaptic-postsynaptic this term refers to the relationship between any two neurons which link up with each other. Of the two neurons, the one whose axon terminals join up with the dendrites and/or the cell body of the other is called presynaptic while the latter is called postsynaptic. For example, in figure 2, (p.175), neuron n-1 is presynaptic to neurons n-2a and n-2b which are postsynaptic to n-1: neuron n-2a is presynaptic to neurons n-3a and n-3c which are postsynaptic to n-2a, while n-2b is presnynaptic to n-3b and n-3d which are postsynaptic to n-2b, and so on.

Neurons, postsynaptic see neurons, presynaptic.

Neurons, sensorial these sensory neurons whose excitation results in the symptoms of the various senses - hearing, sight, kinaesthesia and so forth.

Neurons, sensory all types of neurons which are interposed between the receptors and the central motor neurons.

Neurotransmitters biochemical substances which are secreted into the synapses and either transmit the excitation of a presynaptic neuron to postsynaptic neurons or inhibit the excitation of the latter.

Non-striated muscular fibres a special quality of muscular fibres with which the internal organs and the various glands are endowed.

Phenomena the results of the excitation of effectors, which can be perceived by an observer either with the naked eye or through the use of apparatus which shows the frequency of the heartbeat and respiration, the degree of blood pressure, the diminution of the skin's electrical resistance and so on.

Primitive terror the chaotic fear felt by the Rejected during their intra-uterine rejection and/or the rejection of their expulsion-birth.

Psychotic S & P the permanent symptoms and phenomena which traditional psychiatry characterizes as psychotic.

Psychoticlike S & P the periodic symptoms and phenomena which traditional psychiatry characterizes as psychotic.

Psychotraumatic stimuli see rejecting stimuli.

R the letter 'R' symbolizes any one of the 16 Rejected individuals of Table 1 (p.18). When referring to a specific Rejected person, his or her individual number is written beside R.

Realization (realize) the subjective emotional-intellectual understanding of the content of the unconscious and the motives of behaviour.

Receptors special peripheral sensorial organs of various quality (acoustic, optic, tactile, kinaesthetic and so forth).

The Rejected the 16 individuals of Table 1 who have the unconscious and sometimes also conscious feeling that they were rejected by the womb as a foetus (intra-uterine rejection) and/or as a foetus/new-born (rejection of expulsion-birth).

Rejecting stimuli or psychotraumatic stimuli the stimuli which oppose R's existential identity/self-preservation and/or his sex and which cause him unconscious and sometimes also conscious fear. Rejecting stimuli tend towards reactivating or actually reactive primitive terror.

Rejecting womb the foetus' subjective feeling during his intra-uterine life and/or expulsion-birth that the womb (that is, his external environment) rejects him.

S & P symptoms and phenomena.

Session written with a capital S the word refers to an autopsychognosia session with psychedelic drugs.

Sex identity the subjective sense of maleness or femaleness which R has in relation to the quality of his or her gonads. From the subjective point of view, this feeling is morbid or non-morbid.

Stimulus any form of energy - chemical, mechanical, biochemical, electromagnetic and so forth - which is produced in R's external or internal environment and which acts upon him.

Striated muscular fibres a special quality of muscular fibres which constitute the skeletal muscles. (The cardiac muscle consists of a particular quality of striated muscular fibres.)

Symptom the subjective state - unconscious and/or conscious - which accompanies the excitation of sensory neurons.

Synapse the space of a few A between the axon terminals of a presynaptic neuron and the dendrites and/or cell body of a postsynaptic neuron. (1 A is equal to 10-10 metre.)

Unconscious (partial meaning) the sum total of the 'memory traces', which are preserved by the neurons of a nervous system, of stimuli which had excited the neurons. Also included in the unconscious are 'memory traces' inherited from ancestors.

The Unwanted the individuals in Table 1 who are stimulated by rejecting womb messages-stimuli during their foetal life.

The Welcome the individuals in Table 1 who are stimulated by accepting womb messages-stimuli during their foetal life.

INDEX

A

Accepting stimuli 219
  for the Welcome after expulsion-birth 180, 181
  for the Unwanted after expulsion-birth 182
Accepting womb 186, 200, 233, 243
  revival of in sessions 170
    reactivation of in everyday life after expulsion-birth 200
'Activation' 217, 218, 219, 221–222, 224–226, 237
  and 'memory traces' 224
  and biological significance of stimuli 219
  and identification and projection 185–186
  and S & P 225, 233, 237
  R's 'activation' by rejecting stimuli, outlines 222
  R's 'activation' by stimuli, outline 221
Ancestral memory, see Heredity 162
Anger 200, 231–232, 245
Anxiety 162, 174, 232–235
  and neurotic S & P 233
Aplysia Californica 202
Autopsychognosia 187, 243
Autopsychognosia sessions with psychedelic drugs (pharmaceutical) 188
  aim of 187
  definition 187
  doctor's role during
    from doctor's point of view 197
    from R's point of view 197
  duration of 189
  environment for 189
  experiences during 196
  phases of 190
  preparation for 190
  resistance to 193
    causes of 193
      neutralization of 195
  selection of cases for (indications and contraindications) 190
  therapeutic results of 155
    criteria for prognosis of 156

B

Behaviour 220–223
  'most appropriate' 221–223
  hypocritical 161
  overprotective (parents') 183–184
Bernard, Claude 217
Biochemicophysical substances-factors 200, 218, 224
Biological needs
  and rejecting or accepting stimuli 219
  direct 218, 221–222, 243
  indirect 218, 244
Biological significance of stimuli 202, 203, 219
  and heredity 201

C

Cannon, W.B. 175
Castration 184, 233
Compact system of rejection 161, 183
Conditions-stimuli
  (see also Accepting stimuli;

Messages-stimuli; Rejecting stimuli; Stimulus) 243
Confusion, under psychedelics 162
Constitution, R's individual 224
Conversion hysteria 235

D

Dematerialization of the body, subjective sensation of 162
Depressivelike S & P 236

E

Effectors 157, 219–223, 235, 243
  foetal 157–158
Emotions 200, 215, 218
Environment
  (see also 'Activation') 217–224
    individual constitution 224
    individual heredity 224
    external 217, 243
    for foetus 165, 168, 200, 217
    for foetus/new-born 165, 175, 217
    for new-born 175
    R's 217
    internal (R's) 217, 224, 244
    internal disturbance and restoration of equilibrium of 218
Existential identity
  (see also Psychoticlike S & P) 243
    consciousness of 216
    detachment of, subjective sensation of 162
  Existential identity/self-preservation, disturbances of 175
  foreign, imitation of 231
Expulsion-birth
  and repercussions of in everyday life after expulsion birth 180–181
  revival of in Sessions 171

F

Father, as womb substitute 186
Fear
  (see also Anxiety; Primitive terror; Specific fear) 174–175.
  (see also Neurons, limbic)
Fixation, to womb, see Womb 180, 182
Flashback 164
Frontal poles 215

H

Hallucinations/Hallucinatory like S & P 235–236, 238
Hartline, H.K. 203
Heredity
  R's individual 162, 201, 224

I

Identification 185–186
  and womb substitutes 177, 185, 186
  functioning of 174, 185, 186
Immortality 176
insecurity 164, 181
intra-uterine life
  (see also Accepting womb; Rejecting womb) 167–168, 200–233, 246
  means of describing 201
  reactivation of by psychedelics ,- 166

K

Kandel, Eric 202
Ketamine xvi, 157, 239

249

L

LSD
LSD- (see Psychedelic drugs)
viii, xiv, xv, xvi, 160, 161, 162, 163, 164, 165, 166, 188

M

Maniclike S & P 237
masochism 230
Melancholia 236, 237
Memory traces 156, 162, 164–165, 168, 171–172, 175, 180, 183, 189–190, 197–198, 200–201, 218–219, 224
and heredity 224
Mental clarity, under psychedelics 162
Mental disturbances
classification of the suffering from 226
clinical pictures of
definition of 226
types of 226
definition of 226
duration of 226
mechanism of development of xvi, 157, 230
mechanism of subsidence of 157
phenomena of, definition 227
symptoms of, definition 227
Messages-stimuli n. 217. (see also Accepting stimuli; Rejecting stimuli; Stimulus)
for foetus 168, 200
Metabolism, role played by in threshold of neurons 215, 218
Mother, as womb substitute 180

N

Nervous system 202–203
Nervous tension 229, 231
Neuro-hormones
and pregnant woman's emotions 200
Neuron 202
existential 216
homogeneous 201
limbic 175, 200–201, 215, 220
motor 157–158, 215, 220
foetal - 157, 221
postsynaptic 202–203
presynaptic 202–204
sensorial 215, 220, 222
sensory 218–219
Neuronal excitation, 'storage' of in foetal neurons, 157–158, 201
Neuronal excitation, transmission and end result of
(see also 'Activation') 202
and chronological order of stimuli 211–214
and intensity of stimulus 203, 211–214
and pause between stimuli 203
and quality of neurons 209, 215–216
and subjective judgement of quality of stimulus 203
and threshold of neurons 204, 215–216, 218
Neurotic S & P 228, 233–235
Neurotransmitter 200, 204
and pregnant woman's emotions 200

O

Obsessional acts 233

250

Obsessional ideas 234
Optic symbols 167
Organ of direction 221
Orgasm. (see Sex)

P

paranoiaclike S & P 238
Pavlov 185
Phenomena
  definition of 219–220
Phobias 234
Pregnant woman
  and sexual intercourse (including rape) 172, 182, 239–240
  emotional disturbances of 169, 172, 183, 200
  mechanism of transmission of emotions to foetus 200
Primitive terror 162, 168, 171, 183, 246
  and psychoticlike/psychotic S & P 230, 235
Projection 185
  and womb substitutes 186
  functioning of 185
Psychedelic drugs 188
  harmful? 188
  pharmacodynamic activity of 160–164, 188
  neutralization of 195–196
  therapeutic dosage of 188
Psychic functions 161
Psychological problems
  parents' ignorance of offsprings' 184
  parents' ignorance of own, and subsequent effects on offspring, 184
  R's ignorance of own, prior to Sessions 192
Psychometric tests xv

Psychosomatic S & P 233, 235
Psychotherapeutic sessions
  non-pharmaceutical - xiii
  pharmaceutical. (see Autopsychognosia sessions with psychedelic drugs)
Psychoticlike S & P 235
Psychotic S & P 235
Psychotraumatic stimuli. (see Rejecting stimuli)

R

R,. see Rejected, the
Rape. (see Pregnant woman: and sexual intercourse)
Realization
  emotional-intellectual 161, 166, 187–188
  intellectual, n, n 187
  emotional and intellectual impasse resulting from, n, xii
Receptors 218
Reconciliation with environment 181
Rejected, the 229
  classification of - 171, 226–229
Rejecting stimuli, and mechanism of activity
  (see also Mental disturbance) 179
  basic rejecting stimuli 183, 235
Rejecting womb 171, 200
  and primitive terror 168, 171, 175–176, 183, 230, 233, 235–238
  reactivation of in everyday life after expulsion-birth ,as 'life' 175, 176, 181, 182, 236
  revival of under conditions of autopsychognosia -, 168–171

Rejection
  the compact system of 183
Resistance. (see Autopsychognosia sessions with psychedelic drugs)

S

Sadism 231
schizoaffectivelike S & P 237
Schizophreniclike S & P 236–237
Security, intra-uterine 56, 57, 61, 62, 63, 85, 88, 89, 90, 144, 170, 176, 178, 180, 240
Serenity, intra-uterine 162, 170, 240
Session (with capital S),. see Autopsychognosia sessions with psychedelic drugs
Sex
  as effort to revive accepting womb 180, 181, 182
  between parents, effects on R 183
  symbolism of 117, 176–178, 180–181
    effects of. (see Sexual problems; womb substitutes)
Sexual Problems 178–179
  repercussions of 179
Sex identity, disturbances of (see also Psychoticlike S & P) 178–179
Sight (see Symptom) 215
Social code, rejecting effect of 184
Specific fear 174
  and nervous tension 231
Stimulus
  (see also Accepting stimuli; Messages-stimuli; Neuronal excitation; Rejecting stimuli) 217
  external stimuli for R 217
  and memory traces 218
  individual stimuli for R 226
  internal stimuli for R 217, 218, 219
Suicidal thoughts 236
Supernatural powers, subjective sensation of having 163
Symptom(s) 219
  definition of 219, 220
  of mental disturbance,. (see Mental disturbance)
S & P. (see Symptoms; Phenomena)

T

Threshold of neurons 215
Touch. (see Symptom)
Tuke, H. 228

U

Unwanted, the 163, 168–172, 175–177, 180, 182–184, 247
  and creation of rejecting conditions after expulsion-birth 177, 182
  and efforts to create or revive accepting conditions after expulsion-birth 177
  and reaction to accepting stimuli after expulsion-birth 183
  because of their Sex 169
  existentially 168–169
  Hereditarily 170
  Periodically 169–170

W

'Wandering Jew' 182
Welcome, the 170–173, 176–177, 180–181, 243, 247

as Rejected 171
Constantly 170, 173, 176–177
Periodically 169
reaction to accepting stimuli after expulsion-birth 181
reaction to rejecting stimuli after expulsion-birth 180
Whore, emotional meaning of 7, 27, 45, 47, 64, 68, 78, 122, 133, 152, 179, 180
Womb
  'return' to through sex 176, 181
  as permanent base of reference (fixation to) 180
  as second existential identity 235
  as superpower 26, 168, 235–236
  deification of, -, 230
  fixation to through womb substitutes 178, 180
  repercussions of fixations to, for the Welcome, for the Unwanted 180, 182
Womb acceptance (see Accepting womb) xv, 200
Womb rejection (see Rejecting womb) 171
Womb substitutes 59, 176–178, 180–181, 186, 233, 237

ABOUT THE AUTHOR

The Greek psychiatrist Athanassios Kafkalides (1919-1987) was a leading researcher during the 60'ies and 70'ies in the field of the psychotherapeutic application of psychedelic drugs.

His major work THE KNOWLEDGE OF THE WOMB, (*first published in Greece in 1980*) was written after many years of clinical research carried out into the unconscious and the causes of mental disturbance. It is based on the experiences and conclusions of 16 individuals who relived the conditions of their intra-uterine life and expulsion-birth during sessions with Lsd-25, Psilocybine and Ketamine Hydrochloride